Chicano Politics

Chicano Politics

Reality and Promise, 1940–1990

JUAN GÓMEZ-QUIÑONES

The Calvin P. Horn Lectures
in Western History and Culture

UNIVERSITY OF NEW MEXICO PRESS, Albuquerque

In memoriam
Professor Federico A. Cervantes

Library of Congress Cataloging-in-Publication Data

Gómez-Quiñones, Juan.
  Chicano Politics: reality and promise, 1940–1990. /
Juan Gómez-Quiñones—1st ed.
      p.   cm.—(The Calvin P. Horn lectures
in western history and culture)
Includes bibliographical references.
ISBN 0-8263-1204-7.—ISBN 0-8263-1213-6 (pbk.)
1. Mexican Americans—Politics and government.
2. United States—Politics and government—1945–
I. Title.
II. Series.
E184.M5G634   1990
973'.046872073—dc20
                                                    90-31486
                                                    CIP

Contents

1

Mexican American Politics

Purposes

The transfer of political experience from one generation to another is important to the success of the polity—thus, this book. This volume seeks to place in historical perspective the political experience of the Mexican people north of the Rio Bravo.*[1] It does this through narrative and interpretation. The narrative is chronological, topical, and thematic; it combines summary and analysis. The discussion moves through five decades and with several foci of analysis. People of Mexican descent comprise a distinct native group not solely because of ethnicity. They are a separate economic sector, a community that receives disparate treatment, and they have been concentrated for generations in a particular geographic area, what is today the United States Southwest. They have shared in governance and been denied participation in it. They are socialized both internally, or within the group, and by the dominant society. Moreover, examining the politics of Mexican Americans implicitly entails discussing their uniqueness as a group, and thus their exceptionality as compared to other groups. Yet as this is acknowledged, so, too, do the similarities to other political groups become evident.[2] Academic interest has increased in both the areas of a reinvigorated political history and in the role of the ethnocultural communities within larger societies.

*The terms Mexican(o), Mexican descent, Mexican American, Hispano, and Chicano are used in an interchangeable way and also in distinct ways. The context in the narrative should clarify the usage.

1

This study is within the scope of critical historical political studies and, as such, certain intentions are embodied.[3] One intention is to reconstruct the relations of power, its exercise and sufferance, and relate them to a study of governance and civil society. Power both reflects and shapes what is social, the relationships between the economy, the family and community, the means of communication, the legal system, and institutions. That is, a number of areas of study and experience are subsumed. Power reflects the history of relationships of classes, relations of the state, and dissonance as opposition.

These are dialectical, not linear. The development of a political culture, social ideas, and context is noted. This development combines the political and social and is to be evaluated normatively, or rather, what is observed are structural aspects and purposeful behavior. This requires the study of many disciplines and how they relate to one another. There is only one history of society, and politics are part of this history. The basis of this study is inquiry into the social relations of production. Political practice, thought, and institutions are no less substantive than other aspects of social life. History, as the most encompassing of social sciences, the science of human societies, is the most useful in the study of the political, strengthened by contributions from all the other sciences and humanities. Political history may emphasize the behavior of elites, but it is the mass context, impact, and consequence that are significant. Political history involves breadth, scope, and depth. The intent is to elucidate reality through empirical investigation. The history of society requires new and established models and techniques suitable for the study of the individual and the mass, the present and the past. A critical outlook is indispensable to the narrative, but more importantly there is a need for a critical scrutiny involving judgment and comparison, a questioning of hypotheses, their context, and the investigator. Facts, events, discourse, and the world are dialectical—and so must be their study.

This political history relates details of evolving events and generational participants pertinent to power relations between community (society) and governance (the state).[4] Attention is focused on selected problematical areas of political activity—forms, organization, leadership and ideas, and their context; the minority and dominant societies; and the behavior of the state and its adaptations: conscious intent and action, power relations as perceived by actors, and the factors involved in stability and dissidence are adaptations of the state.

In this section, pertinent generalizations are made about the features of these problem areas, politics in general, and the perception of politics. The narrative relates a rich story; this introduction provides its punctuation. It marks both the constraints and the possibilities of political activity. To begin, two questions are in order: what is "politics," and what is the "group"?

A Politics and a Society

Politics among Mexicans follows some general patterns common to all national groups, but particular constraints have also evolved within distinct applications.[5] From one benign point of view, a political system is a pattern of reinforcing beneficial relations, limited or extensive, pertinent to governance. More inclusive is the notion of power. At the center of politics, power involves authority or rule over the allocation of resources, the validation of groups to share in resources, and the allocation of surplus. In general and specific situations, the economic, social, and ideological matrix both underpins politics and is expressed through them. Among many definitions, politics represent the pursuit of group or individual material interests in the public arena by addressing government and using group mobilization to influence policy and other civic aggregations. In reference to governance, this is most often primarily an elite activity that is a negotiation between those who already have surplus and the authority to distribute it; presumably there are those outside the negotiation who require access. Distribution or redistribution entails conflict, and this elicits a rhetoric to obscure or enhance conflict as well as a need for supporters in order to predominate in the conflict.

Political practice is also a social expression of the group, which, through engaging in this practice, exhibits its defining and identifying attributes.[6] These are, in turn, conditioned by degrees of equality or inequality of political players and members of society at different historical instances and periods. A cohesive element among these players is the particular political socialization fostered among them, a teaching of conformity to values and modes that promote cooperative group living. In the case of Mexican Americans, there is internal and external socialization, what the group promotes and what is imposed upon it. The "consent of the governed" is in fact premised on an earlier enforced consent of beliefs. This is not episodic, but continuous, and generationally transferred. Political activity is both an expression of a collective social intent and an affirmation of the community. This social intent is informed by perception of relations and consequences—a judgment process mapped by negative and positive reinforcements. All this means is that politics, a materially premised activity, is endowed with notions of beauty and the ideal good and involves choice and responsibility.

The Mexican population in what is now the territory of the United States is both a varied indigenous group and an immigrant one whose political history has yet to be closely examined.[7] Dominated and discriminated against, they represent to the larger society not a moral or constitutional dilemma, but a psychological symbol, an economic utility, and a political problem. This trinity may elicit negative and positive responses that can be identified in the historical record. The historical record of Mexican political activity has yet to be developed fully, however. To reveal the record, and in order to understand political activity, certain questions may be posed. How have government, institutions, and society evolved? What is the pattern of governmental, institutional, and social relations? How is power exercised, how is consent engendered, and what is opposition? How do politics reflect socioeconomic competition? What group consciousness is exhibited? What goals, organizations, and leadership have developed over time? How does class consciousness interact with group consciousness? When do they combine? What historical political tendencies are discernible? What forms of struggle are visible? What are the characteristics of Mexican politics? What have been the successes, the failures, and the legacy? What forms of struggle, what political arguments, have acquired the most significant support; which have been the dominant forces; and which have been the most successful? At present, these questions cannot be dealt with exhaustively or definitively. Nonetheless, it is important that they be asked, and there are data available to suggest tentative answers. One question, however, overrides the others: Is there a cohesive political tradition subject to critique? The answer would be evident in the continuity of ideologies—ways and means to secure survival that a community consciously expresses as a political goal.

Achieving survival and equality for Mexicans, most of whom are wage earners and members of an oppressed ethnic community, has

meant a complex political history whose successes have been uneven.[8]
The political realities Mexicanos faced have been both internal and
external. Consequently, the history of political organizing in the Mexican community has been heroic, varied, and tenacious, as well as
frustrated. Clearly, when politics has "failed"—that is, when no beneficial negotiation for resources has ensued—the most important reason for failure has been a hostile and repressive society; in effect, the
objective elements for politics are objectively denied. This failure,
however, was often facilitated by unresolved dilemmas within community politics. Periodically, group unity and resistance have been
expressed sufficiently to defend and advance group interests. More
often, however, class divisions and negative negotiation have intertwined to mitigate political gains. Mexican politics has clearly experienced problems. Some of these are elements common to all politics:
numbers, resources, organization, skills, leadership, institutional access, and allies. What makes them distinctive is the particular historical configuration of their context and content.

History, class, politics, and ethnic composition contribute to their
special nature.[9] The primary elements of Mexican history north of the
Rio Bravo are the formation of the Mexican nation and its initial
exercise of state sovereignty. Thus, the historical record antedates the
present borders of the United States, simply because Mexicans and
Mexican-settled land were incorporated north of the Rio Grande by
U.S. annexation. There is a considerable period prior to U.S. annexation that must be taken into account in explaining the community's origin, diversity, geographic location, and cultural differences
from and its unities with the United States and the core Mexican
societies. This previously ongoing process of national formation was
halted by the United States–Mexico conflict from 1836 to 1846, and
the consequent annexation by the U.S. of Mexican land and people.
However persistent it has been in retaining its distinctiveness, the
community has increased its numbers through natural growth; through
inculturation of a few others; and most significantly through migration.
In effect, its legacy of objective and subjective formation is distinct
within the United States. Nevertheless, the growth and development
of the United States as well as the pervasive negative social views
fostered in the nineteenth and twentieth centuries have shaped the
community and impelled its growth and diversity. This particular political heritage, which is both negative and positive, also includes a

pathology; that is, external pressures and values have distorted political values, behavior, and evolution to the extent that this political legacy includes counterproductive tendencies. One result of historical circumstances is that the community was both a native and an immigrant one, identified as recognizable ethnic group and nationality. It was stigmatized and denied, but also asserted itself. What it called itself, and its public statements of group consciousness, reflected all of these elements.

Identity as Consciousness

Group consciousness is an expression of historical identification and class and cultural allegiance. Politically, it attempts to comprehend the group interests and their relation to the individual's circumstances. There is an evolving refinement of consciousness and its expression under conditions of colonial status, sovereignty, and forced annexation. When the result may well determine marginalization, or integration, the assertion of identity by the disadvantaged becomes a politically charged matter. Nationality, or cultural consciousness, refers to ethnic banner—the cultural practices pursued by the individual in daily life as well as the specific social universe in which the person lives and which provides the context for both individual and organized political action. Though conditioned by a number of variables, the primary relationship remains a dominant culture versus an oppressed culture.

As the community has evolved historically, it also has been under assault socially and spatially, the target of a continuous attack that has impinged upon its sense of identity.[10] Questions of private and public self are interrelated with, and are as problematic as, aspects of class, ethnicity, and political posture. The name of the group speaks to the group's consciousness and its will for survival, yet the formal name for the community has often involved some controversy. A name has significance to self-perception as well as group cohesion; it proclaims cultural heritage and invites a particular acknowledgment. As group consciousness is heightened, the designation takes on psychological, political, and ideological ramifications. Since the period from 1836 to 1846, when hostile attitudes were pervasive among the larger society, there have been differences of opinion as to what image to project and what cultural heritage to claim according to class and region; more crucial, however, has been the debate over what are the desired common ends. The larger society campaigns for the least threatening and least distinctive name, the one which is the most self-effacing. There is an apprehension of the Mexican, which is based primarily on psychological rather than objective factors. Because of U.S. society's preeminently European roots, it fears that its claims may be illegitimate and it experiences guilt over the means of its rise to power. Ambivalence results for the oppressor as well as for the oppressed. In 1830, there was a specific identification—Mexicano; though it persisted in 1980, it was no longer universal.

Mexicano is the historical and most general identity, and the most inclusive term for the people. It refers to ethnic and cultural identity as well as to a political consciousness that developed as the result of a historical process in a particular region. Allowing for time and economic changes, cultural adaptation, and the impact of domination, the majority within the base culture is Mexican—despite denials, obfuscation, or idealistic inventions of the larger and dominant society. Various designations in the past have had special historical roots and meanings associated with particular periods, classes, and regions. *Mexican American* is an adequate general descriptive term which refers to cultural and ethnic identification as well as to residency and citizenship status. *Chicano* is an abbreviation for *Mexicano;* it is an in-group term with connotations of peer fellowship. In the second half of the twentieth century it also has been used to distinguish people of Mexican parentage born north of the border. However, wider public usage of the term as the self-designation for the community appeared in the sixties, when it was given political connotations by young activists. Preference for the term was defended on the grounds that, as a statement of self-assertion, it speaks to what is autochthonous as well as syncretic in the historical experience. For some it included Mexicano; for others it provided a way to deny Mexican identity. In any case, the group has experienced repeated assaults on its designation even in the late twentieth century. Such attempts at establishing a counter-identity are indeed political. Certainly, to be consciously involved in community politics underscores the fact of being Mexican as well as choosing to be Mexican, although this does not include all persons who are of full or partial Mexican descent. This choice takes place within the context of social relations—classes. Class membership and

identity are an integral part of politics within the dominant society
and its politics; and in the dominant society, class plays an important
role in the political–ideological differences within the community. But
class composition changes over a period of time.

Classes

Mexican classes appeared during the sixteenth- and seventeenth-
century colonial economy and took on some institutionalized forms
by the late colonial period. Classes are interactive social groups, subdivided according to material interests. Classes have affected political
actions through periods of national formation, sovereignty, and annexation. Similarly, over time the ideological expressions of these
relationships juxtapose their sustaining rationalizations against their
negative alternatives. With annexation, however, the class relationship becomes both internal to the group and external to the larger
society, and is mediated by pejorative distinctions between "Anglo"
and "Mexican" which are social and economic. Within capitalism there
are potentially or actively two class positions: workers and their allies
versus the upper classes and their allies; and the ethnic impacts upon
both. In political practice no simple polarities exist; however, these
opposing positions are the result of a history that began in the sixteenth
century, and over time the specific expression of class articulation
changed in tandem with the governance forums. The basis of the
economy also changed from precapitalist to postindustrial. What did
not change was the general class premise of politics.

For generations in the Mexican community, class has produced a
social relationship between people which is based on their location
in the economy.[11] Though income, status, livelihood, and education
of individuals are visible and measurable, classes are not invariably
equated with income and education. These attributes may be part of
what identifies class, but more crucial is the power related to the
individual's or the group's economic standing within the larger society.
The small upper class, which is defined by very large income derived
from investment and ownership, potentially has greater and more
direct access to political influence. The larger middle class, which is
identifiable by medium income derived from professional expertise and/
or business and is paid in salary or in profit margin, is subdivided into

two subgroups: the upper middle class and the lower middle class; and the difference between the two groups in relation to politics, society, and income is considerable. The upper middle class may exercise influence or delegated authority, while the lower middle class facilitates and articulates the real or potential power of others. The third class is composed of workers and wage earners, the largest and most important group both numerically and productively, and one which contains several subgroups. Its potential power is actualized on occasion, but more often it is impeded. Finally, there are the lumpen groupings, which combine several characteristics. They are the nonworkers, the perennially unemployed, the severely undereducated, and the deculturalized; and often they are part of, or at the margin of, the criminal world. Among these four classes, each one containing at least two sectors, the major dividing line with regard to access to political influence in the dominant system may exist between the upper class, the upper middle class, and the others. These upper classes may exercise qualitatively stronger influence than the others.

The historical evolution of interactive class relationships north of the Rio Bravo was shaped by different stages of domination: as a colony under the Spanish empire; during the period of formal sovereignty under the Mexican republic; and by the hegemony of the United States. Whatever the optimum possibilities were under these governances, Mexicans living in the far North—now the United States Southwest—had less means in all classes. Over time there have been a handful of very wealthy Mexican individuals and recently a growing number of the wealthy, but their participation in power has varied from the decorative to the modest. Now as then, the two privileged groups, the upper and the upper middle classes, advance their interests through the advantages inherent in their class positions; and they also advance their interests by forging a temporary and expedient alignment with the force of the popular mass which, when it does gain concessions, shares its benefits.

Forms

In measurable terms, politics is the exercise of power to achieve ends or to prevent the opposition from imposing its ends through specific means.[12] As a struggle for equities and against domination, politics involves class and ethnic assertion at any given time, at several levels, and in different ways. Evident in the historical record of the Spanish colony were a variety of political expressions. Twentieth-century Mexicans in the United States do not have a state structure of their own; consequently, their politics exist in a dependent relation to a state whose principal instrument for dominating the Mexican community is this very power relationship. Mexicans have three initial options: to challenge, to appeal, or to incorporate. There is also the more prolonged option of enlightened, directed, and measured contestation. How politics is expressed and given shape will vary within these options, but there is still no recognition of Mexican politics *per se* within the government. In each instance, political assertion has different forms: spontaneous or conceptualized, legal and/or extralegal, massive or exclusive. These forms may emphasize or encompass economic, juridical, social, electoral, cultural, and ideological efforts, and the tempo of their recurrence will change as time passes. Political assertion or contestation is not limited simply to the politics of protest, to electioneering, or to advocacy by organizations. Rather, political struggle encompasses broad dimensions; namely, democratic rights and self-determination, which are subsumed, in general, by conscious and unconscious affirmation of group survival and, in particular, by the struggle for equities or gain under specific leaderships.

Leadership

Various types of leaders at various levels of society were present throughout the colonial period and later.[13] During settlement, leadership was based on land production, military rank, civic office, or clerical status. In the nineteenth century, while these criteria continued to be employed, they now also included commerce, inherited and diversified wealth and professional skills, and organizational recognition. Leadership has changed according to internal changes within classes, but generally, it has been drawn from the three major classes, and predominantly from the middle. Leaders have encompassed several normative types. Autochthonous leadership was integral and organic to the local community; but under domination, increasingly leaders were externally imposed, and frequently chosen because of their loyalty to the grantor. Accountability is a continual problem. The dilemma for leaders became the conflict between their own interests, the interests of the community, and the demands of the dominant power. Community interests could be implemented only to the extent that they did not threaten larger interests.

Minority leaders comprise a spectrum involving gender and generational and occupational diversity. Obviously, the worst leadership is ignorant, incompetent, authoritarian, and weak; while the best leaders secure and affirm the survival of their minority constituency. Generally, however, leadership acts in behalf of its own interests, which are veiled by the employment of both self-righteous rhetoric and a manipulation of the public's general interests. Most often, the leadership which survives is moderate and administrative, rather than charismatic or radical. Because of its need to survive, a leadership is often involved in two discourses: one with the powerholders and another with its constituents. To remain in power, leadership must conform to the norms of the dominant society while simultaneously providing benefits to its constituency. While the cultural, social, economic, and political spheres of society possess their individual leaders, the transference of leadership from one sector to another frequently occurs. In any case, political leadership focuses on community ends inherent in group activity, while servicing individual needs.

Organization

Organization is a structured means for expressing social concern or for achieving a common purpose. While organization was generally evident during the period of settlement, specific organization for social and political purposes, combined with civic attributes, emerged in the colonial period in response to local needs and ends, both objective and subjective. Mexican organizations have been simple and single focused, multiple and diverse, short-lived and continuous.[14] Lack of structure and/or programmatic goals as well as overly complicated efforts have resulted in organizational failure; other organizations have been weakened by restricting their focus to single-issue or crisis-oriented politics and personalistic leadership. Organizations with an appropriately formal structure and clearly articulated goals generally have been more successful. Democratic leadership, family participation, and bilingual latitude, as well as the use of cultural symbols, join with elements of communal mystique and varied functions of membership to contribute to organizational stability. There have been both successful and unsuccessful precedents of working-class and middle-class, rural and urban organizations; and in all of these organizations, mastery of the Spanish language or a bilingual ability have been crucial. Equally important are the content and style of discourse in relation to their purpose within the membership of the organization.

Organizational activity generally emanates from the working and middle classes. But of formative importance is the part played by the dominant sectors and the leaders in these classes in specifically organizing or orchestrating an activity. The upper class has not formed overtly exclusive political organizations, and the *lumpen* has only rudimentary organizational needs; yet the former does have covert and overt forms of organizing, while the latter can develop, on occasion, multifaceted and multilayered organizations. Most important, however, is the effectiveness of the organization in relating its content and context to the achievement of its goals.

Ideology and Goals

Political assertion, in encompassing class, the clash of economic interests, civil rights, cultural rights, and juridical and electoral issues, follows an ideological spectrum.[15] A range of images, opinions, beliefs, ideas, concepts, and plans involve goals that express the limited or extensive ends sought by political assertion. *Ideology* comprises an ostensibly logical set of ideas that serve to advance overt and covert, political and social interests. Mexicans exhibit a wide spectrum of political tendencies from the left to the right, reflecting the social spectrum. Because of the ethnic and class position of the majority of Mexicans in the United States, Mexican politics generally are centrist with a predominantly liberal to progressive tendency, although a relatively smaller moderate to conservative tendency exists as well. Goals and ideologies expressed by Mexicans are indeed related to their circumstances, but they are invariably shaped by forces and articulations outside the community. Thus, as in reference to other political matters, the notional aspect of politics must be seen in reference to the dominated and dominant aspects. Moreover, the minority, for the most part, forms its ideas of political goals and arguments from those that exist within the realm of the dominant society; there does exist, however, counterprocess.

For generations, Mexican people have struggled for rights in the cultural, economic, and political arenas; substantive politics also take place in the less politically charged but emotionally compelling social areas. Circumscribed survival, protection, equity, and empowerment make up the political needs and aspirations of the community vis-à-vis the discrimination practiced by the larger, dominant society. Mexican politics reflect the social and economic basis of society as well as its institutional and political practices. Community progress, in contrast to social advancement for the exceptional few, has been achieved through organized, collective, and conscious struggle. From the settlement period to the present day, the political forms, ideas, leadership, and organization of the Mexican people north of the Rio Bravo have changed according to circumstances prevailing within a broad span of time that may be divided into several major periods. Each period possesses its own social and economic characteristics, and is characterized by certain trends in political ideas, organizations, forms, and organizing efforts which reflect the socioeconomic subordination of the Mexican. Organized articulation, as opposed to one tolerated from idiosyncratic individuals, is tempered by the formal and informal censorship sustaining the system as well as by historical accidents.

A Historical Society and Its State Evolution: Peculiarities and Accidents

Central to the conceptualization of the historical political experience of the Mexican people north of the Rio Bravo is the perception of the Mexican community as a formatively distinct society.[16] The Mexican people north and south of the border are the historical result of a process that began centuries ago and continues today. Culturally and genetically, Mexicans are the inheritors of Indians, mestizos, Africans, and Europeans. Mexicans have experienced a sequence of economic developments common to peoples throughout the world. Mexicans possess a historical homeland, which is one result of their Indian ancestry. The Indian civilizations, and specifically the Mexica, were the historical antecedents to the colonial society in which the Mexican nationality was forged.

In the United States Southwest, the territory and the community are the economic, social, and institutional legacy of war. By and large, the community ethnically is distinct from other sectors of the society. Particular chauvinistic as well as supremacist practices have been directed at the people of Mexican descent. The area of densest concentration perceived as homeland has had a continuing and numerous population. A syncretic Mexican culture has continuously evolved, and over time, intense conflict has marked a wide spectrum of areas of life. The overwhelming majority of the people have been laborers and members of the working class. A predominantly economic immigration from 1848 to the present has been constant, with the community affected by an interlinked and continuing set of relationships between Mexico and the United States involving contiguous land, labor, economy, society, and culture. An immediate proximity exists between many Mexicanos in the United States and those in Mexico. The combination of all these aspects reveals significant differences between the history of the Mexican community north of Rio Bravo and that of other class-ethnic groups in the United States.

Differences exist between individuals and localities, in addition to shared commonalities within the general population. Differences among individuals within the community result from racial characteristics; length of residence; sense of identity and culture; use of Spanish; type of English; acculturation, deculturation, and education; occupation of family and of self; assimilation into Anglo society; urban or rural residence; and experiences of discrimination. Regional and local subgroupings within the community are characterized by length of settlement, type of settlement, and uneven rate of settlement; regional-economic patterns; economic vitality; cultural characteristics of local populations; and rate and manner of displacement by Anglos. Overall sources of differentiation are found in cultural changes in Mexico and in those changes introduced at different times by successive generations of Mexican immigrants and their interaction with local variations. More immediate influences include the different regional and local Anglo political, cultural, social, and demographic complexes within which Mexicans live and work. Differences and commonalities are observable over time; however, commonality generally prevails and becomes manifested politically as action occurs.

Today's Mexican community is the result of the interplay between

economic and state expansion, political dislocation, economic transformation, social changes, international wars, and other causal phenomena.[17] This process has been in motion for several centuries, and
it is related to the process of formation and expansion of the Mexican
nation as well as to the rise of United States capitalism and imperi-
alism. The Mexican community encompasses the formation and recreation of a culture and society whose unity is the result of origin,
time, space, genetic makeup, culture, social relations, historical experiences, and common political interests. Yet the community also
encounters disintegrative forces. From this process of domination there
arise several political circumstances apart from the basic social economic fact of domination itself. One factor is the lack of a cultural
political center, formerly provided by the core area of Mexico; with
annexation, however, the provinces became tangential to one another.
Moreover, domination precluded an autochthonous communication
system; though communication existed, it lacked an internal structure
common to all regions. Overarching institutions, whether religious or
secular for extended periods of time, have proved to be weak or ineffectual in relation to the community. The preservation and conser-
vation of culture becomes a pressing priority, yet under a system of
domination economic and civil aspirations demand change.

Political cohesion is related to authority and rewards, yet often
both have been weak, with no centrally recognized authority and an
often tenuous internal leadership. For the most part, the few political
rewards are controlled by outsiders. The unifying agents vis-à-vis domination have been discrimination, sentiments of nationality, generalized cultural practices, idealized familialism, and class membership—
and all these are expressed in specific local settings. Unity, a strong
but frustrated aspiration, becomes vulnerable to manipulation; yet, in
most given situations, the local is stressed above the general. Moreover, there exists no formal or explicit recognition of Mexican political
rights or of any other rights per se. Even as they are ostensibly affirmed,
in reality, rights are denied in a game where gains require their negation. Such distortion is compounded by the encouragement of sup-
plication, betrayal, and violence. A temporal and spatial unevenness
comes to characterize the political significance of the community as
a whole and in its parts. At times the importance is notable; at other
times, it is not. Either case follows certain contours, even as the
community is misperceived.

Commonplace Realities and Stereotypes

Despite a popular belief, Mexican political activity, from the colonial period to the present day, is variegated and has involved both
men and women.[18] Mexican political action in the United States began
long before the mid-twentieth century. In the nineteenth century, for
example, Mexicans ran for office, and episodes of militant populist
organizing occurred. Concomitantly, the practices of the colonial era
became the historical heritage of nineteenth-century politics.

Mexican political action continues to display local, state, regional,
national, and international dimensions. Two aspects of this political
evolution are the prevalence of the majority's denial of recognition,
and the occasional negative views held by the group concerning itself
and its politics. Historical perspective offers a way of evaluating contemporary political activity as well as a means of clearing away mis-
conceptions common in the literature and in political practice. Since
the 1970s contemporary Mexican organizations, whose leaders represent a variety of leadership and economic sectors, have engendered
continually increasing political activity in the barrios. Many observers
representing different political viewpoints agree that the Mexican community has gained potentially significant political visibility. For most
observers this community activism is startlingly new; but slogans such
as "the awakening of the brown giant" and "the siesta is over for the
Spanish-speaking" betray the ignorance as well as chauvinist condescension apparent among members of the Mexican community whose
opinions demonstrate a depreciative mentality, even when presented
in populist rhetoric.

Rather than stereotypes, comprehensible general characteristics of
Mexican politics account, in turn, for their heterogeneity. Politics
stem from national as well as international economics and social reality, while political change either parallels or follows economic and
social change. Individual political action generally reflects a person's
socioeconomic status. Mexicans experience political exclusion, manipulation, violence, repression, and co-optation of their community,
their leaders, and their goals; in short, covert and overt forms of force
and manipulation are used to maintain domination within the political
process. The degree and nature of these forms of oppression vary,
depending on the class identity of the Mexican individual or of the
group.

Because of class and spatial relations, cultural ties, numbers, and the integral economic relationships between Mexico and the United States and Latin America, Mexican politics possess an immediate international context. Significant exchanges within the sociocultural and the political ideological spheres may be called pan-Mexican relations.[19] The clearest material basis of this interactive exchange is the continuous existence, on both sides of the border, of a large Mexican population with a tradition of continuing ties. Politically conscious relations take many particular forms and involve different sectors or constituencies. Two such broad forms now current are the result of (1) efforts in obtaining assistance from Mexico in defense of the Mexican people living under the domination of the United States; and (2) efforts directed at participation in ideological political struggles involving the people of Mexico. Many efforts, however, grow out of neither of these two types of effort. Varying forms of trans-border Mexican political and ideological activity occur concurrently and often interdependently. Relations permeate differing classes as well as class-strata interests of the Mexican people generally and those north of the border in particular. On either side of the U.S.–Mexico boundary, in certain moments of crisis these political and ideological contacts crystallize and assume definite organizational forms that articulate specific socioeconomic interests: some display a defined ideological and programmatic content, while others possess a mass character involving broad sectors of the Mexican people on both sides of the frontier. Thus, Mexican American politics is characterized internationally as well as otherwise by very concrete rather than abstract dimensions, none of which have been readily understood.

The Discourse and Its Failure in Perception

Through its long and varied history, Mexican political activity in the United States generally has been ignored by the public and by the literature of the academy until recently; or if acknowledged, it has been deemed to be of little significance or judged by political observers and academicians to be inherently defective because of certain allegedly negative features.[20] In this liberal–conservative chorus, it is notable that, for the most part, the class aspect is not considered to be inherent to either internal or external politics. Liberals and conservatives dominate the literature, listing negative features and condescendingly offering recommendations for their reform. In the past, Mexican generally were characterized in the literature as a passive, apolitical, politically submerged, and, in the main, nonparticipating group in the political arena of the United States. Such an argument has been used to explain the alleged lack of political initiative and leadership among the population as well as its apparent unwillingness to invest the time and financial resources required to participate in the political process. When Mexicans have been acknowledged as political participants, their activity frequently is viewed as the result of their manipulation by others. A common stereotype is the image of the Mexican being "led" to the polls to vote for a party's candidate.

Mexican cultural behavior supposedly accounts for the development of a subordinated politics and of broker politicians within the community. Both liberal and conservative political observers cite broker-manipulated and machine politics as the bane of the Mexican people, calling for their replacement by majority-inspired reform efforts within the Democratic or Republican parties. Similarly, liberal political analysts within the community believe that Mexicans could improve their lot in society if they would band together and elect their own people to office. According to this argument, effective representation would ensure that the needs of Mexicans would be met at the local, state, and federal levels because "government" is viewed as being not only able but "willing" to take such action, even in behalf of disadvantaged groups. A pluralist myth lies at the heart of this liberal–conservative political assertion,[21] and indeed, liberal–conservative views dominate the analysis of Mexican political behavior. Such views, however, often are not only ahistorical but factually erroneous in their tendency to rely upon a partial analysis; they do not explain why political power continues to be inequitable, nor why the Mexican people in the United States continue to be impoverished; nor do they clarify the nonlinear pattern of political participation among the people.

To answer these questions several replies followed.[22] Such responses were not only efforts in comprehension; they also reflected forms of political advocacy as well as providing, in a few cases, expressions of explicit political practice. As such, they proved to be contributions which, in some cases, significantly extended the horizon of political understanding. Not surprisingly, initial criticism of the dominant views emphasized discrimination and electoral imperfections,[23] noting dominant and minority views and historicizing their analyses. Thus was orthodox liberalism extended to Mexican politics. In their haste to replace the dominant liberal interpretation with a more profound one, some social scientists proved to be too facile in suggesting an "internal colonial model," emphasizing a discrimination related to economic structures, and later suggesting consciousness and language as explanatory factors.

Drawn primarily from the African experience, the internal colonial model purportedly explains the histories of Indian, Black, and Mexican populations in the United States;[24] but to apply it to the Mexican people in the United States is to simplify and vulgarize their history in much the same way as the liberal, pluralistic, cultural-conflict explanations. The model emphasizes statistics selected during specific periods, pertaining to particular parts of the work force and its conditions and wages; and this critical economy is interspersed with stereotyped assertions drawn from the negative liberal literature. Though ostensibly concerned with the overall structure of domination, at the explanatory core of this model lies its belief in "racism" as a determinant factor. At best, a colonial model may apply to a few parts of the southwestern United States during the period of military and territorial administration. Ignoring the differing relationships of exploitation and character of institutions, the absence of a continuously formal segregation or of separate legal systems, and the rights to citizenship and the vote, the heterogeneity of Mexican political activity, as well as the unevenness of the political process, vitiates the internal colonial model. The model also suffers from an imposed structuralism which was derived from traditional social science and lacks a dynamic explanation for change. In addition to a tendency toward determinism, it incorporates an idealist emphasis on psychology through asserted psychological constructs and mind-set explanations. The colonial model is a descriptive generalization, a deceptive metaphor rather than a theory. For all its weaknesses, this model does underscore a structure of domination, the importance of labor and consciousness in political analysis, and the normative aspects of the paradigm of assimilation and integration. Because its imperfections have been noted even by its proponents, other efforts have succeeded.

Laudably, another series of attempts question how people think about reality as a means of understanding and ultimately changing their actions. The influence here was drawn from the debate between structuralism and poststructuralism, from the generational narcissism, and from postmodern anthropology, ethnography, and literary criticism as an exercise in self-reflection. The view of Chicano politics as "consciousness" is propounded by exponents of "language critical theory."[25] According to this mode, domination is primarily ideological in the realm of values; hence, political thought and activity are to be examined not by studying politics per se, but by studying "categories" of politics in general and as ascribed to mind-sets. In stressing language and communication, the interpretation is often couched in terms of an already superseded literary criticism. At worst, the emphasis deteriorates to an examination of the absence of consciousness among the dominated, focused epistemologically on the admonition of a need for consciousness, and on the study of critiques of power and those who hold it. To date, this kind of analysis has little to say about the political activity of the community—the so-called masses—other than to dismiss it as "false." For the realist, however, "politics begin where the masses are," and conventional descriptions and proscriptions for political activity exist side by side with others that pose an ongoing challenge to them.

In the 1980s, analysts generally sought to know politics both more extensively and more minutely, and to inform the political dynamic. Whatever their shortcomings, behavior-centered efforts, such as electoral studies and demographic analyses, had an immediate utility and method, chiefly due to their avowed emphasis on social science behaviorism. One such approach is the "scientistic" or positivist enumeration of empirical data, specifically statistics, which, it is argued, are the primary source for political analysis as a means of understanding immediate problems and avoiding the biases and disputation of interpretive discourse.[26] Voting figures and opinion surveys provide knowledge judged to be the most useful data concerning political empowerment. Such compilations of data are indeed useful, although they are also limited. While they illuminate a brief and limited point of a universe, it is, however, a multidimensional one. Yet they do not provide a basis upon which to judge the data they contain as either meaningless or meaningful.

Another modest trend is the insistence on examining the Chicano political experience in reference to civil rights organizations and their stated goals as a way of advising activity.[27] Indeed, this is a mode of looking at indigenous responses, governance practices, and public impact. What is claimed as unique is objective measurement and/or a harsh scrutiny of positive progress in statistically measured indicators on the quality of life or the espousal of assimilation and accommodation versus something which presumably is qualitatively different but unspecified. Ostensibly description is decried, as is the recording of pro-Mexican rights activity, although such a method provides the grist of these "studies," however selectively they approach their subject. This approach has been practiced by both conformists and nonconformists to system-centered activity. Often, the result is enumeration and ambiguous reporting. In all cases, however, the sum total of information and tentative interpretations has increased.

In the aftermath of the failure of the internal colonial framework, there were continued attempts to elaborate data by organizing frameworks dealing with race–class dichotomy. One such effort is the "race–class–ethnicity" shell game,[28] with the insistent attempt to fit the Mexican experience into a "race" paradigm and then, through sleight-of-hand rhetoric, to deny the importance of race in favor of the abstract category of class. Then when class is found wanting, the game returns to race, which is now referred to as ethnicity. Class analysis, however, must focus on class; hence, this shell will win the game, although much political reality may be left outside the shell. In part, this is a response to a perceived social dilemma—whether to stress culturalism or assimilation. There is also an ideological conundrum—reformism versus utopianism. Within the analytic discourse there was an ironic divergence. Those who were more conventional seemed closer to actual political practice, while those who were more structural and historical were farther from the political practice. Direct experience and reflection led to analyses premised on a critique of capitalism and ethnic pathology, while accounting for the dynamic to extend the space and activity for an evolution toward greater governmental and economic democracy for individuals and groups—for the Mexican community as well as the larger society, with both avowedly centered around the work place and the residence.[29]

Past and Current Political Models

Mexican politics need to be seen both as a phenomenon in itself and in its relation to the dominant society; also crucial is the way in which such seeing takes place. Both minority and majority societies form the context of Mexican politics. As both ideologies and theories, general frameworks for interpreting human society and its political sphere have implicit and explicit values.[30] Political thought and action are preeminently normative, as are political theories which interpret facts within the context of ideological assumptions about people and society as well as indicating class interests, falsifications, and ideals. Two types of normative theories govern interpretations: one stresses order, the maintenance of stability, while the other stresses conflict, or contradiction in the existing society. In the case of Mexican history, the concept of order would stress accommodation, assimilation, rewards, and mobility; the concept of conflict would stress resistance, assertive negotiation, exploitation, and insurgent culture. Both concepts provide explicitly long-range views of social change. To be sure, there are several theories of historical social change, but the most pertinent today are those that deal with equilibrium and conflict; both presume progress as the enhancement of the potential for perfecting the human condition. Equilibrium theories emphasize the maintenance of the system or of social order through functional integration, interdependence, and designed mechanisms; they view change as incremental and adjustive. Variant theories of conflict consider change as endemic to society, suggesting that it can be accomplished politically through conflictual mobilization and stressing structural innovation related to economic organization and an increase in communications, urbanization, and industrialization. Both conceptualizations are ideological attempts to explain the forces of political change over time; the elements within their typologies are not absolutely in contradiction, nor are their elements exclusive to one and not to the other. Both may be viewed, too, in relation to powerholding and the act of challenging power.

Standard explanations of Mexican politics and political behavior go beyond culturally or historically static paradigms or empirical measurements; they offer proscriptions, which are projected through the theory of equilibrium, or the liberal looking-glass. From the eighteenth century to the present, liberalism has been the dominant social and political ideology evident both in the literature and in the expression of public values that expound a real as well as a preferred economy and class position.[31] Ideas currently ranging from conservatism to liberalism comprise both the right and left wings of the spectrum of one general ideology that draws from theorists ranging from Hobbes, Spencer, and Bentham to Parsons, Samuelson, Friedman, and Lipset. Their theories stress stability and order, evolutionary incremental change, and an unchanging, self-centered human nature; and pose solutions to competition among different interests. They posit capitalism and plural representation as the best of all possible economic and political systems. In the domestically focused literature of political science in the United States, this interpretive mode, this set of beliefs, is known as pluralism, a set of ideological tenets which, not surprisingly, legitimize the practice of U.S. institutions, while also idealizing them. Thus, pluralism is partially an approximation, and a fiction; for some it offers a complete ideological and political scenario, while for others it provides a theology. In any case, it is, to date, the most prevalent practice as well as the prevailing interpretation.

Indeed, liberal pluralism partially corresponds to the image of the social order as well as to the social order functioning at the very general level.[32] Here, there exist eight suppositions: (1) the political system is separate operationally from the social structure and the economic system, though it does interact with both; (2) the government manages the society as an independent power arbitrator, and is determined in the aggregate by a "free" interplay of interest groups who are potentially empowered equally, while the majority of the electorate constitute "the people"; (3) power is distributed diffusely among many different branches, agencies, committees, and interest groups, and every significant interest can at some point gain access to the political system; (4) there is no "finality" in decision-making, and there are no permanently proscribed interests or groups; (5) the formation of an elite is based on a merit system, and the elite sector is as accessible as the system itself; (6) bargaining, compromise, and negotiation between competing elites are important; (7) those elected to governmental positions are attuned to the wishes of the electorate; and (8) there is a positive and adjustive ebb and flow between periods of consolidation and reform. All of these suppositions, of course, are based on others, two of which are particularly pertinent and need to be examined: the legitimacy of democracy and of pluralism in the dominant society.

While liberal pluralism serves a state and a particular sector of the society, it ill serves the study of politics, Mexican or otherwise. It not only stresses *order* as the norm; it advocates order because, simply put, order best serves so-called society. Society itself is viewed as a system

of enhancing action that is unified on a general level by a shared
culture, in which there exist communication, agreement on values,
and benefits for those within the political organization. Not surprisingly, *functions* that maintain the system and keep it in balance are
viewed positively, while success is defined as the maintenance of the
status quo. Balance, stability, authority, harmony, and equilibrium are
all emphasized. Empirical research derived from natural science measures gains and problems in relation to "ideals"; the ideal is, in short,
continuation. More pervasive is the class and culture bias of liberal
pluralism, which is clearly ahistorical and presents an idealized gen-
erality: supraindividual maintenance of the present system and status-
quo relationships. Here, there are said to exist no structural inequities,
only social "problems," or deviations and aberrations to be adjusted;
admittedly social "problems" may promote an imbalance in social organization and the possibility of threatened social control. At the
social level, individuals who fail to meet the maintenance needs of
the social system become "problems," deviations, so many abnormal-
ities. Ameliorative action in response to social problems extends political control through administrative solutions carefully confined within
the boundaries of the established political system. Change is advocated
through sanctioned reformers, reforms, and incremental adjustments.

The implications for United States class and minority relations
are clear. Appropriately relative equality becomes the optimum reward
based on conformity to the dominant set of values and behavior within
the system. Containment is achieved through socialization to dominant values created to maintain a class system; and the transition from
segregation to integration occurs within the generally sanctioned class
system. Minor differences are allowed only within the accepted framework of consensus. So-called "democratic," "elitist" or "cultural" theories of liberalism are all variations of the basic theory cited above,
and all are applied to the governing and economic system of the United
States. With varying emphases, they point to latitudes provided in
choosing candidates or parties; they argue that political equality is
"relative," that democracy does function on a participatory basis, that
the elite is based upon a meritocracy, and that cultural differences are
tolerated even though cultural homogenization is the ideal. Warnings
are delivered, however, to those who fail to conform. The alternatives
to the preferred game include a harsher domination through nationality as well as class mechanisms, or when nationality disintegrates,

through class exclusively. Liberal pluralism evolves as much as its system does. Derived from idealizations and the practice of groups favored within the United States, system-biased frameworks do bear some correspondence to various aspects of Mexican politics, though much of the relationship depends upon the historical reality of the United States and the role, perception, and assigned position of the Mexican in North American society. Such oversights may be summarized tentatively in a harsh but realistic set of generalizations that provide an alternative scenario of the context of Mexican American politics.

Real History, Real Understanding

To view the Mexican, it is necessary not only to examine the evolution of the United States, but to make an approximate historical interpretation of its political system.[33] English settlement on the northeastern coast of North America occurred at a time when European expansion was fueled by the competition among European states for wealth and power. The English established colonies that were so many smaller extensions of England itself. European settlers displaced, removed, or killed the native inhabitants, retrospectively proclaiming themselves a "new" people in a "new" and "empty" land. From the first, an economic, political, and ideological elite, standing distinctly apart from others, supervised the enterprise. There was also a subgroup composed of those who articulated and rationalized the views of the elite. Parallel to this group were the settlers themselves, the productive adjutants of the elite, as well as an indentured work force of whites who were not "free." Aggrandizement was the settler colony's overriding purpose; in practice, this meant relentless territorial expansion and the displacement of the Indians. Aggrandizement also required a large investment of labor, which was secured by the theft of people from Africa; their enslavement provided "free" labor in the colony, and this work force increased to major proportions. In status, free settlers were distinct qualitatively from both Blacks and indebted whites in their economic prerogatives and civil liberties; the latter meant that a person was free from encumbrances but not necessarily free otherwise. The colony was ruled by an economic and cultural elite, which sought further prerogatives to enhance its standing and wealth.

Upon attaining independence—which was not supported by over half
the population—political rights were explicitly restricted, with only
a minority allowed to vote; and the government was divided into three
branches, with the executive and judiciary permitted to veto or to
change the agreements reached by the legislative branch, the third
and relatively more representative but also more contentious and clum-
sier body. The judiciary was appointed for life by an executive who
could veto the acts of the legislature. Changes through amendments
of the basic government guidelines favoring the privileged were ex-
ceedingly difficult to achieve. Judges were not the only ones with no
ready accountability; a sector of appointed officials owed their appointments to others who held office and were not readily accountable
either. Furthermore, the republic was subdivided into a hierarchy of
units which safeguarded privilege at all levels, thwarting change except
in the most mundane matters. Four demographic sectors particularly
excluded were Indians; Blacks; the white and disgruntled poor, who
were accorded recognition even if negative; and women, who were
denied a civic presence. As it accelerated, aggrandizement required
infusions of extra labor from immigrants; and as Black free labor diminished and the need to maintain supportive sectors increased, international expansion also gained momentum. The need for stability
led to an overlapping, biparty electoral system which was dominated,
in effect, by interrelations among the elite. The majority of persons
were incapacitated politically; elected officials were not directly responsive or even informative to the minority that had elected them,
readily violating the pledges they had made to the limited electorate.
From the first, there were no "free" elections, and perhaps there could
not be, because they were controlled and manipulated, and often
fraudulent; the question was who would control, and the answer was
one or another faction of the elite. Sometimes these factions needed
support from the disenfranchised, and at other times they were excluded to win over their competitors. Crises also proved conducive to
dispensation. An immediate option for the disenfranchised, excluded,
and exploited was disruptive violence, which was engaged in repeatedly to gain, for the most part, only minor concessions. There were
concurrent efforts, in effect, to secure greater benefits, service, or
accountability from the government. Two avenues lay open for individual or sectoral amelioration: one was education, an effort in

changing class position; the other, the extension of suffrage, the attempt to become participants.

At the time of the Mexican "acquisition" in 1848 a restrictive
government characterized the United States: a very imperfect suffrage
system; government by regional and local oligarchy; an enormous slave
sector set off by race, with half of the population politically excluded
by gender and severely limited in its legal recognition. It was a society
of endemic violence, exuberantly obsessed with expansion, power,
and profit. It also had developed and inculcated a set of self-righteous
myths concerning its origins, destiny, ethos, governance, and economy, and providing ideological rationalization for the way it was. It
was also a deeply racist, discriminatory society. Yet even more important was its commitment to expansion. The Mexican was fitted
into this scheme and dealt with in a particular manner as were other
discriminated groups. Political response and change were produced by
crises and mobilization, and this evolution could be explained through
an examination of history; in particular, political history.

A satisfactory approach to political history, like general history,
interrelates a multiplicity of aspects and allows for their perception
and explanation,[34] taking into account contexts, perceptions, communications, governance, numbers, values, mobilization, advocacy,
impact, and responses. The whole is viewed as interdependent and
interrelated. The point of departure is the total historical record and
an evolving system, and ultimately the focus is the entire environment.
In effect, there exists a dialectic of need and response, organization
and thought. A more conventional and reductionist heuristic device
would include an interactive communication system premised on social
aspects of advocacy (inputs) and governance (conversion) responses,
that is, policies (outputs) which impact, in turn, on the society.
Ethnicity, class, and culture determine that the majority of the Mexican people exist in a special relationship to the larger society of the
United States. A system of domination involves and is expressed in
labor, in socialization, and in governance entities. Forces active within
the community contribute to a particular dynamic within it, and whose
most salient characteristic is its persistent, if assaulted, consciousness.
Certainly, the Mexican community lies within the larger context of
United States society, and is organically a part of its economy and
intellectual climate. On the other hand, there are influences and
conditions not only related to Mexico in particular, but with broader

international phenomena that have impact on the community: migration and its ramifications, ideas, the economy, and political events. The Mexican's status in the southwestern United States, a minority territorial enclave, is analogous to several generally similar situations in different parts of the world. What this situation produces and the actions it engenders are important in the community's historical formation, in its historical patterns and in politics, including socioeconomic relations, forced deculturalization, class and caste features, institutional oppression, and the historical movement of ethnic resistance and assertion. The complexity of this historical experience makes it unique in the historical analysis of minority groups. In any case, its actions and the actions of the dominant society are both real and rational.

Real Politics: Guiding Generalizations

Mexican politics is an expression of conscious economic and cultural struggle, a conflict of interests engendered by exploitation and a conflict stemming from the group oppression under which Mexicans live. Persistence is facilitated by oppression. Historically and operatively, there exists in the United States an undeniably stratified class structure. The economic class structure is one characteristic of a private enterprise, corporate capitalist economy. A high level of integration and interpenetration exists between the economic and political spheres; and language, communication, and education are manipulated to maintain the structure and its system.[35] Public policy is developed through the relationships of powerful groups that share economic power and a general consensus on values and priorities; they share resources among themselves and provide for others. The system propels the politics of self-interest, a conflictual and elitist situation requiring exact and increasingly costly resources and thus further delimiting its practicing players. As grievances arise, preservation of the system compels occasional and circumscribed adjustment. At play is an aesthetic vision of community as the ideal society, whose achievement involves stratagems as well as a way of acting within and judging them.

Politics may be understood amply through historical analysis because its presentation of the dynamic for change is more comprehensive. The record, however, is at its core—the documentation of human action. Historically, the relation between the dominant political system, its fostered socialization, and the economy translates for the dominated into a nonconforming consciousness and the active conflict of insurgent politics, while for the dominant it means an adjustment to ensure their continued power.

Society is an arena of conflict whose principal characteristic is an unequal distribution of resources. A strategy incumbent upon the ruling group attempts to ensure an inequality among social sectors and component elements of the society which is concurrent with the rationalization necessary for more effective control. Conflict arises in response to the status quo, generating calls for positive change. Such action attempts to move society toward qualitative growth. While political demands are universal human needs they are also relative demands made by particular contenders for power. Social inequities and problems arise from the exploitative practices of the dominant groups, therefore reflecting the deficiency of society as well as impelling change. Inevitably, the legitimacy of existing practices and values is questioned to some extent. Inequities and problems may be identified potentially in such a way that would require a radical and structural transformation of existing patterns of society rather than conformity. The practice, however, elaborates adjustments which are considered only when the demand for change is unavoidable. Political action aims at the redistribution of resources, which, in turn, involves questions of power and control in the social structure as a whole and the relationship between dominant and subordinate groups.

The premises for the relationship between dominant and subordinate groups are explicit in the economic relations and the concomitant institutional patterns of society. Changes in the economy and its general character are basic to political changes, and who rules over all is key. The important decisions are economic ones; they are pervasive in the governing process as aspects of both appeal and response. The elite also undergoes an internal transformation that bears a changing relation to direct economic activities as well as to direct political responsibilities. Equally significant is the evolving differentiation of the other classes—particularly the wage earners and middle-level sectors—as they confront their subordination. A particular subordinate–dominant relation and its ongoing contention is but a scene in a world drama. Society ceased long ago to be merely local; it is international, and the international system of the nineteenth through the late twentieth centuries impacts on domestic politics.

Real politics involves conscious individuals acting rationally in pursuing their interests through serious engagement over substantive issues in the multifaceted public arena of the masses. The areas of dispute are economic, cultural, governmental. Political struggle and politics stem from acts upon the society and its sustaining economy. Political interplay may subsume economic and ideological conflicts, but its causes are multiple. Politics can purposely direct both quantitative and qualitative change. Multiple variables which intersect the community political struggle group into areas of class, ideology, and identity, each of which interacts and crosscuts with the others. An examination of the political struggle in the Mexican community, then, focuses on the assertion of and adjustment to social and economic forces expressed politically by subgroups and their leaders, and according to evolving goals, strategies, and organizations. Within this interplay lies a historical memory as well as a partial vision of a future—the negation of what is oppressive in the past.

2

The Promise and the Reality
from 1941 to the 1960s

The War Years and the Needed Minority

From World War II to the 1960s the acceleration of Mexican
political activity resulted from the changes and contradictions particular to the wars of the time as well as, of course, changes in the
economy and the demographic increase in the community.[1] The continuous Mexican impetus sounded a major part of the tempo, which
was also quickened, slowed, or interfered with by government, creating
a context for political advocacy and activity. Obviously, the expanding
economic and political process antedated World War II; and in the
past, results were uneven. As the national economy grew, so did
government, and the expansion in both areas coincided with population growth. Between 1940 and 1960 the community doubled in
size, from approximately two and one-half million to five million; yet
regional and subregional concentration continued. Though the majority of the members of the community were native-born, a significant
number were under voting age while, just as crucially, many adults
were immigrants. Politically, the community continued to be affected
by anti-Mexican sentiments, lower incomes, and lower levels of education. While Mexican culture did not impede political participation,
the culture of the dominant society did. Despite obstacles, telling
changes occurred: more Mexicans attended schools, more spoke English, more became citizens, and more lived in large urban concentrations.[2] There were also net gains for some in income, education,

and occupational diversity as well as relatively more geographic dispersal for the community as a whole.

And as in the past, class and organizational diversity and vitality continued.[3] Organizationally, while *mutualistas* and previous service groups persisted, new ones emerged. Socially, a variety of subsectors were contained within the parameters of the community. Apart from the six or more layered class configurations were the subsectors of the multigenerational elite, the prominence of middle-class exile families, the industrial workers, the rural communities in contrast to the urban, and the slightly better off native-born in contrast to the poorer recent immigrants. Also continuous were exploitation and poverty and their consequences, as well as large-scale deportations. The review and treatment of Mexicans were revealed in the Zoot Suits and Sleepy Lagoon incidents.

Communication remained less than adequate. Compared to the past, publications declined in number and quality. The two major Spanish-language newspapers, *La Opinion* (Los Angeles) and *La Prensa* (San Antonio), were moderate in their views and less compelling in their writing than in previous decades, and the former did not survive. Except for their greater sympathy, the smaller local papers, such as *El Sol* (Phoenix) and *El Universal* (Corpus Christi), were not markedly different in their views than other local English newspapers. Mexico City–based publications, such as *Hoy* and *Siempre*, circulated in southwestern communities. Obviously some changes in communication were significant for the future. Commercial English-language radio providing music became part of the household and did much to stimulate English among the young; on the other hand, Spanish-language radio increased its audience and helped to make up for the decline in readership of Spanish-language journalism. For the most part, however, radio was owned outside the community. The new medium, television, was at first exclusively English, and only later did Spanish-language programming become available. Television's tremendous impact, however, soon superseded print and audio as the means for knowing events; and the medium was wholly controlled outside the community. Politically, while it brought into the home visually national and international events as well as political personalities and occurrences, it also made local political networks and leadership less important as conduits and organizers.

The ongoing evolution reflected previously uneven impacts in other

ways.[4] For Mexicans, reform movements of the Populist–Progressive
and the New Deal eras had only a modest impact, with the latter
excluding many who were farm workers or were not citizens. War had
a much greater impact, greatly enriching corporations and weakening
the militancy of labor; and Mexicans suffered the consequences. From
1932 to 1952, Democrat liberals dominated the executive branch, and
for an even longer time, they were potent in Congress. This partisan
government was responsible for the state of Mexicans in America.
Furthermore, United States trade unions, even though they were at
their zenith, did not support Mexican improvement either proactively
or extensively. Not as strong in political influence as their numbers
deserved, unions were important nationally though not necessarily
comparable in the Southwest. Unionization among Mexicans did increase, and electoral benefits were combined with others which ac-
crued. Unions, however, were negatively affected by domestic Cold
War politics and rhetoric, and Mexican members felt the consequences. The Mexican government, another erratic but potential source
of support, did move adamantly to protest persecution, discrimination,
and wage despoliation in a number of instances, but not to the extent
warranted by circumstances. To be sure, the United States government
ignored the admonitions of the Mexican government whenever it
chose to do so.

Shared experiences, an improving economy, a massive formative
process for many, and propagandized appeals were all part of the war
and postwar periods.[5] Despite wartime social tensions and continuing
discrimination, the ideological climate of the war, which pitted democracy against fascist tyranny, begged questions on the extent of
electoral, economic, or social democracy within the United States.
For those who experienced persecution, exploitation, disenfranchisement, and discrimination firsthand, the extent of democracy was limited; and many also questioned the Western powers' foreign policy in
general, given their avowed commitment to retain their formal and
de facto colonies. Despite the less than optimum conditions, Mexican
organizations, the Mexican community, and Mexican servicemen
overwhelmingly supported the war effort; and therefore, because of
their evident contribution, they expected equities. Their political
legitimacy was viewed as fortified. Wartime promises of equality led
to a new optimism in the Mexican communities of the United States
regarding the postwar period. Things would be different, better, after

the "war for democracy" in which perhaps 400,000 Mexican Americans served in the armed forces. Not one was charged with desertion or treason, and they suffered casualties above the proportion of their number. They were awarded a notable record of commendations and no doubt earned more than they received, given the attitude of Anglo officers. The rule was frontline duty for Mexicans. "Mexican Americans," to use the term which was first popularized at this time, had proven their tenacity in every major battle of the war. Axis troops never had reason to doubt that they were "American troops," and it was hoped that Anglo Americans might recognize them as fellow citizens. However exceptional their attitude may have been, many Mexicans in leadership possibilities had learned to view themselves as the dominant society saw them and to understand that progress meant adjusting to its demands and parroting its values. Because their politics were shaped by and were a reflection of the larger, dominant society, their leadership on the whole remained marginal and, with a few exceptions, was viewed as such, no matter how hard it tried to please.

Neither Services Nor Employment, But Some Attention

Massive wartime publicity campaigns for "democracy," the avowed commitment to equal citizenship, and the manipulative promise of continuing economic prosperity following the war also led Mexicans, along with most other North Americans, to anticipate a kind of post-war economic utopia.[6] At the same time, there was a limited but significant change in the policy of some federal government agencies toward Mexican Americans. In 1941 President Franklin D. Roosevelt had issued Executive Order 8802, which asserted nondiscrimination in war industries. A Fair Employment Practices Committee (FEPC) was appointed. For the first time, through the Fair Employment Office and the Coordinating Committee on Latin American Affairs, there was a limited recognition by the federal government of the Mexican community in a positive sense. Previously, Mexican Americans had been considered by federal policymakers in the contexts of the debate over the Treaty of Guadalupe Hidalgo and statehood for southwestern territories, and in the context of the immigration debate of the 1900s within which they were considered as a basically foreign rather than domestic population.

The economic, production, and social demands of World War II required wartime policies for efficient utilization of labor resources and for minimizing dissidence; these policies implicitly included Mexicans, Blacks, Indians, and other non-Anglo Americans.[7] At the same time, the leaders of Mexican organizations and the few elected representatives who were Mexicans actively sought equal employment opportunity and an end to discriminatory hiring policies. Efforts by Mexican American organizations ranging from the steadfast, rising League of United Latin American Citizens and the erratic Alianza Hispano-Americana to the dwindling Congress of Spanish-Speaking People had begun before the war when Mexican Americans had sought access to New Deal employment programs. However, not until additional labor was urgently needed by wartime industry did a few government officials become seriously interested in the issue of employment discrimination. A related concern was the public relations problem posed for wartime cooperation with Latin American states by the widespread reality of anti-Latin American feelings manifested directly by domestic discrimination against Mexicans, Puerto Ricans, and other Latin Americans in the United States. Most immediately, anti-Mexican prejudice had posed an obstacle to the proposed negotiation of the labor agreement with Mexico which would become the Bracero Program. Suggestions for a program to improve Anglo American–Mexican American relations surfaced in 1941 with the establishment of the Office of the Coordinator of Inter-American Affairs (CIAA), headed by Nelson D. Rockefeller. As noted by Carey McWilliams, first an observer and then California's Commissioner of Immigration and Housing, he and a number of others, including Dr. Joaquin Ortega of the University of New Mexico, Dr. George I. Sanchez of the University of Texas, and Arizona legislator C. J. Carreon, made similar suggestions for an educational program to improve these relations.

In April 1942, after a field survey in the Southwest conducted by an aide, Rockefeller acted to establish a Spanish-Speaking People's Division of the Office of Inter-American Affairs. The division's initial phase was, however, something of a farce, and as observed by McWilliams at this time:

In many ways the division acted as though it wanted to frustrate any real efforts on the part of Spanish-speaking people to improve their lot. Some of the field representatives seemed to be actually afraid of Mexican Americans, for they insisted on working with the least representative elements in the various Spanish-speaking communities.

On the board of the Southern California Council on Inter-American Affairs, subsidized by the CIAA, not a single Spanish-speaking person appeared although a local Mexican Affairs Coordinating Committee was set up to advise the council. This cleavage perpetuated, of course, the basic fault in Anglo-Hispanic relations.[8]

It was not until the crisis of Anglo violence in the Zoot Suit Riots was reportedly exploited by German shortwave-radio broadcasts to Mexico and Latin America that modest efforts were made by the CIAA to work with Mexican American organizations and educators.

In Mexico, which was one of the United Nations allied with the United States against the Axis powers, concern with anti-Mexican prejudice reached the point that official strong protests were made to Washington.[9] Prominent Mexicans, including the noted diplomat Jaime Torres Bodet, formed the "Comité Mexicano Contra el Racismo" to demand that the U.S. government guarantee the human rights of Mexican nationals and Mexican Americans in the United States. Action stemming from the Mexican government provided significant leverage in ameliorating a "plant" situation of prejudice. This was possible because of wartime exigencies placed upon Washington and because there was a will among some Mexican officials to exert pressure while they had leverage, which they did, in regard to discrimination, violence, and wages. Later, however, they lost that leverage.

Between 1943 and 1945, the CIAA's Spanish-Speaking People's Division was revamped to support educational efforts designed to improve Anglo American–Mexican American relations and to support selected community and youth programs. A series of unprecedented national conferences were funded by the CIAA, in cooperation with the National Catholic Welfare Conference.[10] The first such meeting was the seminar on "The Spanish-Speaking People of the Southwest and the West," held in San Antonio, Texas, in July 1943. These conferences involved the active participation of Mexican American educators and elected officials. Among the most influential Mexican American participants were Senator Dennis Chavez of New Mexico; Dr. George I. Sanchez, a professor at both the University of New

Mexico and the University of Texas; Dr. Carlos E. Castaneda, Professor of History at the University of Texas; the veteran San Antonio attorney Alonso S. Perales; and Los Angeles civic leader Eduardo Quevedo. Later, the "First Regional Conference on Education of the Spanish-Speaking People in the South West" was held at Austin, Texas, on December 13–15, 1945. School segregation and curriculum bilingualism were major concerns.

These conferences were an effort to bring together a group of prominent Mexican American civic and education leaders with their Anglo American counterparts to discuss issues over a nonpartisan table. Especially significant was the effort by Mexican Americans from Texas to influence legislative action to guarantee civil and human rights. Active in this regard were the Tejanos, Alonso S. Perales and Dr. Carlos E. Castaneda, who worked with such Anglo Texans as the Roman Catholic Archbishop of San Antonio, Robert E. Lucey. Their efforts, together with the publicly stated threat by the Mexican government to bar Texas from the Bracero Program because of anti-Mexican prejudice, prompted the governor of Texas in 1943 to form the Texas Good Neighbor Commission to improve relations with Mexico and those between Texas Anglos and Mexican Americans. Encouraged by the possibility of profit losses, this committee provided an early precedent for later trans-border committees; however, its origins and focus intertwined the domestic and foreign in an unsatisfactory way.

The efforts of Texas Mexicans and a few sympathetic Anglo Americans resulted in a few significant works and several magazine and newspaper articles exposing discriminatory practices against Mexicans.[11] Unfortunately, the Texas Good Neighbor Commission was never intended to possess sanctional or investigatory powers, and thus politically it was viewed by state officials and the legislature primarily as a public relations effort. Antidiscriminatory measures recommended by the commission—by leaders such as Alonso Perales—and supported by the League of United Latin American Citizens (LULAC) would never be acted upon. It would take a more broadly based civil rights and legal effort, spearheaded by postwar membership groups such as the American G.I. Forum, to advocate more effectively the enforcement of basic civil rights for Texas Mexicans.

In California, despite efforts by Mexican organizations to address

the issue of employment discrimination, CIAA, state and local government efforts emphasized youth activities because of the public media
perception of a "problem" of Mexican juvenile delinquency, which
was associated with the image of the "Pachucos" and the "Zoot Suit
Riots."A student and young adult organization dating from the thirties,
the Mexican American Movement (MAM) had its own explanation
and solution:

The neglect of these sociological problems can be traced back to the first
days of Mexican immigration to the United States. The failure of our
institutions to assimilate the Mexican citizens into the channels of
American citizenship laid the first foundation to recent troubles.

As leaders of the Mexican-American Movement, we are interested in
improving the general conditions of the Mexican-Americans living in the
United States. We assume the responsibility because we see the lack of
leadership among our group.[12]

Integration and citizenship were mentioned, but what drew attention
was the "problem." Particular attention focused upon youth programs
and, apart from formally funded efforts, a variety of social and recreational youth groups appeared across the Southwest, at high schools
and on playgrounds or in association with churches and the civic
organizations with larger memberships. Though the problem lay not
in the youth but in the discrimination they endured, in any case, the
result was in some much needed funding for youth recreation programs
that involved visible civic activists such as Eduardo Quevedo, who
became the president of the Coordinating Council for Latin American
Youth in Los Angeles, California, while attorney Manuel Ruiz was
named executive secretary. In Colorado, CIAA field workers were
involved in the organization of the Latin American Service Clubs in
1944, a community service–type organization. Efforts also extended
to the Midwest, where Frank Paz (Pax), president of the Spanish
Speaking People's Council of Chicago, sought to focus on fair employment in the defense industries.[13] Centered in Southern California
and drawing from several colleges, MAM, though it often disparaged
youth or depreciated the community, was one youth and young adult
association with several dozen members which continued to be active,
though sporadically, from the thirties through the fifties. Laudably, it
focused on educational and leadership enhancement, and for a few
years it published its bulletin and held occasional conferences.

An Economic Notion

Soon after the establishment of the President's Committee on Fair Employment Practices (FEPC) in June 1941, Mexican elected officials and organizations sought to obtain federal action against the virtual exclusion of Mexican Americans from employment in certain war industries and in certain categories of employment.[14] New Mexico's Senator Dennis Chavez, the only Mexican American member of the United States Senate, was a spokesman in the debate for fair employment legislation. Senator Chavez was also especially active in holding Senate subcommittee hearings on the Fair Employment Practices Act, which focused upon discrimination against Mexicans, Blacks, and other groups. Because of White House inconsistency, FEPC suffered from inadequate funding and its organizational status, and hoped for compliance through informal negotiations. The FEPC was stymied frequently. In 1942 State Department pressure cancelled the scheduled FEPC hearings on "Spanish Mexican" discrimination. In 1944 southern senators launched a major attack that intimated its director. Senator Chavez was among its few main defenders.

Dennis Chavez worked in consultation with many of the same civic activists involved in CIAA, including Dr. Carlos E. Castaneda, Alfonso Perales, Eduardo Quevedo, Samuel Paz, and Ignacio López as well as Ernesto Galarza, who was a staff member of the Pan American Union Labor Secretary. As with the CIAA, the Fair Employment Practices Committee practically ignored the concerns of Mexican Americans about widespread job discrimination until 1943. The most successful efforts, not surprisingly, were in FEPC Region 10 (Texas, New Mexico, and Arizona), whose regional director was Dr. Carlos E. Castaneda.[15] In California, FEPC officials apparently made little or no effort to publicize the program of the agency to the Mexican community. In spite of this lethargy, Ignacio López, who was appointed a Special Examiner, attempted to persuade the FEPC to use radio advertising to reach the community. Given the size of the Los Angeles war industry, it is ironic that many of the same employers who recruited and job-educated hundreds of thousands of Anglo war workers from the East Coast openly declared that they would not hire Mexicans because white employees would not work with them: "it is not the policy of the company, but the inability of the workmen already in their employ to get along with Mexican laborers, that dictates refusal

to employ them." In fact, job discrimination in skilled industrial occupations would continue throughout as well as after the war, and
until technological change demoted these skills. Only in New Mexico,
and then only with pressure from Senator Chavez, were significant
efforts made by the state to place Mexican Americans in the war
industries. In 1945 FEPC was defunded, and at its end the dwindling
staff prepared a report that recommended (1) public informational
outreach and adequate enforcement; (2) adequate reporting by agencies of employment within industries and occupations, and (3) a permanent FEPC. Discrimination in employment, housing, education,
and services was yet to be effectively addressed.

The strategy and tactics of Mexican American organizations during
the war emphasized working in cooperation with authorities and institutions because of the dedication to the allied war effort expressed
by Mexican American community spokespersons.[16] Thus, for a period
of years, leaders and groups practiced primarily a cooperative mode,
holding to the expectation that rights would prevail through the good
sense of Anglo administrators. Prewar Mexican American community
activists, such as those in the Congress of Spanish-Speaking People
and the Mexican American Movement, were especially committed to
the war effort. There were, of course, exceptions to the acquiescent
mode, and these were reflected by the strike activity of Mexican trade
unionists such as the International Union of Mine, Mill, and Smelter
Workers—whose employers tried to take advantage of the wartime
situation to increase profits at the expense of safety conditions—and
the Agricultural and Citrus Workers Union. Unfortunately, public
officials and institutions did not view Mexican American sacrifices as
equities and failed to respond in substantive ways to ensure equality
in the workplace or civically. To Anglo elites, problems of discrimination against Mexicans, as well as their poverty or disenfranchisement,
were to be dealt with only partially, and then only as aspects of other
concerns. An appearance of harmonious civic relations led to emphasis
on youth clubs, youth counseling, and youth recreational facilities.
In education, segregation was addressed because it interfered with
assimilation; but parents were advised to conform to school administrators, and vocational classes were the rule. Employment opportunities meant going to work in housing projects or, at most, as riveters
or sheet metal handlers—rather than employment in skilled industrial

tasks. Ethnicity, minority status, and Mexican origin were again deemphasized. Mexicans were asserted to be white, Latin, or Spanish Americans, and negative disassociation from Blacks was part of the package. Mediator or buffer groups, such as the Coordinating Council for Latin American Youth in Los Angeles, were less urgent or useful at war's end; in Los Angeles this group held a "Postwar Congress" during October 1945, where it released a set of resolutions and apparently dispersed.

Actions by government agencies of the more traditionally negative variety did not cease.[17] Police agencies, prosecutors, and the courts proved to be as harsh as they had been before the war. Incidents of police brutality occurred continually throughout the postwar years. Significantly, police surveillance of even moderate and conservative groups became a practice, while efforts to disrupt the organizing of Mexican workers through public agencies also continued. Immigration, border, and customs agencies conducted massive campaigns against Mexicans; and those functioning under the rubric of "Operation Wetback" committed appalling violations of human and civil rights. In the forties, fifties, and sixties, government agencies also removed Mexicans from their homes, a consequence of "urban renewal." Government services often were either indifferent or actively hostile to Mexicans, and the attempt to bring about a change in this practice became part of the agenda of every Mexican American group.

Continuing Issues, Advocacy, and Figures

After World War II several incremental changes occurred in the Mexican community. The demand for labor by an expanding wartime and postwar economy quickened Mexican urbanization, with more workers than ever before entering skilled and semiskilled positions.[18] There was also a noticeable increase in the educational achievement levels of some Mexicans. The G.I. Bill aided many Mexican veterans in gaining a college education. While the economy was generally prosperous and expanded throughout the 1950s and into the 1960s, the political climate was adversely conditioned by the Cold War, the Korean War, and the drive of the United States for world hegemony. Within a context advocating conformity, optimism, and consumerism, Mexicans formulated and sought to defend their political goals and

interests, which were influenced greatly by the particular discrimination they endured.

Goals and ideology reflected experience as well as the possibilities
available. Pauline R. Kibbie stated for Texas what were, in fact, the
particulars of the negative case for Mexican Americans across the
entire Southwest during the midforties:

Economic Discrimination. (1) Unfair employment practices forcing low
economic status upon the majority of Latin Americans. (2) Discrimination
exercised by both management and Labor unions in the admission and
upgrading of Latin Americans. (3) Exploitation in agriculture. (4) Demand
of growers for cheap labor carried to the extreme of favoring illegal
seasonal influx workers, thereby denying employment opportunities to
resident workers.

Inequitable Educational Opportunities. (1) Arbitrary segregation in public
schools. (2) Inability of working children to attend schools. (3) Lack of
interest of school administrators in enrolling Latin American children and
encouraging attendance. (4) Improperly trained teachers and inferior
buildings and equipment.

Social and Civic Inequalities. (1) Refusal of service in some public places of
business and amusement. (2) Denial of the right to vote in some counties.
(3) Denial of the right to rent or own real estate in many cities. (4)
Denial of the right to serve on juries in some counties. (5) Terrorism on
the part of law-enforcement officers and others.[19]

Underpinning such issues was a poverty that observers such as Robert
Coles found appalling nearly twenty years later. A set of common
attitudinal experiences was also evident. Prior to the war, Manuel
Gamio had found:

The darkest-skinned Mexican experiences almost the same restrictions as
the Negro, while a person of medium-dark skin can enter a second class
lunchroom frequented also by Americans of the poorer class, but will not
be admitted to a high-class restaurant. A Mexican of light-brown skin as a
rule will not be admitted to a high-class hotel, while a white cultured
Mexican will be freely admitted to the same hotel, especially if he speaks
English fluently.[20]

A young college graduate said to Ruth Tuck:

Discrimination? Of course, all of my life, since I was a little boy. I make my way, I enjoy myself, I have good Anglo-American friends, in spite of it, but I never forget.[21]

There were variations, however. An older, and by Mexican standards, successful man told Ruth Tuck:

I don't know why it is, but I've had to fight ever since I first crossed the threshold of a public school. Even now, I seldom sit down in a restaurant without expecting the waiter to come up and say, "Sorry, we can't serve you." I'm careful to go where I know such things won't happen, but I still half expect them.[22]

And the optimistic belief of the time was expressed by an ex-serviceman:

I'm glad I'm going to have one of those little [service] buttons to wear in my coat. And a flock of foliage to put on my uniform for Armistice Day parades. I'm going into politics. There's seven or eight of us, all from Southern California, who've talked it over. Things are going to happen in these colonies [barrios], and we're going to see that they do.[23]

Economic and social progress for the Mexican was identified primarily with combating discrimination in employment, schools, public facilities, and housing, and in registering large numbers of people to vote, people who in turn would elect as well as influence the appointment of effective representatives.[24]

The focus on integration into conventional United States institutional practices, especially when unattended by aggressive activity in social and cultural matters, weakened the thrust of civic and electoral activism. Although Mexican immigration continued to increase, there were no major efforts to incorporate immigrants into the process of community activism; there were, however, concerted attempts to persecute Mexican workers which were combined with anti-Mexican propaganda campaigns and police actions. It was also a time of conservative, stable, and markedly pro-U.S. administrations in Mexico, where the left, with several notable exceptions, had no significant outreach to immigrants, and both implicitly and generally deemphasized politically the "Mexico de Afuera." Integration and participation were the norms governing Mexican political ideas in the United

States as well as a set of ideological tenets associated with the term "Mexican American." Ideally, political behavior would be cooperative with supportive elements, with liberals, and naturally with the fallacious expectation that this would provide leverage and space to maneuver. Overlooked was intentional exclusion by liberals and the lack of constituency organization by Mexicans. In practice, Mexicans increased their close relationship with the Democratic Party; and members of the middle class, particularly businessmen, continued to stress their right to leadership.

The Pan American Progressive Association (PAPA) of San Antonio, formed in August 1947, as well as burgeoning or newborn Mexican or Mexican American Chambers of Commerce, attested regionally to political practices.[25] PAPA stressed economics and leadership:

We believe that a foundation has been laid and that the time has come for *concerted* effort of Mexican-American people to gain the economic security and higher standards of living necessary to attain social equality. WE ALSO BELIEVE THIS EFFORT MUST COME FROM WITHIN OUR OWN GROUP.

Like many other "new" Americans, Mexican-American people have been undergoing a turbulent process of acculturation to the American social system. Our people are faced with the "acid test" of social adjustment and they are therefore in great need of the assistance that can be furnished by experienced leadership. Their abilities and potentialities are great—they must be guided and trained.

The PAPA is in strategic position to provide this Leadership and Guidance.

PAPA exhibited a structural twist. It was constituted by a contributing board of donors from which a ten-person executive council was chosen. They hired an executive secretary. Others could join on an at-large basis, and several dozen did. PAPA was motivated by felt community needs, but it failed because of its attempt to advance such needs too adamantly, in the judgment of some members.

Ironically, the politically repressive environment of the McCarthy era and the more moderate milieu of Eisenhower's second term and Kennedy's administration were addressed by the Mexican leadership with nearly similar political ideas and behavior.[26] As they acted to protest discrimination, they demonstrated a defensive commitment to expressing loyalty and patriotism; a fear of addressing any problem that might cast doubt on the community's or individual's patriotism; and zealous devotion to staying within the conventions and accepted norms of behavior of the society and its institutions. While institutional loyalty was often expressed as patriotism, there was also negative self-assertion, with Mexicans projecting stereotypical faults as a way of explaining themselves and of revealing alleged failings to be corrected by becoming more culturally Anglo. These self-limiting attitudes and beliefs exalting the value of traditional politics shaped Mexican organizational behavior. One extreme pronouncement referred to the colonization of California as memorable because it had stopped the Russian threat 150 years earlier. What was expected and what was accepted was ideological loyalty to the existing order, not simply patriotism vis-à-vis an enemy at war. For a person to be Mexican and radical was to be doubly suspect; thus, assurances to the contrary were common in the rhetoric of community representatives.

The Mexican political experience in New Mexico continued to be unique in comparison to other states. Because of the state's relatively large percentage of Mexican American population, Mexican politicians could wield significant political power at the state and federal levels of government.[27] In New Mexico, Mexicans were actively courted by both parties because occasionally in the past they had provided a swing vote. Furthermore, leadership tended to be both continuous and stable. Voter turnout was enhanced by the greater percentage of adult citizens and local vote-delivering networks.

New Mexico was the only state with a Mexican American U.S. senator, Dennis Chavez, who served in the Senate from 1935 to 1962.[28] As a Democrat and a member of the New Mexico House of Representatives during the 1920s, Chavez reflected the shift of Mexican American voters away from the Republican Party. From 1930 to 1935 Chavez served in the U.S. House of Representatives as one of New Mexico's two congressmen. He was reelected to five terms in some bitter and closely contested electoral campaigns; particularly fraught with charges was the election of 1952, which he won by five thousand votes. Arguably, Chavez was the most influential federal official until the late twentieth century. His most memorable interventions involved the establishment of the Fair Employment Practices Committee and the National Labor Relations Act. In foreign relations, he was a strong advocate for mutually benefitting Mexico–United States relations, and he was recognized for this stance by the Mexican government. At his death he was the fourth-ranking member of the Senate; more importantly, he was the most active advocate for Mexican Americans nationally.

In addition to Chavez, New Mexico continued to elect other Mexicans to Congress.[29] In 1942, former New Mexico state representative Antonio Fernandez eventually succeeded Chavez in the U.S. House of Representatives. Fernandez, who gained a reputation as an efficient but moderate congressman, was reelected a total of seven times and served until his death from a heart attack in October 1956. The next Nuevo Mexicano to serve in the U.S. Congress was Democrat Joseph Montoya, descendent of a settler family. The son of a deputy sheriff from Peña Blanca, Sandoval County, and a law school graduate of Georgetown University, he was elected to the House of Representatives in 1957 in a special election to fill Fernandez's former seat.[30] Montoya was first elected to the New Mexico State House of Representatives in 1936, when he was still a law student and too young to be able to vote himself. Eventually, he became Democratic floor leader. From 1941 to 1946, when he served in the New Mexico State Senate, Montoya was the only Mexican legislator who did not support a state FEPC. Between 1946 and 1951, Montoya served two terms as lieutenant governor of New Mexico. Because of a limitation on two consecutive terms, he served another term as state senator between 1953 and 1954, and he was elected to a third term as lieutenant governor in 1954.

After Montoya's election to the U.S. Congress in 1957, he served in the U.S. House of Representatives until 1964, where he was a member of the influential House Appropriations Committee. Following the death of U.S. Senator Dennis Chavez in 1962, Montoya was viewed by some as his logical successor, and according to the so-called gentlemen's agreement by which one of New Mexico's new U.S. Senators would be a Nuevo Mexicano. However, Anglo American Republican Governor Edwin L. Mechem, as others before him, did not follow this unwritten agreement, and took the U.S. Senate seat. In any case, Montoya was an unusually experienced elected official, and in 1964 he was elected to the Senate; later he was reelected for a second term. He served on the Appropriations and Public Works committees and on the Select Committee on Small Business. His initial emphasis was consumer protection pertinent to toys, articles, and fabrics; he was best known in the community for his lead coauthorship of the Bilingual Education Act (1968), for the bill establishing the Cabinet Committee on Opportunities for Spanish-Speaking Americans (1969), and for the resolution initiating the National Hispanic Heritage Week (1976). He played a modest role in Mexico–United States relations, and became a moderate critic of the Vietnam War; but he received the most attention for serving on the Senate committee investigating the Watergate affair. In 1976 he was defeated for reelection by astronaut Harrison Schmitt, an electoral novice but one who enjoyed great publicity. Moreover, Montoya's base had eroded due to the changing economy and to his own inattentiveness, but also because the type of voter who had supported him previously now came to the polls in fewer numbers. With the election of Republican Manuel Lujan to Congress in 1968, New Mexico had two Mexican representatives in Washington, D.C., for a few years.

Both Montoya and Lujan arose in New Mexico politics at a time of demographic shift and ethnic tensions.[31] There was apprehension that Hispanos were losing ground. In 1948 Dennis Chavez declared that unless a Hispano was elected governor the community would decline politically. In a dramatic response to this call, Ralph Gallegos ran in the Democratic primary and Manuel Lujan in the Republican, with Gallegos losing. In the general election, influential Hispanic Democrats supported Lujan in his battle with an Anglo Democrat, but Lujan still lost. In 1950, U.S. District Court Judge David Chavez, the brother of Senator Chavez, ran and lost in a bitter campaign. In other state politics, fortunes were better but still provided a cause to worry. New Mexicans had run for governor in three highly charged contests in 1948 and 1950, and had lost all three. However, several Nuevo Mexicanos served as lieutenant governor of New Mexico between 1940 and 1960: Ceferino Quintana, from 1939 to 1942; Joseph Montoya, from 1946 to 1951 and from 1954 to 1956; and Tibo J. Chavez, from 1951 to 1954, as well as serving in the House and Senate and later as a federal district judge.[32] During the same period, over one hundred Nuevo Mexicanos served in the state Senate and House of Representatives, about two-thirds of whom were members of the Democratic Party. On a few occasions, Mexicans served as speakers

in the assembly and as Senate leaders. Almost all of these state legislators reflected moderate political perspectives ranging from the liberal Democrat to the conservative Republican. While progressive groups,
including the Independent Progressive Party, ran Mexican candidates
for state office during the period, no Mexican American progressives
were elected to state office. The notable number of Mexican State
legislators was explained by the high percentage of the state's Mexican
population. However, before 1940 it was over 50 percent; thereafter
it declined, and by 1960 it was between 30 and 40 percent; a shift
due to increased Anglo American immigration.

Arizona and Colorado had vocal though small representation, but
it was larger than the number in California and fairly proactive in
comparison to Texas.[33] In Arizona, C. J. Carreon served as a member
of the state legislature in 1941 and was active in seeking federal action
to guarantee fair employment in wartime industries. In Texas, Au-
gustine Celaya served in the state House of Representatives during
the forty-seventh legislative session, 1941, having served four prior
terms in the forty-third, forty-fourth, forty-fifth, and forth-sixth ses-
sions as the representative from Cameron County in south Texas.
Celaya was also identified as the chairman of the Committee on State
Affairs and as a member of the Oil, Gas, and Mining Committee.
Celaya was directly associated with real estate and farming interests.
Also, a Texas state representative in 1941 was the one-term representative John C. Hoyo, an attorney from Bexar County. For the so-
called native counties in Colorado, at least one to two Mexican Americans served as state legislators each term between 1940 and 1960,
including Herman Atencio who served as state representative from
Archuleta and Conejos counties. In 1956 Bert A. Gallegos was the
first representative to be elected from the city of Denver. During this
period, a much larger number of Mexican Americans ran for state
political office in these and other states than were elected.

Civil Rights Dismantled

Perhaps in response to a self-conscious, assumed need to learn to
act within the acceptable parameters of moderate protest both to
enrich the legacy previously acquired and to secure support, several
community groups sought advice outside their circle in an attempt to

improve their efforts. For example, the Latin American Research and
Service Agency in Denver, Colorado, which was supported in part by
the Mile High United Fund, focused on community organizing. It
should be noted that this counsel was sought for efforts in nearly all
cases already under way, that is after they had begun. The organization
goals, methods, and tactics associated with Saul Alinsky—especially
as they were taught by Fred Ross—provided guidance to efforts by
some Mexicans seeking to participate in pluralist and traditional advocacy and electoral politics.[34] The major issues included restricted
housing practices, police brutality, segregated schools, inequitable judicial practices such as exclusion from juries, and exceptionally harsh
sentences and discriminatory employment practices. Ostensibly, the
Alinskyean approach disavowed ideology, and through accepted advocacy and neighborhood resident organizing, it emphasized the
achievement of minimal equities that were recognized but denied.
Mexican organizations met with varying success in dealing with such
issues; and notably, these have continued to be specific and central
issues for decades, although there have been significant changes in
approach and emphasis. For example, efforts to bring about changes
in schooling could not be limited in the same way they were in
implementing the goal of integration through the tactics of lawsuits
and petitions to administrators and elected officials. A rallying issue
in New Mexico was the effort to form a permanent FEPC that would
involve unions; Black, Jewish, Protestant, and Catholic organizations;
liberal legislators and Senator Chavez; and the LULAC and the G.I.
Forum as well as local and state organizations.[35] Though the federal
effort had proved ineffective, it did provide a focus on employment
and discrimination as well as stimulate state legislation. Among several
successful state efforts was the one in New Mexico. An FEPC bill
introduced by state Senator Tibo J. Chavez in the 1949 legislature
addressed employment, membership and advertisement, and a commission to implement the laws; and its major supporters included the
G.I. Forum, LULAC, the NAACP, B'nai B'rith, the American Jewish
Congress, and the clergy. Debate became intense, the rhetoric of both
opponents and proponents grew unabashedly self-righteous, and "freedom" and "communism" were mentioned often. All Mexican legislators
stood in support of the bill, and finally its passage was secured by one
vote. In exchange for their support, Mexican legislators agreed to

changes in reapportionment that were real while the bill was symbolic
and implementation weak. However, alongside this victory and the
frustration that arose during this period as it had in others were contrasting political currents or approaches to issues.

Radical and moderate tendencies continued into the forties and
fifties—some independent, others associated with the Communist Party
or the Socialist Workers Party.[36] Most prominent among these were
the Progressive Citizens of America, the Independent Progressive Party,
and the Committee for the Protection of the Foreign Born. For the
most part, these groups organized those already committed to a progressive viewpoint and, in a variety of cases, active before as well as
during the war. Mexicans were sought by these organizations, included
in their membership, and even modestly given prominence, but they
were not promoted to positions of leadership and were, in fact, often
treated with condescension. An unprecedented effort was the 1959
petition to the United Nations arguing that the treatment of Mexicans
in the United States violated the Declaration of Human Rights. An
ethnically targeted effort which was encouraged and supported by the
Communist Party and its intellectual and labor allies was the Congress
of Spanish-Speaking People of 1939, an organization intended as a
coalition with a purported coordinating structure. This Congress was
as notable for what it was as for what it was not. It issued a programmatic statement addressing many issues representing a multiethnic
perspective, but its organizing ambitions were not realized; nor did it
harness major figures or organizations in the Mexican community. Its
significant activity took place in Los Angeles for a few years, and the
most noteworthy leaders were Josefina Fierro and Eduardo Quevedo.

The progressive organization which drew the most participation
was one that not only focused upon, but was based on Mexican Americans. This was the Asociación Nacional México Americana (ANMA),
formed in 1949 in Grant County, New Mexico. ANMA was a national
advocacy organization dedicated to the attainment of democratic and
economic rights for the Mexican.[37] The national organization was
declared at Albuquerque, New Mexico, in August 1949, and was
moved later to Denver. Based primarily in the Southwest, ANMA's
thirty chapters were noticeably progressive and international in their
perspective, oriented toward trade unions and labor in regard to membership and issues, and claimed a national membership of four thousand in 1950. Major figures included Alfredo Montoya, a long-active

trade union organizer, and the organization's national secretary Virginia Ruiz. Between 1949 and 1954, ANMA was involved in campaigns against police brutality, housing discrimination, Immigration and Naturalization Service deportation raids, and the media stereotyping of Mexicans and other Spanish-speaking people. ANMA publicly opposed the Korean War, U.S. support for Latin American dictatorships, and the interventions in Guatemala and the Middle East. ANMA leaders also worked to develop coalitions with non-Mexican groups such as the Independent Progressive Party, the Committee for the Protection of the Foreign Born, the Progressive Citizens of America, and the Civil Rights Congress. In a significant ANMA effort, Josefina Fierro, a veteran and a former member of the defunct Congreso, ran for Congress in 1951 on the progressive platform.

Positions taken by ANMA and by its newspaper *Progreso* became increasingly adamant at the very time that the national political mood was growing unusually conservative. In 1954, ANMA was placed on the U.S. Attorney General's list as a subversive organization and a Communist Party "front." While members of the Communist Party were influential within ANMA they were also numerically few and may not have comprised its most radical element. In fact, most ANMA members who were attracted by the organization's defense of Mexican American civil rights did not necessarily possess a previously radical background. After the organization came under attack as an allegedly subversive group, it gradually lost credibility both outside and inside the Mexican community, mainly due to the intense antisocialist, anticommunist propaganda of the time. The Independent Progressive Party, which sought to include Mexicans to a limited degree, quickly faded. Progressive politics coincided with and often were integral to electoral and civil rights efforts, and case after case revealed political roots that led back to the thirties.

More pervasive than the individual linkages was the impact of dogmatic neopatriotism and procapitalism, anticommunism and antiunorthodoxy.[38] For decades, Mexican activists had suffered the consequences of being charged as foreigners who turned radical and disloyal in any number of efforts to secure equities. Persecution rationalized through such biases were the order of the day in U.S. politics. Persecution was lauded and institutionalized, and its denunciation was surprisingly sparse given the size and sophistication of the liberal sector in the U.S. The liberal practice was to acquiesce or to join the denunciation. For the most part, liberals protested the practice only when they were included. Equally noticeable was the near collapse of the left wing in the United States in the face of a rhetorical, legislative, and judicial confrontation. To Mexicans, all of this experience underscored the lessons of the twenties regarding the narrowness of the permissible in United States political practice. Mexican left-wing activists, and particularly those in labor, were harassed, persecuted, and, in some cases, deported. This lesson was quickly absorbed by the community's liberals and moderates, and in some of their worst moments they joined the chorus of denunciations. For nearly fifteen years, left-wing public dialogue was quieter in the community than at any time since the turn of the century.

During the 1940s and early 1950s the Civic Unity Leagues of Southern California achieved some success in electing a handful of Mexicans to local office and in mobilizing activists in a number of small towns in an area where negative relations between Mexicans and Anglos dated from the nineteenth century.[39] Two aspects set the Civic Unity Leagues apart somewhat. They were intended to attract local residents, not activists per se, and they were willing to consider direct protest. The Unity League was organized in 1947 by Ignacio López, a veteran of the wartime Office of War Information. Efforts by him and by others were at least ten years old and stemmed from activity associated with the newspaper *El Espectador,* founded in 1933. Its editor, López, was a graduate of Berkeley with an M.A., and a major promoter of civil rights efforts in the region. With membership congregated primarily in the eastern part of Los Angeles County—the politically and socially conservative Anglo communities in the Pomona Valley area and in San Bernardino, Riverside, and Orange counties—the Unity League campaigned vigorously against blatant discrimination in the area in housing, cemeteries, theaters, restaurants, police services, judiciary, schooling, and public accommodations. Anglo–Mexican relations were as negative in this part of southern California as they were anywhere. There was, however, a small Mexican business sector and an extensive network of organized groups. Partly because López used effectively the Spanish-language newspaper, *El Espectador,* in the Pomona Valley and was supported by an aggressive and conscientious attorney, Richard A. Ibañez, who eventually became a judge, the Unity League was able to publicize issues of concern to a growing suburban Mexican community and to promote economic boycotts of businesses that discriminated. Throughout the late 1940s and early 1950s the group scored several local successes, and Ignacio López demonstrated extraordinary leadership. Members were especially successful in San Bernardino County in winning lawsuits against segregated schools and swimming pools. Prejudice directed at Mexicans was publicly demonstrated in situation after situation. By 1949, the Unity League had helped to elect Andres Morales as the first Mexican member of the city council in Chino, California. But throughout the eighties, electoral rights for Mexicans in that area of California remained insecure.

Services and Electing Our Own

In the immediate postwar period, there emerged two major organizations—one regional and the other national—which would continue: the Community Service Organization (CSO) and the American G.I. Forum. Both reflected the conditions of the period between the end of World War II and the rise of the 1960s civil rights movement. Originally designated as the Community Political Organization (CPO), CSO was founded in September 1947 by an energetic group of Los Angeles businessmen, unionists, workers, and veterans.[40] The CSO developed out of its founding leader Edward R. Roybal's unsuccessful 1947 campaign for the Los Angeles City Council: the CSO's founding members came from the Committee to Elect Edward Roybal. In the aftermath of the election, a committee formed to consider future plans, to write a constitution and bylaws, and to raise funds began to hold open meetings to discuss educational reform, police malpractice, and unresponsive municipal government. To implement their belief that electoral power was basic to change, they received counsel from Fred Ross of the Industrial Areas Foundation (IAF), and for several years they were funded by the IAF, focusing on major voter registration drives in East Los Angeles while also conducting drives in other major pockets of concentration. In the impact of their success, these efforts were relatively unsurpassed in the Los Angeles area. Eventually, CSO increased its membership to three thousand and succeeded in registering and educating over forty thousand voters. Its regional and

local office was situated in East Los Angeles. CSO considered expanding further, however, and although multiple chapters were soon
established across California they eventually closed. Memorably, CSO
was successful in helping to elect Roybal to office, thus playing a major
role in building a continuing political network.

Eventually, Edward R. Roybal, a native of New Mexico and CSO's
founder, was acknowledged to be the single most important Mexican
elected official in California during the post–World War II period and
the hub of a network that lasted more than forty years.[41] A graduate
of UCLA and a veteran of the Second World War, Roybal was a social
worker and the former educational director of the Los Angeles County
Tuberculosis Association. Above all, he sought to advance the political
interests of the community and insisted that social problems facing
the community could be ameliorated through the actions of government. After his defeat in 1947, Roybal and a group of his supporters
reconstituted the election committee as CSO. Their aims were
straightforward: they sought to challenge effectively the social problems plaguing the city's Spanish-speaking people and to provide the
community with a level of political representation which it had lacked
for three-quarters of a century.

Roybal's defeat had served to underscore for the group an important
reality: Mexicans who were not registered to vote could not contribute
to the election of sensitive representatives to positions of local influence. Consequently, CSO's first major undertaking was to ensure that,
in the next election, the community's numerical strength would translate into voting influence. A large-scale voter-registration campaign
emerged under the leadership of Henry Nava; and the group effort was
supported by several Mexicans unionists, by clergy at St. Mary's, Our
Lady of Talpa, and Our Lady of Lourdes, and by some members of
other ethnic groups throughout the city. Over sixty Deputy Registrars
were recruited, and in 1948 fifteen thousand new voters were registered. By 1949, CSO had registered thousands of voters in the city's
Ninth Council District; and when Roybal challenged the Ninth District's incumbent council member, he won by a two-thirds margin,
becoming the first Mexican to serve on the city council since 1881.
Roybal's victory, of course, meant even more credibility for CSO. The
organization continued its effort; and by 1950, with the aid of 150
Deputy Registrars, it claimed 32,000 new Mexicans had been added

to the registration rolls, thus contributing to the election of businessman Ernesto Padilla to the San Fernando City Council.

Next, CSO turned its attention to civil rights and the defense of Mexican immigrant rights, and to the control of chauvinist police brutality as exemplified in the "Bloody Christmas" and David Hidalgo cases, where police officers were found culpable for the first time. CSO and the new member of the city council, Roybal, led many of these activities, particularly those focusing on police harassment. In fact, they demanded the removal of a number of police officers with anti-Mexican reputations. CSO also led the battle against housing discrimination, which was only partially successful. A series of CSO-supported litigation and complaints eventually forced specific real estate agents to sell homes in Montebello and in several other suburban communities to Mexicans. Nevertheless, not until the 1960s were restrictive covenants categorically struck down by the courts. Courageously, CSO initiated a campaign against police brutality and won significant cases. CSO increasingly emphasized programs suitable for public funding as well as cooperative ventures, citizenship classes, and a savings and loan institution. In 1962 the organization had twenty-two chapters principally in California but also in Arizona, and it conducted lobbying in Sacramento. It recruited, among others, a young Cesar Chavez, who proved to be an effective director. Apparently, CSO became relatively insular and cautious in its emphasis on organizational survival, pragmatic results, and economic efforts. On the other hand, CSO leadership was active in founding the American Council of Spanish-Speaking Organizations, an ambitious undertaking. By 1965, when CSO was in decline, it had become a service organization providing benefits to a reduced clientele who were now isolated from the radical currents it had helped to introduce. In the late sixties, CSO announced plans to inaugurate an electoral organization to endorse and supply candidates, but the effort had become somewhat redundant by this time.

With Anthony Rios, who had worked with unions during the early 1950s, as its most influential leader, the Community Service Organization eventually changed its orientation and abandoned electoral politics in favor of direct modest-scale service programs such as pilot housing projects, health maintenance, credit unions, buyers clubs, citizenship classes, and leadership training, and launched campaigns to secure pensions and to beautify neighborhoods.[42] A guiding logic was to consolidate CSO and to avoid factionalism. The change in CSO policy was conditioned partly by the McCarthy era, and indeed it faced severe local red-baiting; but it was more directly influenced by the changing emphases of its leadership. Between 1955 and 1964 sharp internal discussions were complemented by overt community criticism. While the general membership continued to be composed of the urban working class, the leadership increasingly became circumscribed and cautious, rather than either lower middle class in orientation, overly ambitious, or indifferent to specific membership needs. As the most visible organization in the largest urban community, it was expected to be everything; thus, it eventually chose a direction both understood and appreciated, mutual aid. The leadership showed less concern for the importance of organizing in Mexican culture or for needs inherent in the membership's working-class nature such as relations with trade unions. It was more interested in allegedly "developing practical solutions to practical problems." This meant services rather than mobilization, which may have been no great matter for some other organization that began as a service one, but CSO's prominence was linked to advocacy and not to services. The CSO commitment to social services and its practicing nonpartisan lobbying accounted, to some extent, for the organization's decline in public political importance. CSO's refusal to remain politically oriented and to diversify its activities into rural organizing led Cesar Chavez and a few others to leave it in order to organize farm workers. And the political leaders of the next generation came to see CSO as marginal rather than central, and to view it as a negative example of what happens to an organization that abandons agitation for services. Clearly, its membership in Los Angeles dropped. However, the funding for its consumer education and youth programs during the 1960s war on poverty made staffing possible and renewed its vitality regionally. Nevertheless, CSO was superseded. At its peak, CSO was a dramatic example of successful Mexican political organizing in California, with a laudably impressive record of contributions.

Contemporary with Roybal and CSO in California was the postwar political career of Henry B. González and the building of organizations in Texas.[43] González was the son of prominent middle-class and provincial Mexican exile parents; his father, Leonidas González, was the mayor of Mapimi, Durango, when the 1910 insurgency swept them north and into Texas. After the family immigrated, his father became

the managing editor of San Antonio's major Spanish-language newspaper, *La Prensa*, in 1913. Heavily influenced by his father, González
attended the University of Texas at Austin and then transferred to St.
Mary's University Law School, from which he graduated. Due to a
temporary eye illness, he was unable to complete his bar examinations.
In 1943, he began an extensive career of social service as a juvenile
probation officer. In this position, González gained extensive community contacts and visited thousands of homes. In 1946, following
a conflict with a biased judge, González resigned after he was ordered
to segregate a Black employee from other workers.

Consciously or circumstantially, González laid the foundations for
a unique political career. In 1947, the Pan American Progressive
Association (PAPA), the newly constituted organization of Mexican
American local businessmen, employed González as their executive
secretary.[44] In this position, González involved the organization in
support of efforts to gain basic municipal services for San Antonio's
west-side Mexican and Black communities, which included involvement in the 1947–48 "Puente Case" against restrictive housing covenants prohibiting Mexicans and other non-Anglos from buying homes
in white areas. While the case proved to be a victory for PAPA and
González when the courts ruled against the restrictive covenant, González's activities reportedly also caused friction within PAPA that culminated in his resignation from the organization in 1948.[45] González
established a translation business and secured a part-time position as
the educational director for the International Ladies Garment Workers
Union (ILGWU) in San Antonio and, as part of his work, he taught
English and citizenship courses to immigrants. The electoral efforts of
two Mexican American candidates in 1948 are said to have influenced
González to seek elected office. One of these was the unsuccessful
campaign of LULAC veteran activist Manuel C. González (no relation) for state representative. Although he lost, Manuel González
secured an unusual amount of support from areas outside the heavily
Mexican west side, including labor endorsements. The other campaign
was attorney Gus García's bid to become a trustee of the San Antonio
School Board. The popular and respected García won largely through
a coalition of Mexican and Black voters. After analyzing both campaigns, Henry B. González decided that a winning electoral strategy
could be devised for a Mexican American candidate in San Antonio

that would appeal to a broad constituency including Mexicans, Blacks, Anglos, and labor voters.

Although González eventually established a notable record in a series of elected offices as well as a distinguished style,[46] his early career was riddled with setbacks. In 1950, González mounted his first campaign for public office, running for the Texas State House of Representatives. As a result of his varied career in community work, González gained endorsements from the Mexican and Black communities, but he was nearly always discouraged from running by white activists who believed that a Mexican could not win. His campaign was endorsed by LULAC's founder, the attorney Alonso Perales, and the newspaper *La Prensa*. Running against a conservative Anglo opponent, González achieved a runoff election. In the runoff campaign he allied himself with the liberal, Maury Maverick, Jr., and made a strong showing, losing by a narrow margin of two thousand votes. From 1950 to 1953, González worked with the San Antonio Housing Commission in developing low-cost housing. In 1953, a conflict between the mayor and the San Antonio City Council over annexations of land to the city provided González with his next opportunity to run for public office. González was approached by the anti-City Council group of candidates calling themselves the "San Antonians" to run on their ticket for city councilman. González accepted this unique invitation and became the only Mexican American candidate on the nine-member "San Antonian" ticket. Running against another Mexican American, George de la Garza, an automobile salesman, González was elected by a large margin along with the other "San Antonians." In recognition of his important contributions to the "San Antonian" slate, González was elected Mayor Pro Tem under Mayor Jack White. As City Councilman and Mayor Pro Tem, González soon came into conflict with the other "San Antonians" over issues which included the defense of civil liberties, the desegregation of parks, and lower water rates. Tellingly, in the next election he was the only incumbent to be reelected. During his six years on the City Council, González gained wide public recognition as a competent, if often controversial, councilman who could be not only a strong aggressive liberal, but also one who was not timid in taking a conservative position, and yet able to do both outspokenly.

In 1956 González resigned his City Council seat to run for the Texas State Senate. In a hard-fought campaign, he defeated a conservative Republican opponent by thirteen thousand votes. As the first Mexican member of the Texas State Senate since statehood, González gained a reputation as a champion of civil rights for his opposition to legislation designed to encourage *de facto* segregation and to encourage slum clearance—that is, the removal of residents. In 1957, González and fellow state Senator Abraham Kazen gained national attention by mounting a thirty-six-hour filibuster on the floor of the state Senate against a segregationist bill that entailed ten specific measures. González's prompt action resulted in a partial defeat of the racist legislation and prompted a series of articles in national publications including *Time* magazine. As a result, he was granted the NAACP Citizenship Award. Later, he could denounce sales taxes as biased against the poor and also condemn the use of poll taxes. Next, he filibustered alone but unsuccessfully for twenty hours against three conservative bills, which eventually passed and were signed by the governor; however, this independent action increased his stature. He then took on the governor, even though he faced certain defeat.

In 1958, Henry B. González became the first Mexican American in Texas to campaign for the office of governor in the Democratic primary, challenging the seemingly powerful incumbent Democrat, Price Daniel. González was encouraged by liberal democratic defections from Daniel, but he failed to win the support of Democrats of Texas (DOT), a counterpart to California's CDC (California Democratic Council). In the primary, González was defeated while receiving a commendable 19 percent of the statewide vote, finishing second in a field of three candidates and behind the incumbent, Daniel, who, in winning, received 60 percent of the total votes. Nevertheless, this campaign had a tremendously positive impact for Mexican Americans. In 1960, despite heavy opposition, González not only won reelection to the state Senate but played a key role in the John F. Kennedy victory in the Texas election for president of the United States. In 1961, Kennedy reciprocated by supporting González's bid for the open position of U.S. congressman from Bexar County, and González won the election with a total of approximately fifty-three thousand votes. As an elected official, González earned the reputation for being a hardworking congressman who handled committee assignments well. During the late 1960s and 1970s, Congressman González, in contrast to his earlier opposition to the red-baiting of the 1950s, moved conspicuously to a conservative posture in an effort to distance himself

from more militant Mexican Americans, and yet he still retained his
position at the center of Mexican American politics, particularly in
Texas.

Signs of the Times

In Texas, concurrent with developments elsewhere, was the organization in March 1948 of the American G.I. Forum,[47] which exemplified the postwar optimism and confidence based on earned equities.
As occasionally happens, the organization was galvanized to move
beyond its initial stages by a specific and pejorative incident. In early
1949, a funeral home in Three Rivers, Texas, refused burial services
for a Mexican veteran, Felix Longoria. Anger over this act of discrimination led to the establishment by Dr. Hector García, attorney
Gus Garcia, and a group of Mexican veterans of the G.I. Forum, a
well-structured and well-led organization, with formal membership
initially offered to veterans. Mexican Americans had been members
of veteran groups since the nineteenth century, but Anglo veteran
groups displayed no specific interest in them. The constitution of the
American G.I. Forum stated the group's goals and purposes, as follows:

[to] strive for the procurement for all veterans and their families, regardless
of race, color, or creed, the equal privileges to which they are entitled
under the laws of our country. . . . To foster the training and education of
our citizens in order that a true and real democracy may exist in the
lowest as well as the highest unit so that our loyalty to these principles
may never be questioned.

As loyal citizens . . . we sincerely believe that one of the principles of
democracy is religious and political freedom for the individual and that all
citizens are entitled to the right of equality in social and economic
opportunities and that . . . we must advance understanding between the
different nationalities.

The G.I. Forum was dedicated to assisting Mexican veterans, providing services and leadership, ending discrimination, and maximizing
Mexican influence in government. Organizers approached their task
with almost missionary zeal; founders traveled from community to
community to form new chapters. Effectively, they argued pride *and*

benefits. A tireless worker in this initially primarily male organization was the national organizer Molly C. Galvan. During the organization's early phase, chapters were grouped within geographical districts and the districts placed under a state Board of Directors.

The G.I. Forum made major contributions during the 1950s, when even mild reforms were stigmatized in public as "un-American." The Forum utilized United States patriotic symbols and rhetoric, and therefore occupied a secure position in its attempt to defend Mexican civil rights, representing a constituency with undeniable claims and demonstrable supportive needs. While seeking to increase the impact of Mexican American voters in the 1950s, the G.I. Forum initiated, with some success, "pay your poll tax" and "get out the vote" drives. The G.I. Forum extended its organizational interests to encompass some of the immediate problems faced by the Mexican community; for example, job training, schooling equities, judicial rights, and bilingual education programs. Though intended to serve veterans primarily, the Forum was multifocused and later included non-veterans, women, and youth. Its membership was largely wage-earner in origin, and its leadership generally middle class in orientation. Eventually, the Forum was labeled as moderate, but it was still highly respected. Initially, its chapters were located only in the five southwestern states; then it spread into twenty-three states, where highly active youth and women subgroups were combined with a membership that hovered around ten thousand in the midsixties, then reached twenty thousand and later increased twice over. Usually, the Forum has been credited with a strong internal democratic vitality, the result of its access to the services of several talented leaders.

As a national congressman, Henry B. González endorsed the expansion of the American G.I. Forum while overlooking other groups. He argued strongly that the G.I. Forum was by far the only organization which provided an effective and cohesive effort in behalf of progress for a large and numerous group of Americans who had been hindered in their effectiveness and articulation by a lack of organization. Significantly, in 1965 the Forum received a five-million-dollar grant for job training through Service, Employment and Redevelopment (SER), and was instrumental in establishing the Inter-Agency Committee on Mexican American Affairs as well as organizing the threshold 1967 national El Paso conference on Mexican Americans. From the first, the G.I. Forum implemented a multipronged effort pertinent to improved schooling, which involved litigation, parent and student motivation, protest at specific schools, and raising scholarship funds. Its work in relation to immigration was a mixture of the negative and the benign, of supporting curtailment but denouncing abuses. Through the years, the G.I. Forum has maintained an ostensibly nonpartisan but active electoral stand, and its influence increased during the Lyndon B. Johnson and Richard M. Nixon administrations as did that of the older organization, the League of United Latin American Citizens (LULAC).

Along with the G.I. Forum, LULAC stood as an important Mexican lower middle-class membership organization. Its organizational interests and overt nonpartisan politics were generally similar to those of the Forum. However, the Forum was more aggressive, more service-oriented, and more willing to confront unfair practices. LULAC, however, also included some remarkable figures. Alonso Perales continued to be active until his death in 1960, as did J. T. Canales. In addition, George Sanchez, Ben Garza, and Carlos Castaneda were outstanding, while Senator Dennis Chavez provided key support as a LULAC member.[48] Near the end of World War II, LULAC amended its program by visualizing broader and more intense action, but still within the parameters of its founding views. Its aim, as amended in 1944, included, among others, the following:

To eradicate . . . discrimination. . . .

To use all the legal means . . . to the end that all citizens . . . may enjoy equal rights, the equal protection of the laws . . . and equal opportunities and privileges.

The acquisition of the English language. . . .

To define . . . our unquestionable loyalty to the ideals, principles and citizenship of the United States of America.

We solemnly declare . . . to maintain a sincere and respectful reverence for our racial origin of which we are proud.

By all lawful means . . . we shall assist in the education and guidance of Latin-Americans. . . .

This organization is not a political club, but as citizens we shall participate in all local, State and National political contests. However, in doing so, we shall ever bear in mind the general welfare of our people. . . .

With our vote and influence we shall endeavor to place in public office men who show by their deeds, respect and consideration for our people.

We shall pay our poll tax and urge all our fellow-citizens to do likewise. . . .

We shall endeavor to secure equal representation for our people on juries and in the administration of Governmental affairs.

We shall resist and attack energetically all machinations tending to prevent our social and political unification.

By 1960 LULAC had in place over 150 councils, in contrast to the 46 councils extant in 1932. LULAC gained from the national political activity during the fifties and the seventies.

With an experienced but cautious leadership and a more evolutionary approach, LULAC viewed the conventionally moderate advocacy process and the selected use of the judicial systems as effective means to redress the problems of the Mexican community. For example, in relying on a moderate approach in Texas, members failed to secure an anti-discriminate measure; in 1949, however, they contributed to enacting the New Mexico State Fair Employment law through a more aggressive campaign. With the Salvatierra desegregation case in Del Rio, Texas, during the 1930s serving as a precedent, LULAC contributed to several schooling and anti-segregation precedents, including *Mendez, et al.* v. *Westminister School District* (1946), and *Delgado* v. *Bastrop Independent School District* (1948). In the 1950s and early 1960s, "the Little School of 400" was a significant effort in education; and LULAC formed a partnership with the G.I. Forum in founding SER, a significant job education program. LULAC support helped to make possible the landmark 1953 Peter Hernández case, which recognized Mexicans as a discrete and discriminated sector. Yet rifts occurred between the older and newer leaders; while LULAC grew slightly and continued to do important work, there were many who considered the organization's ways to be out of date and pretentious. In its attitudes toward immigrants, for example, LULAC frequently and, for many, too often voiced the conservatism of the right.

Older than LULAC was the Alianza Hispano-Americana founded in Tucson in 1894 and an organization that had gone through its own period of difficulties.[49] It was organized as a *mutualista*, and at its core financially were the provision by members of benefits and regular payments to the insurance fund. From the first, it had been a more salient advocate than most *mutualistas,* and at one time in 1939 it had reached a membership of nearly eighteen thousand. Although its membership declined, it remained the second or third largest group throughout the forties and fifties. Before it diminished greatly, it undertook a number of precedent-setting activities in relation to civil rights and regional coordination. Eventually, both the G.I. Forum and LULAC became better organized, larger, and in possession of more resources than any other organizational efforts, and both also enjoyed some ties with the churches.

The Catholic church also involved itself with the Mexican community more than in the past, stressing church-centered activity for all facets of life, civic participation, and anticommunism.[50] Its strongest effort came in San Antonio with the establishment of The Bishops' Committee for Spanish-Speaking, beginning in the late 1940s. During this time, the Cursillo movement became popular among Mexicans in Texas and in the rural sectors of the Southwest. At its core was a series of religious retreats for lay persons. In some communities *cursillistas* were dedicated to enhancing their religious practice through social action. The *cursillistas* worked to alleviate the problems of the Mexican community and, not so incidentally, to foment anticommunism. Throughout the 1940s and 1950s the Catholic Youth Organization (CYO) conducted leadership development work among Mexican youth, instilling in them religion and ethics, but also at its best, providing them with a Catholic social-service ideology and the opportunity to develop organizational skills and leadership. At its worst, the CYO peddled a parochial Catholicism, reactionary political ideas, and a ridiculous social snobbery. In some limited ways, a few clergy in San Antonio and Los Angeles supported liberal electoral politics. In San Antonio this involved the archdiocese, while in Los Angeles it involved a few pastors and other religious but was counter to the archdiocese's preferences. The political relationship between the liberal Catholic church clergy and the activists of the Mexican community was reminiscent, in some aspects, of an incipient Christian Democratic tendency occurring at that time in Latin America. Through its growing school system and other outreach programs, the Catholic church undoubtedly continued as a major ideological influence, but liberal exceptions aside, as a decidedly conservative force.

As the Catholic church was becoming less indifferent in a few islands, Protestant churches intensified their interest in the Mexican ministry even more so than in the past.[51] There was a difference, however: Protestant churches reduced their hostile "Americanization" policies and increased their tolerance and even encouragement of Mexican culture by considering community preferences in language, prayers, and music, as well as providing for Mexican pastors and nondenominational community activities. Protestants also became much more willing to take up civil issues and to integrate Mexican pastors and community needs into their agendas. Most active were the Presbyterians, Methodists, Baptists, and Episcopalians. A major source for the Protestant funding of community activity was the National Council of Churches. One focus was on blue-collar and agricultural workers.

Mexican workers and their political votes were of concern to some leaders of trade unions.[52] The majority of workers remained unorganized, but many were members of unions. Among the unions most notable for their activism were the mine and smelter workers, the steel and rubber locals, and the teamsters and auto workers. A major AFL–CIO-sponsored effort was the attempt to organize farmworkers in California. Ernesto Galarza believed that a union not only would improve wages but empower agricultural workers; unionization, however, failed. In fact, during the postwar period many unions increased their institutional presence in community affairs beyond labor organizing; in many cases, this was accomplished through Mexican American representatives who enrolled in organizations, helped to initiate them, participated in community activities, and made representations to public bodies on the assumption that they were representative of both the community and specific unions. Though in some cases Mexican trade union leaders held positions to which they had been elected by Mexican members, more often they were appointed by Anglo or Jewish labor leaders. In several instances, they contributed crucially to political activity in the Southwest and the Chicago area. In 1956 the AFL–CIO formed and funded its Committee on Political Education (COPE), which conducted voter registration and voter turnout drives as well as supporting specific candidates and holding training and informational conferences. These were all efforts that underscored the importance of coordination.

In May 1951 there was formed the American Council of Spanish-Speaking Organizations, a coalition of representatives from groups in Arizona, New Mexico, Colorado, Texas, and California; among them were the Alianza Hispano Americana, the G.I. Forum, LULAC, CSO,

and the Unity Leagues.[53] Individuals involved included George Sanchez, Ignacio López, Gregorio García, Ralph Estrada, Bernardo Valdez,
Tibo Chavez, Tony Rios, and others. Chavez, who was at that time
the lieutenant governor of New Mexico, was elected president, while
Dr. George Sanchez was named director. The organization's purpose
was to eliminate public school and housing segregation, to increase
participation in juries and public offices, and to end discrimination in
employment. Efforts were particularly visible in Arizona and California, and especially active was a resurgent Alianza Hispano Americano
based in Tucson and led by Gregorio García and attorney Ralph Estrada. Appeals for convicted Mexican prisoners were undertaken; threats
of legal suits were made to desegregate public facilities, such as swimming pools in Arizona; and several segregated schools were denounced
in both Arizona and California. A small grant was received from the
Robert Marshall Foundation. In 1955 the Alianza established a Civil
Rights Department to be directed by Ralph Guzman of East Los Angeles; and a series of cases in cooperation with the National Association
for the Advancement of Colored Peoples (NAACP) followed. In effect, the 1951 coalition, however erratic and vulnerable, offered the
experience of operational cooperation across state lines; and in the
late fifties, members of the coalition were emphasizing electoral participation and would soon cooperate as individuals in organizing Viva
Kennedy groups as well as the attempted electoral organization known
as PASSO, the Political Association of Spanish-Speaking Organizations.

Electoral Organizations: Taking Off the Gloves and Putting One of Them Back On

Toward the end of the 1950s, a modest wave of political liberalism
arose across the United States; the McCarthy furor was subsiding and
the United States' social conscience was aroused by the burgeoning
Black civil rights movement.[54] For their part, Mexican organizers and
politicians began to glimpse the potential power of their constituency.
This realization focused on numbers, for the community was the largest
minority group in the Southwest. They watched with great interest
as the Black community gained widespread media coverage through
its public struggle against discrimination. The new political opening

was initially explored by some of the better positioned Mexican politicians in the southwestern states.

California was the most promising as well as frustrating situation. At the time, there were no California Mexicans in the state legislature or in the U.S. Congress, and Roybal was the only notable elected Mexican official. Overall, organizations were not at par with the needs; CSO was in retreat and the Mexican American Political Association served at best as a modest vehicle for electoral advocacy in California. Earlier, in 1954, Edward Roybal had sought the nomination for lieutenant governor. In 1958, Hank Lopez campaigned for the Democratic nomination for California secretary of state and City Council member Roybal ran for the Los Angeles County Board of Supervisors. Both candidates lost, but not by much; and in Roybal's case, the result was extremely close. In fact, some observers believed that it was only because of voter intimidation that Roybal's opponent, Ernest Debs, managed to squeak through. Reportedly, some of Debs's supporters challenged the qualifications of Mexican voters at the polls. A darker possibility was a conspiracy by Democratic and Republican leadership as well as by county and city officials and the moneyed interests of Los Angeles; in this case, the effort to deny Roybal the city office extended even to the possibility of someone engaging in fraud. Boxes containing hundreds of votes from East Los Angeles were "lost." Previously, when Roybal in 1954 and Hank Lopez in 1958 had been defeated in their respective races for state office, the Democratic Party had failed to support fully their candidates, although both had won the Democratic Party primary. Lopez, a Harvard graduate, an author, a successful attorney, and an attractive and articulate candidate who ran for secretary of state, was the only Democrat to lose for state office in 1958, although the margin of loss was close.

By the late 1950s, the need for distinctly Mexican electoral organizations was evident across the Southwest. To fill the void in California, the Mexican American Political Association (MAPA) was organized by 150 volunteer delegates at Fresno in April 1959.[55] Notably, this organization would stress ethnic identity, direct electoral politics, and electoral independence. In addition to this platform of principles, all of which augured well, an initial strength of the organization was its chair, Edward Roybal. Organized as a primary was in process, MAPA declared, from the first, that its basic aspiration was to become the political voice of the state Mexican community; its slogan was "Opportunity for All through MAPA." Frustrated by the Democratic Party's disregard for the Mexican community and by the defeats of Mexican office seekers, and anticipating the national elections, Eduardo Quevedo, Frank Casado, Ed Roybal, Alex Zambrano, and others formed MAPA to work for the election of Mexicans to office, regardless of party, by uniting urban and rural activism under one organization. The major figure was Roybal, who represented a significant constituency in the major area of demographic concentration, urban southern California. Initially, the organization's lower middle-class leadership effectively identified with the Mexican culture to attract and receive blue-collar support. Because its organization coincided with the primary, MAPA received a major impetus during the 1960 campaign. MAPA chapters were strongest where the membership was mostly working class, aggressive, and locally rooted. Several women—for example, Francisca Flores, Grace Davis Montanez, Julia Luna Mount, Ramona Morin, and Dolores Sanchez—associated with MAPA forged new constituencies in the sixties and seventies.

Though it continued throughout the eighties, the peak years of MAPA visibility came between 1960 and 1965. In the sixties, its California organization was divided into northern and southern sections and fifteen chapters. MAPA contributed partially to the election of two assemblymen, one congressman, and six judges; that is, it endorsed and publicized these candidacies, but local supporters made them possible. Ostensibly nonpartisan and rightfully resentful of the Democratic attitude, MAPA was linked in a dependent relation to the party. Despite its many political veterans, it did not maximize its power resources or votes, except in 1960. Significantly, between 1960 and 1966 the total number of Mexican votes declined in California. From the first, the organization was loose, subject to divisions between moderate and progressive factions and power struggles between competing leaders. It was often accused of not having a sharply informed and well-reasoned position, of reacting too late and too ineffectively to issues, of uninformed spokespersons, and of a leadership that diverted the voiced populist concerns of the membership to the careerist interests of the officials. The last followed from the avowed ends of emphasizing recognition for its spokespersons. Furthermore, MAPA was one more organization without resources or effective outreach. More positive were MAPA's actions in defense of the community in specific local cases where membership pressure was effective in the issues of immigration, police brutality, discrimination, and education. Reportedly, its charitable efforts were helpful to many. Its predominant activity, however, was the endorsement of candidates and the advocacy of appointments, preferably its own members. Large-scale registration or precinct work was an aim that remained unfulfilled. Events clearly revealed the weak Mexican position in conventional California electoral politics. Here, for example, MAPA was unable to prevent Mexicans from becoming the victims of gerrymandering when, in 1960, the Democratic-controlled legislature reapportioned the state's political districts. This was one more example of the Democratic Party's disregard for the Mexican community and its political organizations. The lack of funds and the poor electoral results of California Mexican candidates were partially offset by the key role played by the Viva Kennedy clubs in the 1960 presidential election; yet John F. Kennedy lost California. The frustrations suffered by MAPA in state contests as well as the promises it offered in local elections caused some of its members to consider new political tactics.

Local as well as interstate mechanisms were in order, and they arose nearly concurrently; they were often in communication, and always through persons who had been active previously. The Political Association of Spanish-Speaking Organizations (PASSO) was organized in Texas in 1961, and was followed closely by attempts at establishing groups in Arizona later in 1961.[56] Initiated in Victoria, Texas, under the rubric of Mexican-Americans for Political Action, PASSO sought to take a more direct political stance while bringing together Mexican advocacy and membership groups; it also hoped to create a multistate political organization. Explicitly if ambitiously, the organization was proclaimed as the representative of a community dedicated "to further the cause of good government." Involved in the effort were several American G.I. Forum and LULAC activists who believed that an explicitly political organization was needed. A constitution and bylaws were adopted and a statewide organizer, Gilbert Garcia of Fort Worth, was appointed. Groups were to be formed and poll tax–paying drives launched. Initially, the organization was generally well received by political operatives. The major tests of the organization were the Texas primary and general elections of 1962. The strategy was for PASSO adherents to present a united bloc in support of candidates; all candidates would be invited by an endorsing committee for an interview and would later be evaluated competitively. It was considered a step forward for Anglo Texas Democrats to compete publicly for the endorsement of a Mexican American political group. A not uncommon question arose, however, which would upset the promising scenario: Do you endorse on the bases of the character of the candidate, his general promises, his specific patronage, his liberal credentials, or his probability of winning? Price Daniel, who made specific patronage promises even though he was considered a conservative, and although he possessed a poor Mexican American record, indicated a willingness to improve, was considered the candidate with the strongest probability of winning; and he was chosen over Don Yarborough, the strongest liberal and the person considered to have the most attractive public and private record. Taunting PASSO, Yarborough said he already had the Mexican vote. Daniel was chosen; several PASSO delegates walked out; and Daniel eventually lost to John Connally, who had made no commitments to the organization. PASSO had grown quickly and encountered difficulties quickly. Members had seemed to act logically and had lost. The group's internal unity had weakened and adherents had been unable to deliver the vote in San Antonio and south Texas, two areas that were central to their own standing.

The PASSO effort stimulated in Arizona was notably successful at first. The American Coordinating Council on Political Education emerged with ten chapters in Arizona, a dues-paying membership of 2,500 located in a majority of Arizona's fourteen counties. ACCPE's most notable contribution was in Miami, Arizona, where five Mexicans were elected to the seven-member city council in 1962. Its nonpartisan character was suitable in local city and school-board races. Partisanship however, was important in county, state, and federal offices; and the party organizations were not to give way before a "new" ethnic effort. Facing a common dilemma, ACCPE could confront and lose to them or endorse *their* candidates. Its electoral constituency was Democrat, and if it made an issue of ethnicity the parties would put forth their own ethnic candidates, capitalizing on ethnic arousal. ACCPE had created space for its efforts, but the conventional rules imposed limits.

Capitalizing on the experience and contacts of the successful "Viva Kennedy" movement of 1960, the Texas leaders of PASSO sought to amalgamate local groups in creating a more effective presence in the state and with an eye toward coordination beyond Texas itself. Thus, individuals associated with the organization embraced groups in Arizona and endeavored to incorporate the participation of MAPA, LULAC, the Alianza Hispano-Americana, and CSO. This "PASSO," then, was an attempt to create an electoral regional umbrella organization. PASSO's overall goal, according to Carlos McCormick, its executive secretary and also associated with the Alianza, was

to improve economic and political opportunities for Spanish Speaking Americans through political action. PASSO feels that participation in government, including non-career, appointive service, is a vital factor in strengthening the overall position of Spanish Speaking Americans. PASSO also believes that the Democratic Party has also benefited from the votes of the Mexican-American, but has taken them for granted and not done enough to further their interests. [57]

PASSO's intended role was to strengthen electoral and civic activity among Mexican Americans by encouraging them to register and vote and to participate actively in politics. Arguments over ethnic designation—"Mexican" or "Spanish-Speaking" or "American"—were rife, but even more telling were a continuing liberal–conservative debate within the organization, the impact of national politics, and the influence of major outside forces. There were two faces of PASSO: one looked toward regional coordination and the other to its logical strength, Texas itself. In any case, PASSO endorsed and supported candidates during election campaigns, and in one of these its promises and troubles collided.

In Crystal City, Texas, in 1963, PASSO seemingly but only briefly proved its political effectiveness. [58] Although Mexican Americans outnumbered Anglos four to one, typically the Anglos had controlled the city. The local white minority attributed its electoral success to the allegedly inactive Mexican American posture toward local politics. In effect, present here was the pattern of token participation by those who worked with the local establishment and the exclusion of others through one means or another, or through the threat or reality of reprisals to those who might consider challenging the existing arrangement. The context was both historical and ethnically discriminatory, and it was heightened by the concern of some trade-union leaders showing their colors. In effect, a local circumstantial and joint effort of labor and reformers took place. Members of PASSO, in cooperation with members of the Teamsters and others, began actively campaigning for five candidates who were representative of the majority of Mexican Americans of the community—the blue-collar, less-educated voters, including women, one of whom, Virginia Musquiz, was particularly active. Perceived or real, middle-class Mexican Americans generally favored the situation as it was; that is, there were worse places to live. By broader standards, teamster contribution was modest but locally important. They paid the salaries of two campaign coordinators and supplied posters and other campaign material. San Antonio PASSO provided the part-time services of a district organizer, material, and some volunteers. Presumably, the Teamsters wished to strengthen their position in Texas and local politics; PASSO wished to strengthen its hand in Texas as well as its voice in Washington, D.C.

The enthusiasm of the Mexican American residents was soon aroused, resulting in the election of the top five candidates, all Mexican Americans. This election marked a victory for PASSO and attracted the attention of Mexicans elsewhere in the country. The election also offered a valuable lesson for Mexican American political aspirants, which was apparently not fully understood at first. First, as the result of an organized coalition effort led by a group such as PASSO, Mexican American residents did rally to support their own candidates and gained a city government whose elected representatives ostensibly would be responsive to their needs. Second, the political future of the Mexican Americans was being tested in the election, and the victory was a positive indicator. Third, this election demonstrated to the country the possibilities of the ballot box for politically underrepresented groups. What happened in Crystal City had its parallels in other areas where a few Mexican Americans were elected to office. Thereafter, however, the limits were demonstrated. Those elected failed to win reelection, in part because they did not or could not meet expectations; they made errors; and their opponents also learned a lesson, counterorganizing an effective Anglo–Mexican American coalition. At the 1963 Waco, Texas, PASSO convention, the more moderate faction headed by Hector Garcia of the G.I. Forum and by Tony and William Bonilla and others in LULAC left; ostensibly, they objected to the Teamster influence in PASSO, but they well may have acted to weaken PASSO and to strengthen their own organizations not only in Texas but in Washington, D.C. PASSO was clearly weaker at the 1964 convention than previously, and it responded poorly to college students who sought to participate meaningfully in the organization's activity. Though the membership age was lowered from twenty-one to eighteen, overly active youth were not encouraged. Despite setbacks, PASSO and ACCPE endured in Arizona and Texas, particpating in several elections and adding to the politicization of southern Arizona and south Texas communities. Elsewhere, further electoral achievements were occurring.

In the early sixties a few significant electoral positions were secured, which provided a voice for and participation in important concerns and issues.[59] As a Los Angeles City Council member from 1949 to 1962, Edward Roybal was responsible for encouraging municipal employment for minority groups, the establishment of a community police relations committee, and the elimination of discriminatory practices in housing. In 1962 Roybal was elected congressman of the Thirtieth District, which was at that time only 9 percent Mexican American; this meant that he represented a multiethnic constituency among whom Blacks and Jews were important; thus, he was elected not only by Mexican voters, but by an ethnic coalition. However, he was not succeeded in his council district by a Mexican American, but by a Black. That year, California also saw the election of the first Mexican state legislators since the 1890s and 1900s—John Moreno and Philip S. Soto; the former, however, was not reelected, and the latter served only two terms. In Texas, Henry B. González and Eligio de la Garza were elected to the House of Representatives in 1961 and 1964, respectively. Thus, three Mexican-American congressmen were all elected within a three-year period, and all were Democrats. Furthermore, Joseph Montoya of New Mexico, already serving as a congressman, was elected in 1964 to the U.S. Senate. One Senate and three House seats were an improvement. In Texas, after years of activity by LULAC, the G.I. Forum, and, more recently, PASSO, Mexicans held only 31 of the state's 3,300 elective posts, and of the 11,800 appointments only 5 were Mexican. Whether at the local, state, or federal level, gains were limited to a few legislative seats and were often partially a result of forces and resources outside the Mexican community. There were thirty-five state legislators in 1965. By the mid-sixties, less patronage existed for officeholders throughout the Southwest. None of the Mexican officials had access to significant resources. There was a limit to what these officeholders could accomplish, but they

did contribute to civil rights, equal employment, and bilingual legislation at a time when these issues were receiving some national
attention.

After 1960, a significant case of tentatively independent Mexican
electoral activity was the formation of the Colorado New Hispano
Party in the summer of 1966 and its limited campaign for state and
federal offices.[60] The formation of the New Hispano Party was the
result of the dissatisfaction of some Mexican political activists within
the two-party system, the result of Democratic and Republican Party
indifference to the Mexican community and its need for political
representation. Frustrated in their attempts to secure the nomination
of Mexican candidates for office by the Colorado Republican and
Democratic parties, the Mexican activists withdrew from the two
parties and formed their own political group, the New Hispano Party.
The New Hispano Party then nominated its own slate of candidates,
including Levi Martinez as candidate for governor; Tom Pino, for
lieutenant governor; and Joseph Lucero, for the U.S. Congress seat
in Denver's Second Congressional District. None of these candidates
were elected in the following November. The New Hispano Party
faced significant opposition from Mexican Democratic politicians, including Rodolfo "Corky" Gonzales, head of the local Denver War on
Poverty, Inc. (DWOP), G.I. Forum member and a major Democratic
ward leader in Denver's Mexican community. The New Hispano Party
was in tempo with the changing times in its emphasis on elected
representation, but it was amusingly out of date in its rhetorical ethnic
references, which came close to suggesting a pseudo pro-Spanish, anti-
Mexican rhetoric.

The motivations of the New Hispano Party's organizers appear to
have been mixed. A significant sector of their number, probably including the major leadership, viewed the party as the focus of a one-
shot protest designed to influence Colorado's Democratic leadership
to give them greater consideration in future elections. However, it
seems that a number of the precinct-level participants viewed the New
Hispano Party as an ongoing political vehicle for the organization of
Mexican people in Colorado, and certainly as more than a temporary
expedient. The composition of party membership, particularly among
the leadership, appears to have been largely professional and middle
class, including some elements from LULAC. Their resentment was
plain, but it was also mixed with an elitist orientation toward what

they referred to as the "Spanish American" community. The New Hispano Party dwindled following its defeat in the 1966 election. Since that time, its few major figures have returned to participation in the two-party system, consolidating their position within the ranks of the middle-class leadership. On the other hand, several of the party's mobilizers continued to work in organizations formed later, such as the United Farm Workers and the Crusade for Justice. While its direct influence subsequently seems to have been limited, the case of the New Hispano Party as a precursor remained open. Between 1965 and 1967, in San Patricio County in southern Texas, the so-called Action "party" actively sought to improve public services. More integrationist and radical were the handful of Mexican activists who participated in the efforts around the National Conference for New Politics in 1966; however, when Mexican-related points were discussed, these were in relation to Mexicans supporting the Black movement and the concern for farmworkers.

Segregated Cities and Counties

An area of Mexican politics which was active and which should have experienced stronger results but had only limited success, was electoral politics at the county and municipal levels.[61] Perhaps the most salient success was Republican moderate Manuel Lujan, who served several times as the popular mayor of Santa Fe. Feasibly, consistent Mexican participation in county and municipal politics has been most extensive in areas with a large Mexican population, especially along the United States–Mexico border. Outside of New Mexico and perhaps southern Colorado, Mexican American participation in county and municipal politics during the twentieth century generally and in the period 1941–1960 specifically was probably most energetically sought in Texas. San Antonio and Crystal City provided the most striking efforts. On the border, the best known figure of the 1950s and 1960s was the former Air Force officer, the conservative Raymond Telles, who had previously served as county clerk and city councilman, and was elected mayor of El Paso in 1957. Though clearly supportive of business, Telles had considerable opposition; yet the overwhelming turnout of Mexican voters made his victory possible. He later served as ambassador to Costa Rica and chaired both the

U.S.–Mexican Commission for Border Development and the Equal Employment Opportunity Commission. In contrast to gains elsewhere, Los Angeles, apart from Roybal's council tenure, displayed mostly a record of defeats. Efforts at incorporation in South Tucson and East Los Angeles attempted to establish a municipal base where demographics were favorable and where previously there had been none, thus making it possible to gain a voice in city governance. South Tucson, a smaller and poor community, secured incorporation while East Los Angeles, a larger and economically more diverse area, did not. There were three Superior Court judges and three mayors in California; while there were two county judges and several mayors in Texas.

The substance of Mexican participation in county and municipal politics has varied widely in content and significance, and according to the way in which elections were established and conducted. Participation has ranged from the manipulation of Mexican voters by political networks, usually controlled by Anglo patrons employing middle- and local-level Mexican ward heelers, to local political "revolts" by independent slates of Mexican American candidates challenging the local electoral establishment. Still another phenomenon has been the support of Mexican American voters for Anglo American candidates who either openly championed issues of importance to Mexicans or were perceived as efficient local representatives who could generate government action on practical issues like increased services to the community.

Local networking, electoral politics dated from the nineteenth-century North American political style which once characterized most local governments, especially those at the county level, and was especially prevalent in the Southwest, in south Texas and northern New Mexico, until well after World War II.[62] In Texas, it represented an interactive exchange system under which a Mexican majority population had formally participated in the electoral process by voting for the candidates of the major and most influential Democrats, in exchange for benefits. In some areas the leaders of the political networks possessed considerable influence over county, city, and special district offices. They used local government authority to provide economic benefits for friends, allies, and other special interests. The role of Mexican American *políticos* varied from loyal subordinates to those with locally powerful influence. The why and wherefore of Mexican participation in such politics was not a dated question, and bloc voting had pluses and minuses in the past that would continue in the years to come. Certainly, if bloc voting is seen as possessing virtues, this, in turn, would be premised on effective and supported coordination. In any case, abuses as well as the organizational example of "boss" politics could and did result either in local political revolts by individual Mexican *políticos* or in the formation of slates of Mexican candidates. The most prominent examples of individual revolt were Texas state Representative José T. Canales's break from the Jim Wells machine in the 1900s, and more recently Henry B. González's challenge to Governor Price Daniel. By the 1940s, machine-style politics of the previous and ruder type was deteriorating, and independent slates of Anglo or Mexican candidates were challenging conventional *políticos* periodically. In the early sixties they still survived, though weakly.

In Chicago, a variation on this pattern reflected shortcomings but also indicated fortuitous results.[63] Apart from *mutualista* organizations in the forties, there were several umbrella or coalition efforts: the Pan-American Council, the Spanish-Speaking People's Council, and the Mexican Civic Committee chaired by Frank Paz (Pax). Elements of all of these organizations were part of the Metropolitan Welfare Council. In the late fifties there were a relatively active Comité Patriótico Mexicano and two newer groups, the Illinois Federation of Mexican Americans (ILFOMA) and the Mexican American Council. The latter two received modest public monies and church support, and were animated by a social work mentality to help the poor in understanding the complexities of city life. They also emphasized the attempt to persuade employers and service personnel not to discriminate. An energetic college graduate and former Marine, Lieutenant Martin Ortiz, was chair of the council. When a police brutality case proved to be successful, a turf conflict ensued over leadership. Demographic concentration in the Irondale and Millgate neighborhoods and in steel-mill or steel-related work led to a modest but growing Mexican base in the union and in the Tenth Democratic Ward, and thus some leverage in union, city, and county politics. The Mexicans faced the dilemma of increasing their own influence while at the same time contending with the currently entrenched leadership, the rising Black impetus, and the liberal opposition to the local *políticos*. Generally, the more acknowledged leader was the unionist John Chico. Though the Mexicans suffered setbacks due to the highly volatile and competitive situation and their smaller forces, they gained precinct leadership and eventually became a force to contend with in future Chicago politics. But in these years Mexican ward efforts faced dilemmas. The incumbent Democrats offered sure but small rewards and insisted on organization subordination. Blacks offered a willingness to confer group recognition, but the Black political and demographic presence was such that cooperation would tend to drown the Mexican effort. Cooperation with the reform liberals offered some resources and plaudits in those circles, but the liberals had difficulty in marshaling their forces, were not strong enough to assure prospects, and, contrary to their statements, would not support Mexicans themselves. The best choices for Mexicans were to seek Puerto Rican and Black support while maintaining relations with incumbents.

In some cases, Mexicans gained by aligning with supportive winning candidates. Perhaps the best known case of Mexican support for an Anglo American candidate viewed as championing Mexican issues was that of Maury Maverick in San Antonio and Bexar County, Texas.[64] Maverick came from an old San Antonio political family which had produced at least one previous mayor of San Antonio. A New Deal Democrat, Maverick's political image was that of a reformer and a champion of the lower middle class and the poor who were hard hit by the depression of the 1930s. Building a political coalition that included Anglos, Mexicans, and Blacks, and challenging the Paul Kilday network, Maverick was elected to the Texas state legislature, to the U.S. Congress from Bexar County, and to the mayor's office. As a congressman, Maverick supported wartime fair employment practices and worked to bring defense facilities to the San Antonio area and to Texas. Possibly, Maverick's coalition building may have contributed to developing Mexican, Black, and labor coalitions of the type that Henry B. González would develop so effectively in his political career. But even though he received the support of Mexicans, so did his opponents to some extent, and eventually Maverick was criticized and abandoned for a failure to live up to his promises. Less known and less ethnically direct, but more protean for the future, was the Mexican support for Lyndon B. Johnson. Apart from his skills and his ability to make his own opportunities, Johnson benefited from the support of many, including the oil, cattle, and cotton interests, John Nance Gardner, Sam Rayburn, and Franklin Roosevelt. He also benefited from Mexican support, which he repaid. On the other hand, Mexicans in California gained a pittance, if that, from supporting such relatively liberal elected officials such as the governors Earl Warren or Edmund G. Brown, Sr., Congressmen Chet Holifield or George Brown, or County Supervisors John A. Ford and (after his first controversial election) Ernest Debs.

Mexican participation in local politics in New Mexico and southern Colorado from the 1940s to 1960s had as broad a range of types as those in Texas. A significant difference was that historically, Mexican political leaders had network-controlled local offices and political organization at the county and municipal level in those areas whose Mexican population was a majority. A related circumstance involved most of the Mexican population in New Mexico and southern Colorado, which was composed of long-term inhabitants who held U.S. citizenship and hence voting rights by birth. However, the demographic impact of World War II, in stimulating a large-scale Anglo American population majority in New Mexico, led to the reduction of the number of counties and municipalities whose Mexican electorate provided a majority. By the end of the 1940s, the number of such counties had shrunk to a rural geographical area in northern New Mexico and a few counties in southern Colorado. By the end of the forties, larger urban cities such as Albuquerque, Santa Fe, and Las Vegas experienced the growth of an increasingly significant Anglo population which hesitated to vote Mexicans into office.

Mexicans in cities and towns with Anglo American majorities during the postwar period were at the time reduced to secondary or tertiary influence, but they strived continually, however frustratingly, to gain influence. One means toward achieving a voice was to organize an umbrella group of Mexican American organizations, offering tentative unity on issues and in coordinating activities, such as had been done in Chicago. This "mesa" or *central* notion was not easily realized, partly because there were differences in views and competing leaderships; but in any case, Mexican Americans floundered because of the lack of resources and activities through which to bargain. A partial example was the Council of Mexican American Affairs (CMAA) in Los Angeles, founded in 1953.[65] It had a governing board of thirteen at-large members and twelve representatives of the House of Delegates which were drawn from forty-four member organizations. These groups ranged from *mutualista* associations or social clubs to veteran and service organizations. The themes were "cooperation" and "unity," and supposedly these were to provide for progress. Mini-conferences were held on issues toward developing a common informational base. According to projections, CMAA was to have an office, a secretary, and director with a budget of fifty thousand dollars. Though CMAA lasted for ten years and did provide some positive contributions, it could not raise money and often there was not a quorum to conduct business or to elect officers, and little substantive political action was realized. Given the notorious incidents of police malpractice and electoral disappointments, an attempt at minimizing Mexican grievances at a 1960 U.S. Civil Rights Commission resulted in a notable reaction, with over five hundred people protesting under the rubric of the Mexican American Citizen Committee; a major figure in such protests for several decades was Celia Luna. As elsewhere in Los Angeles, the ideal of a coordinating structure endured and was reinvigorated with the establishment of the Congress of Mexican American Unity (CMAU), which superseded an offshoot of the earlier Council of Mexican American Organizations. Participants in CMAU during 1967–68 achieved some success, at least to the point of contributing in 1967 to the election of a Mexican to the Board of Education, Dr. Julian Nava, and in providing a forum and a consensual voice during the busy years from 1968 to 1970.

Why and Wherefore

In some respects, the influence of earlier patterns of political organization can be viewed either as prolonging Mexican political influence at the county and municipal levels or as impeding adaptation to changing demographic and economic realities. On one hand, the older continuities of electoral politics developed a group of Mexican political leaders with an electoral power base and the ability to influence blocs of votes at election time. At the state level this was exemplified in the practices of New Mexico, where Mexican leaders had some influence in major elected or appointed offices. On the other hand, the older political style was being preempted by changes that proved to be problematical in urbanizing areas with Anglo American majorities. Media penetration of the home and voter transience made efforts dependent upon political patronage positions resulting from control of local government, as well as accustomed methods of political mobilization, seem dated and clumsy. Difficulties in adapting to new methods of political mobilization stemmed in part from greater costs. Other contributing factors were the need for access to outside expertise and the increasing ability of Anglo candidates to appeal to Mexican voters vis-à-vis the continuing difficulty of Mexican candidates in gaining voter support from Anglos.

Objective aspects that impeded Mexican politicians at the local level while strengthening their Anglo American counterparts included, apart from targeted negative devices, lower levels of Mexican American education, income, employment, media exposure, image, and voter registration as compared to Anglo Americans.[66] Furthermore, in the increasingly large and important urban areas of the late fifties, Anglo political advantages were magnified by the larger scale of the urban political environments. Handicaps in local politics were present in all areas, but more notably so in areas of states such as California, Arizona as a whole, and the areas of Texas, Colorado, and New Mexico in which Mexicans were numerically a minority but a significant population. Mexicans were excluded from political participation almost as effectively as Blacks in Mississippi. Constant harassment at the polls from one end of the Southwest to the other impeded the registration of Mexican voters. At best, in some areas the Mexican electorate had approximately 50 percent registration and a somewhat higher figure for voting, with favorable rural figures lower than favorable urban ones; San Antonio during the fifties and early sixties had the highest rates of voter turnout among urban centers, with over 55 percent. But, in all cases, representation was minimal.

Only in a series of exceptional cases were Mexicans in the 1940s and 1950s able to overcome these handicaps in major urban communities through adoption of target methods of political mobilization and through coalitions with Blacks, labor unions, and other groups, as in the successful elections of Edward R. Roybal and Henry B. González to the Los Angeles and San Antonio city councils and Leopoldo Sanchez to the East Los Angeles Municipal Court. A few years later, Ed Peña and Joe Benal, both from San Antonio, were elected Commissioner for Bexar County and Texas senator, respectively. At another level, in a series of political successes Mexican politicians in a number of small towns with predominantly Mexican populations were elected to office: this occurred, for example, in San Fernando,

Ontario, and Colton, California; San Angelo and Mathis, Texas; and
Clifton and Miami, Arizona. In one case, a Mexican woman, Tina
Villanueva, achieved the precedent of being elected justice of the
peace in Jim Wells County, Texas, in 1966. Soon after her election,
however, her district was abolished. Others, when elected to office in
Texas, were humiliated by their colleagues: two council members were
excluded from council meetings, and a state legislator was pistol-
whipped by Texas Rangers. The respected Californian Edward R. Roybal was also humiliated upon first being elected to the Los Angeles
city council seat, in this case by his own council colleagues.

Both the urban and rural electoral successes of this period provide
examples of extensive grass-roots efforts at urban mobilization; exper-
imentation with a variety of campaign methods; and the involvement
of World War II veteran activists from membership groups. Two other
elements were often present in the urban victories and small town
successes—coalition politics and trade union participation. These, in
turn, were influenced by two most important factors: the change in
popular consciousness and expectations created by wartime prosperity,
and the series of challenges to the government which were publicized
in the media declaring that the United States would indeed become
a less discriminatory democratic society with civil liberties for all,
including Mexicans. Thousands of Mexican Americans were receptive
to these possibilities and ready to cooperate in order to share fully in
both prosperity and the exercise of civil liberties. The "free" exercise
of the voting franchise to secure elected representation was said to be
the "American Way," and Mexican Americans were ready to register
and vote. In communities where Mexican candidates enjoyed favorable
district circumstances, were supported by effective campaign organizations, had a sufficient base of registered voters, and were able to
form coalitions with other groups, they were able to make significant
showings or win an occasional election.

Almost as memorable as the victories in electoral politics are the
defeats; for example, the defeat in California of Ed Quevedo for councilman, Henry Lopez for secretary of state, and Anthony Bueno for
assembly. Obviously, electoral defeats have not been as popular a topic
for reflection and discussion after the event as have victories. By the
score, there were unsuccessful campaigns for office in the period from
the 1940s to the 1960s. Richard Calderon waged major efforts to win
office in East Los Angeles and drew considerable support, though one

MAPA leader denounced him as a communist. A case in point was the state senate primary race between Assemblyman George Danielson and Richard Calderon in 1966. Despite support of much of the Chicano community, as well as of such organizations as the United Auto Workers, the Californians for Liberal Representation, and Women For Calderon, he was unsuccessful in his bid for the Democratic nomination, losing by less than five hundred votes. In the previous year, with Danielson as vice-chairman of the Reapportionment Committee, the boundaries of this senate district, the most populous for Chicanos, had been redrawn, thus removing a considerable number of Chicano voters, eight thousand, to other districts to strengthen Democrats, and making it very improbable that a Chicano would garner enough votes from his community to be elected, especially since Anglos would not vote for one in significant numbers. Yet, as the careers of both Edward R. Roybal and Henry B. González demonstrate, a hard-fought and close campaign could lay the basis for future victory. An examination of close but unsuccessful campaigns for office demonstrates to what extent increasing Mexican political awareness and participation generated, in reaction, the adoption of more sophisticated techniques of electoral discrimination such as increased gerrymandering, at-large elections and negative poll monitoring, the changing of precinct boundaries or electoral districts at the last minute, the failure to mail notification of registration—all tactics used to deny equal voting rights and effective political representation and supplementing the standard and more traditional impediments of poll taxes, residency and language requirements, physical harassment, and so forth. These adjudicated the manner in which the postwar changing political climate affected Mexican electoral politics at the local levels.

Organizations faced a number of common problems which, in fact, stemmed from the discriminatory, impoverished, and disenfranchised state of the community. One problem was a recurring one and posed the question of to what degree it was advantageous or disadvantageous to identify as an ethnic organization in behalf of ethnic interest. Self-proscription by an organization from political participation, though there were possible gains to be realized, meant eliminating organizational resources from the means of addressing directly the governance sources of the problems they were constituted to alleviate. To be not only political and electoral but nonpartisan ostensibly provided maneuverability and a sharper focus to direct energies, but partisanship was a major part of the political arena, particularly if the strength was electoral numbers rather than finances, expertise, status, or publicity. Party politics continued, but party officials were set on not incorporating Mexican leadership, much less providing resources for their activities; nor were they merely upon request to facilitate Mexican candidates and set aside others. The more cohesive organizations at best could raise money for their operating costs and to continue their services, but they were not able to raise funds beyond such a point. These organizations as well as new ones primarily depended on modest dues which were not always collectible. Finances were lacking for an activity, politics, which costs money. The multiple groups were a reality, however, and could be seen as a strength or as a problem. Coordination was a continuing difficulty. The myriad small and specialized organizations providing particular satisfactions were not likely to grow into larger groups, and there were no incentives immediately available to encourage them to make their priority either advocacy or electoral work. Furthermore, coordination proved to be a further burden above those already borne by both leaders and members. Coordinative activity was viewed as important to the more senior and experienced of the larger groups, much less so to others. If intragroup coordination was a problem even for multichapter groups, "unity" alliances and coalitions with others were even more problematic for smaller groups, though it remained a repeatedly expressed aspiration. Efforts at coordination, and certainly those aimed at unity, involve the proposition of compromise at different levels.

Activist Mexicans in a frequently disregarded and unequal position were often loathe to compromise or associate, given that they were inspired to be active because they wished to put their community, their issues, and their leaders first. Partially related to the questions of resources, but more attitudinal was the posture toward youth, women, at-large participation, and immigrants. Organizations did not turn away members, and in major groups such as LULAC and the G.I. Forum there were youth and women branches. Nevertheless, in a decade marked by the growing importance of youth, organizations did not encourage proactive youth or women's participation. Many youth activists can recall one or more experiences of negative interface with the older leadership. The rift between young and old activists would prove to be as weakening as it was seemingly unnecessary. Organizations railed against "apathy" and called for civil and human rights respect; yet political activity was seen as primarily involving leaders and aspirants to leadership. Action too often meant one professional or merchant writing to another asking for a letter to be addressed to an official or a particular office. Given the creditable record of activity between the forties and midsixties, there was more, of course; but for the most part, mass efforts or calls were not made to the at-large community or to immigrants.

Changes in leadership and organizational modes were interactive, and patterns were evident.[67] Elected officials and elected organizational leaders were most widely accepted as formal leaders, and reputational and institutional leaders were acknowledged on the basis of acceptance to both internal and external audiences; leadership combined authoritarian and motivational and ideological aspects. The authoritarian leader forced activity by strength of character, the ideological leader by ideas and insights. The first type eventually caused a negative reaction, but the second persisted longer. The patriarchal or self-proclaimed leader was increasingly superseded. Leaders became more educated and had more income and independence of action than was the rule for community members; and invariably, they were active for several years. They were also more likely to participate in several organizations and civil projects concurrently, to be competently bilingual, church-affiliated, married and with children, and decorous in their behavior. A rule was a pronounced commitment to civic equities and to organizational action. Formal organization was understood to be the basis for the advancement of goals. The practiced mode was negotiation. Among the formal leadership, responsibility, accountability, and public disclosure were consensual duties. Leaders were invariably criticized, but this was part of the leadership experience and a usual part of organizational life. Organizations were not lacking; every community had several while the larger centers contained dozens. A rough division can be made between those that were specifically pro-Mexican—whether general or specialized, expressive or instrumental—and those which were Mexican by virtue of organizational location and membership. Not surprisingly, participants were a minority within the total population; but they tended to be more stable in their employment and their residence and to be more informed than the average citizen in the community. Organizations varied in their focus, of course, as well as in their way of operating. Most were not ephemeral and lasted more than a few years; and a crisis usually revolved around the transition from the founding figure to a more pluralistic and participatory leadership. Most met from once to twice a month, followed well-understood rules of participation, with membership between twenty and fifty persons, modest dues, and activity. Organizations varied in prestige with more respect accorded the more formal groups. They varied, however, in discourse and energy, and obviously organizations were composed of those with strong ethnic concerns. There was an abundance of organizations, led by individuals who understood organizational procedures. Nevertheless, there was a real need for greater organizational skills, compounded by a lack of resources. At one time or another, attempts were made to teach organizational and leadership skills, whether by large groups such as LULAC, the G.I. Forum, the unions, or churches. Though all participants freely chose to become members, those who were more active often comprised the core of an organization. The need was for competent leadership and effective participation as well as for contributing members. Debilitating to the Mexican leadership and to organizational development were two major institutions indifferent to Mexicans: the political parties and the universities; the first inhibited political space, the second human leadership material. Despite problems, however, organizations continued, and coalitions and alliances were formed on an operational or de facto basis.

Laws and Rights

A number of national legislations impacted on Mexicanos.[68] The most obvious bills were Public Laws 45 (1943) and 78 (1950), which created and extended the Bracero Program; the closing of the program (1964) also created an impact. Three measures were particularly negative. The 1952 McCarran–Walter Act worsened labor conditions and the political harassment of Mexicans, particularly progressives. The 1947 Taft–Hartley Act undid much of what had been positive in the mildly prolabor-organizing Wagner Act of 1935. It made stronger the right-to-work laws and management prerogatives, and it limited union participation in electoral politics and furthered the antiradical climate. Beginning in 1949, a series of measures were enacted through the Housing Act that strengthened the right of federal, state, and local governments to eminent domain, which meant, in turn, that privileged developers could profit from others' property, a fact eventually affecting Chicano neighborhoods from the border to Chicago. There were significant and positive legal precedents. In the Peter Hernández case, the Supreme Court ruled Mexicans were "a distinct class" which, under certain conditions, could claim protection from discrimination. Chief Justice Earl Warren argued:

Circumstances or chance may well dictate that no persons in a certain class will serve on a particular jury or during some particular period. But it taxes our credulity to say that mere chance resulted in there being no members of this class among the over six thousand jurors called in the past 25 years. The result bespeaks discrimination, whether or not it was a conscious decision on the part of any individual jury commissioner. The judgement of conviction must be reversed. (Supreme Court of the United States, no. 406, October Term, 1953)

This decision preceded by two weeks the better-known ruling in *Brown* vs. *Board of Education*. Tellingly, the case was made possible by community funds and argued by Mexican attorneys, Gus García and Carlos Cadena. Nevertheless, the Texas police had their say, inducing Hernández to confess. Earlier, the 1946 McCormick decision in California established that there was no legal sanction for public school discrimination. The *Hernandez et al.* v. *Driscoll Consolidated Independent School District et al.* (1957) determined on appeal by the U.S. District Court of the Southern District of Texas that grouping of pupils on the basis of ancestry (Mexican) was arbitrary and unreasonable. Thus, the Hernandez–Driscoll case in the southern district of Texas brought an end to the practice of requiring Mexican children to spend two years in the first grade. Even more far-reaching politically, the 1964 Economic Opportunity Act and the Civil Rights Act of 1965 made a major impact in fueling civic participation and voting.

Despite difficulties and insufficient resources or support, the Mexican community between the 1940s and 1960s expanded its space in several areas of discrimination even as it continued to endure it. Through protest and formal grievances, the more blatant forms of discrimination in employment were ended in principle. Job openings in public employment and in some of the private sector were created. Discrimination in compensation and assignment persisted as did the exclusion from middle and senior positions. Formal school segregation ended, and some educational benefits were obtained through specific community initiatives. Crucially, in 1965 a modest public scholarship funding was made available, and not surprisingly the number enrolling in college began to increase. Exclusion from juries, from voting, and from services was steadily eroded even though much remained to be done. Positive changes included the ending of the poll tax practice and the enabling of grievances with regard to electoral practices and the right in principle to access to the courts for representation. Social discrimination as galling but not as substantive as discrimination in other areas also was legally challenged. Protest and court cases ended formal discrimination against Mexicans in public facilities and through property covenants. These were real accomplishments; the generations following the sixties were not to be born under conditions of explicit exclusion.

1960, and the Answer to Someone Else's Call

The civil rights movement, the Adlai Stevenson campaigns, and the rhetoric of John F. Kennedy quickened Mexican politics; in effect, the Mexican vote was large and dependable enough to be targeted, and television reached everyone.[69] With the beginning of the civil rights movement and the end of the McCarthy era in the late 1950s, reformism was relatively in vogue in the United States; both were stimulated by the candidacies of Adlai Stevenson and John F. Kennedy and both impacted the community, but the latter was more visible. In 1960, John F. Kennedy campaigned for the presidency against Richard M. Nixon, President Eisenhower's protégé. The Kennedy campaign had considerable influence on Mexican American political development through the Viva Kennedy effort to attract the Mexican vote. The election of John F. Kennedy and Lyndon B. Johnson produced a few benefits, and it did lead to more jobs for the enterprising in poverty programs.

In some areas which had participated in elections since the nineteenth century, Mexican votes obviously were important. Prior to the presidential election of 1960, Mexican American and Latino voters had participated in one candidacy or another of both major parties and in several third parties.[70] At the Democratic conventions throughout the 1940s the major elected officials of New Mexico had some voice. Although a few delegates were sent to the national conventions, apart from two or three officials, Mexicans were not widely recognized electorally as a significant factor in the national presidential elections. Mexican American voters were taken for granted as a known but modest part of the Democratic Party constituency. Waging a closely contested race, John F. Kennedy, because of need and probably in part because of the influence of vice-presidential candidate Texan Lyndon B. Johnson, was the first presidential candidate to address the Mexican American voter saliently. The 1960 election campaign and results significantly altered previous low estimations of the vote through the general activity of the Viva Kennedy organization. In particular, the Kennedy electoral victory over Nixon in the state of Texas was seen by some as having been made possible by the margin of Mexican American votes obtained by Kennedy. Some noted these votes were due to traditional networks functioning in Texas.

The Viva Kennedy movement encompassed the activities of Mexican political leaders, including elected officials such as Senator Dennis Chavez, congressmen Edward R. Roybal and Henry B. González, and organizations that included the American G.I. Forum, the Mexican American Political Association, and the Alianza Hispano Americana, represented by Carlos McCormick of Arizona as well as by members of the senior Kennedy staff and, of course, volunteers including a significant number of youth, among them some who would continue on to make political careers of their own.[71] Several individuals claim to have originated the notion of the "viva" club, which became a significant electoral phenomenon in the community, eventually impacting on tens of thousands of lives. The point of targeting Mexican voters was clearly consistent with the significance of large states and the need to target receptive sectors within those states to secure a majority of electoral votes. If, as a consequence, multiplication of votes occurred in contiguous states, so much the better. In any case, Robert Kennedy was operationally in charge of the overall campaign, and Edward Kennedy was director of the fourteen western states which included the Southwest. LULAC and G.I. Forum members were in contact with the Kennedy campaign, as were Edward Roybal and MAPA with their access to a relatively large constituency in Los Angeles, a city viewed as the key to winning California. Mexican leaders including Senator Chavez, Representative González, and Councilman Roybal took the Viva Kennedy concept to Robert Kennedy, who approved it; and these three were named chairs for their states. The first two had available to them established networks to generate the vote, and Congressman González also had the support of Lyndon Johnson as well as the outreach of the G.I. Forum and LULAC. California provided a more problematic situation generally and especially with regard to Mexicans. Immediately after the July Democratic convention and the nomination of Kennedy, Roybal attended a Democratic Party meeting in San Francisco to plan the means for victory in California. Assembly leader William Munnal was to be in charge of California coordination under Governor Edmund Brown, Sr. As the senior Mexican leader, Roybal was assigned responsibility for East Los Angeles precincts, and MAPA was to work with Munnel. Roybal wisely selected Ralph Guzman to head operations, and he recruited an electoral force.

A major effort in targeting Mexicans was undertaken with specific responsibilities to overcome registration and voter-turnout obstacles as well as funding limitations. Guzman and others saw the effort as one which, apart from contributing to the immediate campaign, would be a building block for Mexican political cohesion and influence. Apart from registration gatherings, meetings were held in public and private locales to stimulate electoral interest as well as to provide campaign spots for candidates. Distinctive material and buttons were prepared. On October 12, 1960, Día de la Raza, Chavez, Roybal, and González met with Ted Kennedy to upgrade organization and resources, and Chavez and Roybal were named national cochairs. Representatives of the Southwest Viva Kennedy clubs met at San Pedro, California, on October 17, and amid the gleeful note of the opponents' emulative effort to mount "Arriba Nixon" groups, they agreed on priorities for the last few days. Texas and New Mexico seemed reasonably favorable, and the priority for the last days was California. Los Angeles received candidate stops at Olvera Street; and a major rally was held at East Los Angeles Community College with seats for 22,500, but there were nearly twice as many persons in and around the stadium. Kennedy had achieved unprecedented overt enthusiasm among Mexicans. The opposition's counteroffensive was seen on election day where, through one ruse or another, Mexicans were to be hindered in voting.

Apart from the organizational coordination, candidate actions help explain election results. John Kennedy actively campaigned in Mexican communities and became an honorary member of LULAC and the G.I. Forum, and he repeatedly identified visually with one community aspect or another. Mexican American voters seemingly responded to a candidate who appeared to take them seriously, was charismatic, addressed issues in Latin America, shared with most of them a Roman Catholic religious heritage, and had a wife who spoke to them in Spanish. In fact, they responded to a rhetorical program articulated pointedly by the candidate which addressed somewhat their issues—economics and discrimination. Because of this and the hard work of the Viva Kennedy movement, John F. Kennedy received approximately 85 percent of the Mexican American vote nationally. In Texas and New Mexico, Mexican American voters provided the margin of victory for Kennedy. In Texas, Kennedy won an extraordinary 91 percent of the Mexican American vote, 200,000 votes, which allowed him to win the state and hence the presidency. In New Mexico Kennedy received 70 percent of the Mexican American vote, which narrowly allowed him to win the state by two thousand votes, even though he had not received a majority among Anglos. Kennedy also secured significant votes in other southwestern states with large Mexican populations, including California, Arizona, and Colorado. While he received over 70 percent of the Mexican American vote in each of these three states, the extent of voter registration made this support not as decisive a factor as in Texas. However, the returns in these states made political operatives graphically realize that higher voting rates and higher registration by Mexicans may have altered the outcomes in these states.

The Kennedy election in 1960 signaled a change in the political temper of the Mexican middle class. The organization of Viva Kennedy clubs for the presidential election had tapped the Mexican community voting potential. To reach these voters, traditional middle-class leaderships were mobilized to lead and organize voter registration drives and get-out-the-vote campaigns; in addition, they argued that Mexicans were appointed to some posts, but not without twists. One example was the objectionable appointment of Reynaldo Garza as a federal District Judge for the South Texas District, the first Mexican to serve in such a capacity. His appointment came through L. B. Johnson, but activist Mexicans did not comprise his supporters. Garza had not supported Mexican Americans or other party efforts in the 1950s, and he was seen as a conservative. Raymond Telles was made ambassador to Costa Rica, the first such appointment; and Hector P.

Garcia was named to the delegation negotiating a defense treaty with the Federation of the West Indies. More felicitously received were administrative appointments to positions in programs such as the Peace Corps, the Agency for International Development, and the Alliance for Progress.

Frustrations, Persistence, and Opportunity

As the Kennedy campaign unfolded and its success was recorded— a preeminent example of mobilization for an emphatic white liberal— there loomed the dual need for electoral organizations, statewide and regional, which could negotiate the vote and more effectively run indigenous candidates; such, however, was not to be realized. The prominence of the need did not immediately translate into local electoral organizational strength. PASSO had victories and frustrations, and so did MAPA. MAPA had declared as its overriding concerns (1) "the election and appointment of Mexican Americans and other persons sympathetic to our aims to public office," and (2) the need "to take stands on political issues and to present and endorse candidates for public office."[72] Accordingly, the organization ostensibly emphasized in its statements voter registration, education, and participation, as well as lobbying and antidiscrimination activities focused on police and school practices. Though largely composed of Democrats, Republicans and Independents were also involved in MAPA, and it was hoped that this would strengthen its bargaining power. Though founded with enthusiasm by 150 people, this number did not grow in step with the electoral needs; moreover, MAPA soon began to be viewed as an ineffectual group. There were endorsements forthcoming, but no precinct work or significant fund raising was realized. Materials were comprised, at most, of buttons and bumper stickers, few in number and those not even widely distributed. In retrospect, an organization devoted to enhancing electoral empowerment would be well situated in the sixties and seventies. Indeed, electoral enhancement occurred, but not because of organizations like MAPA.

This as well as other organizations were plagued by numerous and at times seemingly inherent problems. Lack of resources and political differences hindered the effectiveness of these organizations. Leadership conflicts and insufficiently articulated goals militated against broad community support and participation. There was no outreach instrument apart from poorly produced newsletters, and no attempt was made toward conceptualizing a mystique. The unorganized and unnegotiated commitment of Mexican American voters to the Democratic Party limited the bargaining stance of the political organizations, especially since Democrats in the leadership reassured the party operatives that Mexicans would remain in the Democratic Party's column. At the same time, the official bipartisan status of MAPA and others closed some political avenues. The tendency toward *liderismo*, or loyalty to the individual leader rather than to the organization as a whole, was alleged to be an obstacle to the development of a strong political organization. More debilitating was the lack of effective leadership. Leaders could not devote themselves to the organizations full time or, in place of this, afford to hire a competent staff. In addition, leadership was determined through rhetoric and by packing meetings. The effectiveness, vitality, and membership of organizations went through a cycle of highs and lows. A major setback for PASSO was the Crystal City defeat; MAPA's most significant setback was the failure of the campaign to incorporate East Los Angeles in 1961. An effort to incorporate, then as well as later, promised a municipal status for the major urban concentration of Mexican Americans in the country. In its rhetoric, MAPA addressed issues of ethnicity and political office rather than taxes or services, which provided the opposition with its agenda. Poorly financed and coordinated, the effort failed; but the organizational efforts continued and eventually were modestly rewarded.

Opportunities were possible. The Kennedy–Johnson administrations set in motion a diversity of social and economic maximization programs targeted at disadvantaged or discriminated subpopulations, which meant resources, employment, and validation for political leaderships. Blacks benefited visibly, and Mexicans were aroused. "Viva Kennedy" leaders and other organizational leaders felt that they had provided President Kennedy with crucially needed votes in key states in the election (such as Texas). After a Republican administration, these leaders had been motivated by the belief that a Democratic administration in Washington would be more understanding of and accessible to their problems. "Viva Kennedy" leaders had hoped for appointments of Mexican Americans to the new social programs as

well as to major positions in formulating Latin American policy. However, they were disappointed after the election; they believed President
Kennedy did not sufficiently or amply reward them for their efforts in
the form of political appointments.[73] In late 1960 a "national unity"
meeting was called at Phoenix, Arizona, and attended by LULAC,
the G.I. Forum, the Alianza, CSO, MAPA, and others. "Unity" was
attempted but it was not made continuous due to disagreements over
regional, organizational, issue, and ethnic labels. As the numbers
increased and as the community's unrealized electoral potential was
more and more insisted upon, the tangible benefits of coordination
and the joint demands for a fair share of federal funds and projects
encouraged action, and also had unforeseen effects on organizations
and leaderships. Mexicans were indeed not receiving a fair share, and
they were forced to recognize the difference between themselves and
Blacks who were quite visible and seemingly more effectively organized. As sustainers of a Mexican civil rights movement, the leadership
of the forties and fifties sympathized and supported the Black civil
rights movement and its goals; they were not, however, in step with
its ideological or tactical dynamism. They were more perplexed by the
Black power movement, which stressed autonomy in all spheres. It
went against their political grain as much as it did for older and more
moderate Blacks. However, they did understand that identity and
mobilization were resources, and they wanted a share of the more
conventional resources.

As a major civil rights debate unfolded, Mexicans were at first not
well positioned. Several (four) congressmen did not have a major
impact on legislation, nor were they greatly successful with the bureaucracy; but they were a presence and a voice. They also contributed
to the informational and coordinative resources available to Mexican
American organizations. At Washington they performed a range of
constituent favors. Legislatively, they offered opinions and voted on
the key legislation of the time; for example, the Voting Rights Act,
immigration proposals, and language programs. They also promoted
very modestly what few possibilities for employment existed. González
and de la Garza were the more successful politicians in the Washington
maze. From the point of view of their constituents in a period of
national revitalization, they were not present in their home districts
nor visible in Washington; in any case, however, they were rather
conventional players who observed the rules. Older Blacks did not

readily grant existing Mexican American leadership entry; as a case in point, the United Civil Rights Committee of Los Angeles formed in 1963 refused them recognition.

In the early sixties came a loose effort at coordination referred to as National Organization of Mexican American Services (NOMAS) involving members of the larger organizations. The modest objectives included dissemination of information and contact with foundations while eschewing partisanship and advocacy; and apparently no plan or resources existed. More specific were the rudimentary efforts of the Mexican congressmen to maintain liaison with each other. To achieve a fair share was at the core of the insistence on a White House conference. This would be a vehicle for legitimization and the receipt of equities. There was indeed a meeting, the 1965 White House Conference on Civil Rights; however, it was intended primarily for Blacks. In lieu of unmet expectations, the Johnson administration held a meeting with Mexican American representatives and the U.S. Equal Employment Opportunities Commission at Albuquerque in March 1966.[74] There were no Mexicans on the commission, and in any case, only a token representation of the commissioners was present; not even the chair, Franklin Roosevelt, Jr., attended. Such a clear message of rejection sparked a set of demands and a walkout as well as a pledge by those present to maintain unity vis-à-vis the Johnson administration and to continue the pressure.

Underneath all this was the maneuvering to decide who the favored Mexican representatives would be.[75] The G.I. Forum and LULAC maneuvered best. Shortly afterward, Vicente Ximenes was appointed to the commission. A further response was the administration's marked preference for dealing with representatives of LULAC and the G.I. Forum who were known to Johnson, while bypassing others. Between 1966 and 1967 steps were taken which resulted in the Inter-Agency Cabinet Committee on Mexican American Affairs, with Ximenes playing a key role in accordance with the administration. After Albuquerque, the next galvanizing incident was the White House conference planned for El Paso in late October 1967 as an adjunct to meeting with the president of Mexico for the turnover of some land acreage. The conference was intended as a showcase for the new Cabinet Committee, organized by the administration and its chosen insiders, but the planning for the conference as well as the list of prospective invitees angered several Mexican American leaders. Six hundred dis-

sidents met in El Paso to plan their own conference for November in
San Antonio. This conference would focus on protest and condemnation. The result was a commitment to a coordinating committee,
a general platform, and an announcement for a larger conference, to
meet again in San Antonio on January 6, 1968.

But regardless of whether a fair share of federal programs was
obtained between 1960 and 1967, a new element was present in the
community—federal program employees.[76] Whether they came from
activist members of prior existing organizations or were recruited from
the ranks of those primarily active elsewhere, if at all, but known to
Anglo politicians and to the administration, a sector of federal employees was a novel interdiction; so was a sector for whom "representing" the community provided a job with status and the possibility
for more. They were to enhance services through federal, state, and
local government agencies; in fact, they were paid or subsidized by
the Office of Economic Opportunity, U.S. Department of Labor, to
be both intermediaries and formal leaders. Many began to build or to
add to networks as they felt the tension between agency obligations
and constraints and community needs and pressures. Although many
were formally proscribed from direct partisan politics, associated political activity took place nevertheless, whether in Texas, California,
or Colorado; and it involved professionals—in some cases priests—
who were recent college graduates or even undergraduates, self-up-
graded lay persons, former housewives, small-business persons, blue-
collar workers, and others. They had a stake in defending and maintaining their position as well as in enlarging the scope of their activities
based on the unmet equities due to the community. Organized groups
also benefited, thus improving their resources and outreach; among
these particularly were the G.I. Forum and LULAC. An exceptionally
skilled individual was Manuel Aragon, who was appointed to direct
the Economic and Youth Opportunities Agency of Los Angeles (of the
U.S. Department of Commerce's Economic Development Administration); this agency covered three hundred positions and had a fifty-
million-dollar budget. The responsibility entailed relations with the
spectrum of social and economic interest groups within Los Angeles.
With varied experiences ranging from agricultural work to student
body candidate for Slate, the progressive campus party of the University of California at Berkeley, and stints in a variety of campaigns,
Aragon became a major player in the politics of public service. Urbane

and articulate, his personal style prefigured that adopted by other civic leaders during the seventies. He also faced continuous personnel and constituency pressures. Upon the 1973 election of Tom Bradley as mayor, Aragon was named deputy mayor, and later he was among those who successfully entered the business sector. The War on Poverty had a significant impact by circulating some monies, civic experience, and jobs and increasing the participation of low-income people, women, and youth, as well as of those who had experienced difficulties with school or legal authorities.

Debits and Lessons

By the midsixties, nationally the Mexican American community numbered a significant four to five million and one of the major areas of growth was in California and Los Angeles, an undeniably important state and city, where a major civil rights movement occurred.[77] As in the past, in the sixties the leadership of the larger society and the society's institutional representatives had done much to mold the Mexican community and the beliefs of its members; and the social configuration was a reflection of its economic assignment. For some, the perception of the dominant society was a reflection of what the larger society had done to the community and had not done for it. Rather than acquiescence and petitioning, incident after incident in daily life taught Mexicans bitter lessons about Anglos, and each liability they suffered was a result of Anglo action. Reflective of this process were the educational liabilities of youth, and particularly crucial were the whys and wherefores of continuing discrimination in the schools.[78]

An entire generation of activists had endeavored to bring about the change which seemed imminent in 1945, and their slow progress had shaped both them and the lessons to be learned from their experience. The wartime fight for democracy signaled a new promise for the future of Mexican Americans, but in the end the promise failed. Returning veterans of World War II found that rampant discrimination still prevailed on the home front, long after peace was established.[79] In Texas, even a Congressional Medal of Honor was not enough to gain a dead war hero burial in an all-white cemetery or to get a live hero served at a lunch counter in California. Comparatively more superficial forms of racism such as segregated Mexican nights at swimming pools and movie theaters, which were being disavowed in the large cities, still persisted in the smaller communities of supposedly more liberal California. Returning Mexican veterans found that they could not buy new homes in newly developed suburbs because of restrictive housing covenants. While the employment situation had improved due to postwar demand and reconstruction, Mexicans were still excluded from most skilled industrial jobs and white-collar occupations. Educational discrimination including school segregation still prevailed, although it would become increasingly *de facto* rather than *de jure*. Mexican war veterans were also forced to witness police harassment of youth and the degrading brutality of immigration raids that targeted only persons who "looked Mexican." Worst for the future was the inferior schooling and its negative effects on the young.

Probably the most debilitating effect of prejudice, however, was the continued maintenance of the dominant Anglo American attitude of superiority toward Mexicans, a combination of ethnocentrism and supremacism. The dominant society still believed that Mexicans should be grateful for being allowed to live in the United States, and for having any job at all. Though they were native to the continent, Mexican Americans were perceived as foreigners by most Anglo Americans, in spite of an actual history in the Southwest which preceded the founding of the thirteen British colonies that became the United States. The maintenance of an attitude of ethnic and cultural superiority would continue to be the mainstay behind the special set of unequal relationships existing between the two groups.

Interlinked with the Anglo American–Mexican American relationship was the unequal relationship of the United States with Mexico. The subordinate status of the Mexican in the United States had originated in the 1840s with Mexico's defeat and territorial loss. That unequal status and the subordinate relationship of Mexico in its relations with the United States continued to be interlinked and mutually reinforcing, and was perpetuated regardless of whether Mexicans or Mexican Americans wanted it or widely understood it. In the postwar period, immigration and the Bracero Program became the most visible and highly charged fulcrums of the Mexican–United States relationship. Deportations in the mid-1950s of over one million Mexicans from the United States most visibly signaled the continued status of Mexican Americans in the United States and the position of Mexico as an unequal and dependent ally.

Despite the organizational challenge by Mexican Americans to discrimination in the forties, fifties, and sixties and economic gains resulting from postwar economic booms, the unequal position between Mexican Americans and Anglo Americans probably expanded rather than contracted. Mexican advances in education, income, employment, occupational status, and political representation were dwarfed by the much larger gains of Anglo Americans. As the great promise of postwar equality failed to materialize, an attitude of recrimination took shape. Providing an intellectual rationale for this phenomenon, which was somewhat novel in the late thirties through the forties, academically based intellectuals during the fifties and early sixties such as George Sanchez, Carlos Castaneda, Arturo Campa, Ernesto Galarza, Americo Paredes, and Ralph Guzman contributed to a slowly growing contemporary literature of affirmation that kept pace with the tempo of the political evolution.

3

Liberalism: The Chicano Movement and Its Organizations from the 1960s to the 1970s

Introduction

Between 1966 and 1978 the Mexican American community faced, at least tentatively, a juncture between integration or self-determination, with rhetoric highlighting the latter while circumstances spelled out the conditions of the former.[1] This juncture was the result of the intercession of interacting events and inequities. The perceived ineffectiveness of liberalism and the increasing economic and human costs of the undeclared and victoryless war in Vietnam, combined with urban youth dissidence and ethnic protest, were productive of growing social and political unrest. A disillusionment experienced by the Mexican community as a result of the slow and modest economic and civil gains since 1948 was an aspect in the activist politics of the later years of the period. There was change as well as a lack of change. Even though the Mexican continued to enter the skilled labor market, larger numbers were kept poor through discrimination, exploitation, and the social control mechanism of selective and limited mobility. At the same time, a modest economic and political elite burgeoned and solidified. Concurrently, large-scale political organizing with a hitherto unprecedented intensity became evident. In the fifties and sixties, the number elected to office slowly increased, but underrepresentation remained the rule. Electoral political momentum continued throughout the sixties and seventies to be accompanied by slow gains. In comparison with preceding periods, labor organizing continued and increased in the scope of the industries it reached; nevertheless, more

101

people by far were outside the unions than inside them. Explicit discrimination receded in some areas of employment and housing, but it did not disappear. For some activists toward the midsixties, matters compelled a reevaluation of earlier ideological tenets and the development by both older and younger activists of a new style of politics, which was based on wide mobilization and an insistence upon democratic rights. Most importantly, the community grew numerically, including citizens as well as high school and college graduates; growth continued into the decades that followed. As an expression of denials and gains, Chicano politics became increasingly regional and national as well as local.

The Movement and the Mainstream

In 1966, Senator Joseph Montoya (D-NM) told a group of Mexican Americans that if they would organize, work together, and, above all, register and vote, they could become one of the most politically potent groups in the United States.[2] Mexican political activity during the early 1960s entered a new phase. It became increasingly more varied and complex, reflecting all hues of the political spectrum. The origins of the new political activity lie in the political climate and material conditions of the early 1960s. An accelerated increase occurred in the Mexican population which was caused by both birthrate and immigration. As a result, the community aroused some scholarly and political interest; and the contrasting opinions contributed to ideological growth. Mexicans were a little more recognized by the media as the nation's second largest minority, a minority overwhelmingly found to be holding the least desirable and worst paying jobs in the economy, a people who lagged behind the income and schooling levels of both Anglos and Blacks. The social and economic conditions of the Mexican people heightened the national consciousness of political activists. Furthermore, the United States, both socially and economically, was undergoing the impact of the federal programs of the sixties. Mexican contact with government services increased both in relation to services received as well as to services demanded. Past experience with government agencies was a uniquely abrasive one, and Mexicans received the regulatory attention primarily, rather than the service or support aspect, of agencies. As service became slightly more accessible, hostile government attitudes and practices remained the rule and became the focus of protest and mobilization.

Changes in both the domestic and international climate of ideas also contributed to renewed Mexican political activity. The civil rights movement of the 1960s focused attention primarily on the problems of Blacks, while devoting some attention to the problems of other minorities. The Kennedy administration's "New Frontier" and Johnson's "Great Society" environment seemed to be willing to consider the increased demands by Mexicans for equal citizenship rights. Both administrations increased the resources available to community activism. The aftermath of the Cuban Revolution, and later the African and Vietnamese liberation wars, galvanized Mexican consciousness about the conditions of Third World peoples within the United States. Changes in international relations contributed to the development of a nationalist perspective of the Mexican situation in the United States as well as strengthening the civil rights impulse among political activists.

Within the ferment created by changes in the ideological climate and material conditions of the early 1960s, there arose a variegated burst of activity loosely identified as the "Chicano movement."[3] Seminal initiating forces were the Farm Workers Union, the Alianza, the Crusade for Justice, student organizations, and eventually, La Raza Unida. Workers or persons of working-class origin were key to these forces, and women often provided the organizational backbone. Whatever the particular goals and methods of the political activism, the underlying current was disenchantment over the Mexican's political, economic, and social status in an Anglo-dominated capitalist society. Political activists became increasingly concerned with understanding how economic and class exploitation and racism had shaped the Mexican experience in the United States. The struggle to understand the Mexican American experience increasingly focused on questions of alienation, ethnicity, identity, class, gender, and chauvinism. An articulation of a historical understanding of the Mexican experience became a paramount motif, a necessity in the struggle to shape a future for La Raza in the United States.

Although "Chicanismo" was often a loosely expressed concept, it did translate as a radically political and ethnic populism. Chicano politics emerged as a challenge to the assumptions, politics, and principles of the established political leaders, organizations, and activity within and outside the community; and once again the issue of national identity was in the forefront. Although politics in the early 1960s was overwhelmingly liberal and reformist in nature, more radical currents were nascent. However, the dynamic force was often distrustful of known electoral *políticos*. These currents encompassed separatist and anticorporation tendencies. To voice and express hopes and affirmations, and certainly the praxis of an overt identity, there came into use among the youth, the term *Chicano*, a word used as a group referent since at least the turn of the century. Chicano denoted the person and group, while "Chicanismo" referred to a set of beliefs; in particular, a political practice. The emphasis of "Chicanismo" upon dignity, self-worth, pride, uniqueness, and a feeling of cultural rebirth made it attractive to many Mexicans in a way that cut across class, regional, and generational lines. In some way or other, most Mexicans had experienced, directly or indirectly, economic or social discrimination. These negative experiences increased the appeal of "Chicanismo"; it emphasized Mexican cultural consciousness and heritage as well as pride in speaking Spanish language *and* economic opportunity. However, even though it marked a progressive step in the struggle for identity since it denied the grosser aspects of deculturalization, it also became a subterfuge for avoiding identity. The widespread appeal of "Chicanismo" without an explicit class content explains, in large part, how often-contradictory and heterogeneous political elements could identify with the "Chicano movement." With hindsight, one can ask whether "Chicanismo," though a militant force, was, in the context of its identity and ideological notions, simply one more effort to subsume Mexican identity and all of its implications; more accurately perhaps, it came to be such for some but not for others. Clearly, at the beginning "Chicano" was an abbreviated form for Méxicans north of the Rio Bravo, and "Chicanismo" meant a politically charged *Mexicanidad*. Curiously, it was rejected on the right and by middle-class people as pejorative; and at the laboring base it was questioned because "Mexicano" was preferred. But to many of the young, "Chicano" was *the* term and a litmus test for a political frame of mind. Furthermore, enhancing its meaning was an attempt to emphasize not only a "lifestyle" stressing Chicanismo but also the more widely noted features of radical personal values of the late sixties.

Whatever the ideological orientation, confrontation politics and heightened ethnic consciousness characterized Mexican activity. Institutions were confronted through demonstrations, boycotts, strikes, sit-ins, and street fighting. Gradually, a perceptible development in political ideas occurred in the movement from protest over the denial of full and equal civil rights to the rise of a vehement cultural nationalism whose logical culmination would seem to be separatism; then followed on a lesser but briefly growing scale the emergence of a class politics which envisioned radical economic and political change and the development of ties with the working class in both Mexico and the United States. The emphasis was on the conceptualization of identity as nationality and full political rights and economic and social participation, but such emphasis did not become a full-fledged and mass-based nationalist movement. In contradistinction with other civil rights efforts, however, the Mexican movement emerged in relation to labor and land issues, the most basic of equities.

The United Farm Workers

The origins in California of the United Farm Workers (UFW) initially the National Farm Workers of America (NFWA) lie in previous attempts to unionize agriculture as well as the reputed unwillingness of the Community Service Organization (CSO) to commit itself to the task of organizing rural agricultural workers.[4] In 1962, Cesar Chavez left the CSO to begin the organizing work which eventually led to the founding of the NFWA. Between 1962 and 1965 a leadership cadre assembled, dedicated to the effective organizing of agricultural laborers. This effort, obviously based on workers, successfully drew wide support during the midsixties and even more during the subsequent decade. The revitalized struggle in behalf of Mexican farm workers was made public by a strike of grape pickers on September 16, 1965.

El Plan de Delano

A march on Sacramento, California, which began on March 17, 1966, was planned to dramatize the inequities suffered by farm workers.

Out of it came the Plan de Delano, a ringing call for justice and self-sacrifice with echoes from past plans in Mexico, in the Declaration of Havana, and in Catholic pietism.[5] This patently moderate plan was preceded by an effective introduction and consisted of six well-designed points and a conclusion emphasizing, "History is on our side"; although it was later downplayed between 1966 and 1968, this rallying cry was the most effective propaganda statement available to the Chicano community. Between 1965 and 1975 the dramatic organizational struggle of the UFW was a major catalyst in the development of Mexican politics. Support of the farm workers union was a major focus and inspiration for the political activism of the urban Mexican, the vast majority of whom had never been farm workers nor had their parents. From the mid-1960s on, many Mexican activists from the center and left, and regardless of their political affiliation, concurred in supporting the farm worker cause.

The Delano strike, the march on Sacramento, and the 1968 fast gave the UFW union not only visibility and cohesion; their end result was political legitimacy. Militant tactics such as strikes, boycotts, and public opinion, as well as electoral politics and its use of culture to organize workers, enabled the union to succeed in organizing a multinational work force with a Mexican majority. From the first, the base of the farm workers organization has been the dominant Mexican work force in agriculture, a basic industry. At considerable cost, the union withstood the attacks of agribusiness, the political power of the U.S. government, the state government of California, various local governments, and the opposition of one of the country's most powerful unions, the Teamsters, as well as internal and external ups and downs in the UFW's own stability and popularity. To some extent, the UFW raised the wages and living standards of agricultural labor in the United States and made unionism in agriculture a reality. However, its success and reform tactics culminated in the union eventually facing new problems and questions in the Chicano movement as well as in the American left.

Since the 1966 march on Sacramento, the union and Chavez, though they disclaim political leadership, have become a major force in community politics in California as well as exerting Mexican leadership nationally.[6] In spite of their critics, they were accorded influence and stature in national politics. Chavez's support for George Mc-Govern's presidential candidacy in the primaries and the national election of 1972; the UFW's endorsement of Edmund G. Brown for the California governorship in 1974 and 1978; and the union's role in the presidential primaries of 1976 and 1980 all highlighted the national and state influence of the union. If any single organization could be identified as being able to bargain on the strength of its organizational power and public support, it was the farm workers union; and if one person could be identified as a recognized national leader, it was Chavez. Although the union chose to be associated with the Democratic Party, it did not always endorse the party per se, but selected issues, candidates, and elections carefully and with one overriding guiding principle; namely, the furtherance of its organizational goals and strengths. More questionable were its roughshod methods with regard to urban issues, organizations, and leadership, and its oscillating positions on the undocumented worker. There also have been signs of faulty administration, poor decision making, and nondemocratic tendencies within the union. Nonetheless, it has continued as a liberal force, supporting unionization, world peace, the right of people to a decent living standard, and civil rights. In general, it has worked for Mexican political influence. Its salient national and electoral role, rather than symbolizing Mexican political power, may be a sign of the erratic quality of Mexican middle-class leadership and of urban organizations in achieving political efficiency. Given the UFW's social base and its organizational discipline, clear goals, able leadership, and political flexibility, it is not difficult to understand the UFW's success. But by the late seventies and eighties the UFW faced major problems, some of which were concurrent with its overt and partisan participation in electoral politics.

Stimulants

The voting strength of Mexican Americans declined and varied in effectiveness during the midsixties. After the political surge of 1960, a noticeable gradual change occurred, affecting political sentiments of the Mexican Americans for a short period of time. Mexicans did not always support strongly their own candidate or even incumbents; they did not always support someone who had favored them; and they did not always punish those who deserved it. Voter registration and voter turnout were visible weaknesses. When voter turnout increased

in California, greater numbers than ever before, over 20 percent, voted
for a Republican gubernatorial candidate, Ronald Reagan. Instead of
electoral rhetoric and erratic voter registration drives and organization,
a new type of politics, proactive dissent, began to attract the attention
of some Mexican Americans.

As mentioned above, when dissent was already visible in several
areas in March 1966, the Equal Employment Opportunities Commission (EEOC) called a meeting with Mexican Americans in Albuquerque.[7] This commission, headed by Franklin Roosevelt, Jr., had
promised the Mexican Americans "personal" attention to their employment problems. There was no action on this promise, however,
and the commission also failed to include a Mexican member or a
single Mexican American staff person to participate in preparing policy. In attendance at Albuquerque were representatives of LULAC,
the G.I. Forum, the Latin American Civic Association, PASSO, and
others; but Roosevelt and all but one of the commissioners did not
attend. Though the commission promised to call another meeting to
"discuss" problems, the fifty Mexican-American representatives decided to walk out of the meeting; a move later called the "guarache
out." They promptly organized themselves as a new committee in-
tending to deal directly with the Johnson administration. Their first
action was an eight-point resolution asking that EEOC be changed to
benefit Mexicans. Eventually, the Johnson administration established
a precedent by creating an office for Mexican American affairs at the
national level, the Inter-Agency Committee on Mexican American
Affairs.

Rejections signaled a trend in Chicano political tactics. A pending
question for Chicanos was whether there should be one distinct major
political organization; a forceful integration of Chicano politics into
the two major parties; or a multitude of organizations becoming part
of a functional coalition of minority groups, unions, and youth organizations devoted to advocacy and protest. Neither of the traditional
parties was interested in increasing the political voice of the Chicano
community through dialogue with the established leadership; and this
was particularly noticeable in California. The failure of California
state politicians to open government to Chicano representation served
to disillusion some of the activists within the community and to cause
them to consider the possibility of other options for gaining political
leverage. Active in the 1964 and 1966 elections in California were a

group of students who organized approximately one hundred volunteers to do voter registration, education, and mobilization. They pursued their intention of demonstrating the effectiveness of organized precinct work. Though they accomplished their goal, they questioned its value under the circumstances prevailing in the dominant society.

Although they were not yet major factors, dissatisfaction with underrepresentation, the war in Vietnam, and the generational conflicts of the 1960s had begun to influence a small sector of Mexican Americans in creating their stance toward alternative politics. Independent or third-party political activity, however—such as what led to California's Peace and Freedom Party as well as the efforts of the Communist Party (CP) or of the Socialist Workers Party (SWP)—was not integral to the Mexican community. Colorado's New Hispano Party, while claiming to be independent, was more a bargaining maneuver by a few self-appointed Colorado Mexican Democrats to gain concessions from the state Democratic leadership; and apparently there was never any firm intention on the part of the leadership to continue the group, which folded after apparently not achieving its objective.

Plan de la Raza Unida

A major event of 1967, signaling a change in the Mexican American temper, was the development of the Raza Unida concept, which arose in protest of the cabinet committee hearings held at the conference in El Paso on October 28.[8] The salient origin of Raza Unida was the Johnson campaign promise of a White House conference. To fulfill this promise, or rather to placate the protest that had continued since Albuquerque, hearings were held to coincide with the Chamizal land turnover, an event central to Mexico–United States relations. There was considerable debate by Mexican leaders as to whether this meeting should be supported since it was a hearing and not the "White House Conference promised"; and objections arose concerning the selection of the representatives by Washington and the direct or indirect exclusion of many others. Eventually, a larger and self-appointed group was constituted and preliminary-planning meetings were organized. Though some of the senior leadership were complaining, it was pointed out that they were not effective in elections and were also ignoring the youth which constituted a growing force. At El Paso the hearings were protested; and a name chosen in Spanish, Raza Unida, declared the hoped-for embodiment of the effort. Twelve hundred people representing fifty organizations attended a meeting in San Antonio, where Plan de la Raza Unida, a short and basic statement, was generated. Its introduction stressed pride and mobilization as well as "loyalty to the Constitutional Democracy." The plan's eight points emphasized organization, job training, education, housing, political representation, the Treaty of Guadalupe Hidalgo, police harassment, and cultural rights. Present at its creation were representatives of established organizations as well as California and Texas student groups and more senior individuals such as Ernesto Galarza.

Coordination and Support

In the midsixties a tentative coordinating organization, the Southwest Council of La Raza (SWCLR), was established to provide training and funding support for local organizations.[9] The council received funding from the Ford Foundation for its operation and for resources to initiate local projects; and later, some churches and unions contributed modest sums. The organization's initial emphasis was on the coordination and targeting of Anglo power structures as well as neighborhood maintenance and civic organizational enhancement. A council trend soon became the development of fund-generating activity in Oakland, Phoenix, San Antonio, and Los Angeles; while the council contributed concurrently to the development of what came to be known as the Mexican American Legal Defense and Education Fund (MALDEF) and, later, the Southwest Voter Registration Education Project (SVREP). Eventually, both MALDEF and SVREP did yeoman work in reducing barriers to political participation, specifically in extending the provisions of the Voting Rights acts of 1965 and 1970 to the Chicano community. SWCLR reorganized as the National Council of La Raza (NCLR) in December 1972, establishing its national office in Washington, D.C., and its program operations in Phoenix. Under the influence of Ernesto Galarza and directed by a self-selected board, the National Council of La Raza was envisioned as a major facilitator for advocating the integration of Chicano interests into all major facets of society and for providing coordination or clearinghouse activities as well as dissemination of information. There was to be a unique interaction between a national organization council and a network of autonomous local organizations. NCLR was projected as *the* national pan-organizational vehicle for the community and as the major voice of advocacy. Its resources were intended to foment key mobilizing projects at the local level, and to initiate projects as a consequence. Its publication, *Agenda,* offered timely information, especially considering the vacuity of many other Latino publications. Yet NCLR did not possess either the leadership or the funds necessary to realize its optimum vision. Even though encouraged and supported by the Ford Foundation, it was obviously underfunded and the leadership was forced to adjust its plans accordingly. It became more frequently a liaison office for federal agencies, gathering data and issuing statements on current issues or on pending legislation. It concentrated on business projects with potential for development, from mattress companies to franchises, demonstration-housing efforts, an investment corporation, and so forth. Some insiders adamantly believed that "economic" efforts, rather than the organization's more idealistic and overarching goals, were the key to future empowerment. Overlooked were the individual and entrepreneurial basis and ethos of these projects. By the 1970s, under the leadership of Raul Izaguirre, who at one time had been associated with the G.I. Forum, NCLR gained recognition as a lobby and as a mediator between corporations and the community. And as the politics of confrontation were ebbing in the eighties, NCLR was recognized as one of the major organizations.

In a society with a complex legal system which is the product of political and economic influences, litigation is an indispensable instrument in the political mobilization for change. To practice litigation, organizations sought the services of attorneys skilled in specific areas of the law, and preferably experienced and talented ones; they also attempted to establish coordination, informational, and resource capabilities as well as a centralized office with access to legal support from nationally recognized legal collaborators or associates in both national organizations and law firms.

Given the high costs of litigation in the United States, financial resources are also indispensable, particularly in pursuing activity that identifies and diminishes adverse precedent and establishes a coherent and continuous test-case strategy, resulting in success in the high courts of the states as well as in the Supreme Court. In the late sixties, with the founding of MALDEF, sustained litigation yielded results in more areas for more of the subject persons.[10]

In 1967 Pete Tijerina and Gregory Luna, with the support of the NAACP legal section, secured the financial interest of the Ford Foundation and a grant of two million dollars to initiate the Mexican American Legal and Educational Fund. A national board was created, offices were established in San Antonio and Los Angeles, and Tijerina was named executive director while Mario Obledo, then a Texas assistant attorney general, was designated general counsel; also involved in the establishment of the organization were a young attorney Vilma Martinez, Morris J. Baller, Peter Roos, Jane Couch, and the veteran Ed Idar. Two immediate internal issues were the lack of Chicano civil rights attorneys and the enormous demand for individual legal-aid counsel in the lower courts.

To have the desired impact, MALDEF needed national visibility and legitimacy, which required, in turn, board members who could facilitate all this as well as associations with prestigious firms, foundations, and national groups. The initial priorities of education and political rights were later supplemented by issues concerning employment and immigrant as well as women's rights, and developmental activity related to law schools and to leadership.

At all times, intense fund-raising is required to maintain the organization and its activity, which means a working relation with foundations, with the private sector, and with government. As may be noted a number of potentially inherent tensions exist within this type of organization. The organization is governed by a thirty-five member board from different sectors of the community and from the larger society. The board meets once a year, and each member serves a two-year term that is renewable. Its extensive activities have resulted in valuable specific contributions as well as support for other organizations.

Crusade for Justice

The founding of the Crusade for Justice in the mid-1960s did much to provide direction for the politics of confrontation. Its origins stem from urban inequalities, exclusionary Democratic Party politics, and the disillusionment with poverty programs.[11] A specifically galvanizing event was the protest against discrimination by the administration for the city of Denver in April 1966. The Crusade was organized by Rodolfo "Corky" Gonzales, a former liberal Democrat and member of the G.I. Forum who became an influential activist leader and the strongest advocate of "Chicano nationalism." His influence was especially felt among the barrio youth, college students, and the ex-inmate population. Originally, the Crusade's social base was comprised of approximately thirty working-class families, and it was directed by an executive board concentrating on civil rights activity, discrimination in the schools, police brutality, and cultural programs. The Crusade's protests often involved thousands, and it held weekly activities for its members. Particularly visible was the Crusade "assembly." Tentatively, members tried to organize sanitation and postal workers. Crusade remained a single-base organization, and for a few years it was fairly well-organized and developed its own funding. The Crusade for Justice advocated cultural consciousness and the creation of a society based on humanism rather than on competition; it was oriented primarily toward "La Familia" and self-determination. Unlike most political efforts, however, its thrust focused upon the development of alternate institutions. Exemplified by its school, Tlatelolco, and by its newspaper, *El Gallo,* the Crusade significantly denounced the governing system as a monopoly in practice. Nevertheless, it risked a seeming discrepancy by running Gonzales for mayor of Denver and doing poorly in the election.

In providing national leadership for Mexican progressive elements, the Crusade was highly active throughout the Southwest between 1968 and 1978; its activities included the Poor People's March, the Chicano Moratorium of 1970, the building of the National La Raza Unida Party, and a frustrated attempt at welding together a few of the more militant groups in the early seventies. In 1970 the leadership of the Crusade declared the establishment of a Colorado La Raza Unida Party. Albert Garrule ran for governor and received less than 2 percent of the vote. The total impact of the Crusade movement was strengthened through the Chicano Youth conferences held in 1969 and 1970. One of the problems encountered by the Crusade for Justice was harassment and violence by law enforcement agencies, which reduced the Crusade's membership and created tensions and splits among its surviving members. Another factor in the Crusade's waning influence upon later

radical Mexican politics in the United States was its inability to confront successfully, and on a continuing basis, the importance of the
development of ideas, analysis, and membership and organizational
changes.

El Plan del Barrio

In a major multiethnic and multisector effort in 1968, a national
Chicano contingent was organized to participate in Washington, D.C.,
in the Poor People's March initiated by Dr. Martin Luther King. Often
with support from Episcopalian and other Protestant clergy, local dep-
uties of the march organized support groups and volunteer participants;
meetings, rallies, and discussions of demands were held to foment
interest; and several bus caravans were created. Sparking the effort
within the community were the Crusade; the Alianza; defense groups
such as the Brown Berets; unionists; movement newspapers; and student representatives from the United Mexican American Students
(UMAS) and the Mexican American Youth Organization (MAYO).
All of them eventually converged on Washington, D.C., where the
base of activities for Chicanos was the Hawthorne School. Initially,
one strategy was to concretize political unity and economic demands
through Mexican, Indian, and Black land demands. There, Chicanos
issued the "Plan del Barrio."[12] The plan called for the following measures: for housing that would meet Chicano cultural needs; for schooling, basically in Spanish; for barrio businesses that would be owned
within the community; and for reforms in landholding, with the emphasis on restitution of community grant lands. The State Department
was confronted over violations of the provisions of the Treaty of
Guadalupe Hidalgo. The Mexican embassy was asked to intervene on
behalf of Mexican American grievances, and the Southern Christian
Leadership Conference (SCLC) was charged with being insufficiently
attentive to Chicanos. The contingent participated in a wide range
of meetings in Washington throughout the spring and summer of 1968,
with their actions directed at federal offices and intended to bring
about greater understanding and coordination between Black, Indian,
Puerto Rican, and women's groups. Though it did not involve large

numbers of Chicanos, the Poor People's March was a significant and politically enriching experience for the Chicano "movement" as a whole.

Alianza Federal de Pueblos Libres

An organization of seminal influence in the mid-1960s on the development of the Chicano movement was the Alianza Federal de Pueblos Libres, organized in 1962 in Nuevo México by Reies López Tijerina, an uneducated and itinerant Protestant fundamentalist and revivalist from an immigrant family who was born at Fall City, Texas.[13] The Alianza was part of a heritage of efforts to reclaim or to retain the land and/or maintain water rights. A 1960 court ruling had ended the hopes of many heirs because the opinion stated that Congress rather than the courts was the ultimate arbitrator in questions pertinent to issues raised with regard to land rights based on the Treaty of Guadalupe Hidalgo. With its most immediate predecessor, the Abiquiu Corporation, based in Albuquerque, Santa Fe, and Tierra Amarilla of Rio Arriba County, the Alianza was formed to reclaim for descendants of land grantees, both Mexican and Indian, hundreds of thousands of acres of Spanish and Mexican government land grants dating from before the takeover by the United States. These grants had been taken by governmental agencies or by wealthy Anglo individuals or corporations. Initially, the Alianza proposed the courts and public support as a means of securing land rights, raising as demands the guarantees of the Treaty of Guadalupe Hidalgo, which stated that Mexicans in the Southwest were to be given citizenship and rights to their land, language, and culture.[14] By emphasizing land and language, Alianza's demands did much to shape the character of cultural nationalism. Seminally, the Alianza also sought an alliance with Black and Indian groups. In the gist of its advocacy, the Alianza's argument combined references to papal bulls, the laws of the Indies, claims to Spanish descent rights, and biblical references with its own understanding of legal and historical arguments. They were committed to a conviction that these arguments would be compelling to public opinion, to elected officials, and ultimately to the courts. Though Alianza spokesmen often referred to the prejudice of courts in the past, the premise of their legal effort was the hope that a judge and a court would revise the property rights currently held by corporations and the United States government; however, they were unsure as to how they would influence several hundred congressional representatives.

The Alianza was first a movement of self-identified land grant claimants who were among the urban poor of New Mexico, who had been forced off their land, and who later had been supported by the people still on the land and by youth activists. Its followers were persons of all ages, but especially noticeable were older people; and the motivating force was the desire for the land. The Alianza began in the barrios of Albuquerque and Santa Fe, but in 1965 hundreds of farmers and ranchers joined the group, and at its height it claimed a membership of twenty thousand. Initially, it sought support in Mexico City and in the United Nations, and in 1966 a march was organized to call on the governor, who indeed listened to the group. Next, it established a "free state" on federal land and claimed the right to issue visas. The Alianza resorted to attention-getting militant confrontations when trial litigations seemed both frustrated and prohibitively costly. Thus, an incident or incidents was sought that would bring matters into court. Two of several provocative incidents occurred on October 15 and 22, 1966, at the Echo Amphitheater (in the Kit Carson National Forest), which was occupied on both of these dates to illustrate the rights of grant heirs. As a part of this strategy, a forest ranger was "tried" and a Forest Service truck impounded.

The most publicized of these incidents occurred on June 5, 1967, with the Tierra Amarilla Court House raid involving both the citizens and the local district attorney. This incident culminated with a shootout between authorities and Alianza members, which became a part of the legacy of deeds stimulating the Chicano movement. In effect, though Tijerina was either praised or blamed for the incident, the effort was conducted by the more militant local members and Tijerina, although present, did not act in the immediate incident, and in fact, he was nearly repudiated. Tijerina was charged with kidnapping and assault to commit murder, destruction of federal property, and assault on two officials. The Alianza's support eroded even as its visibility increased, and the more established elected officials, with Joseph Montoya at their head, increasingly denounced the Alianza as counterproductive and unethical.

In 1968 the Alianza broadened as Tijerina faced trials.[15] Along with other groups, the Alianza participated in the Poor People's March in Washington, D.C. In the same year, members of the Alianza formed the People's Constitutional Party, based on a populist platform. This party was a coalition of groups and individuals from different ethnic groups and with a variety of political positions. A slate for state offices was agreed upon, and Tijerina and others were ruled off the ballot by Secretary of State Ernestine D. Jones. Other candidates were selected, and though the party was seriously disadvantaged, members were confident of support; but in this and other elections the party received less than 2 percent of the vote. There were two positive, though fleeting, recognitions of Alianza land efforts. Augustus Hawkins, a Black congressman from Los Angeles, introduced a "Community Land Grant Bill," and the Presbyterian Church announced plans to restore some of the acreage that it owned to land-grant heirs.

Efforts to build public support through legal defense activity centered on trials stemming from 1967. Tijerina stood trial for the Tierra Amarilla Court House raid, defended himself, and was acquitted of the charges of kidnapping and of assault to commit murder. On June 5, 1969, with the Alianza looking forward to renewed vitality, the Coyote campsite at Kit Carson was occupied. The Alianza's 1969 efforts were thwarted when, in a subsequent trial, Tijerina was convicted and sentenced to federal prison on charges of destruction and of assaulting officers. Between June 1969 and July 1971 he was at the federal prison hospital in Springfield, Missouri. Mexican activists were convinced that his incarceration was a political jailing to stop the Alianza. Without Tijerina's charismatic leadership the Alianza's efforts were debilitated. However, its leadership and membership structure were more weakened by unresolved ideological and organizational problems. The organization failed to expand its membership in New Mexico or to other states, or to develop ideas beyond those it had begun with, and had never mustered the minimum of organizational discipline, structure, or resources apart from money collected at rallies. Tijerina was placed on probation for five years; and one condition was that he not be active in the Alianza. In any case, the Alianza impacted on New Mexico and the Mexican community and on the public at large. The issues of land and language were dramatized, as was the historical heritage and rural poverty and the role of federal agencies in rural areas whose actions were directed against Mexicans. Effectively propounded was the relation between the displacement of people and the usurpation of their land rights with their deteriorating social, cultural, and political cohesion. Culture and politics were not abstractions; they were related to the economic base of the land.

While he operated most effectively between 1962 and 1967, after his release from prison in 1971 Tijerina was no longer willing to organize in vehement protest of the system's practices. He spoke now of "brotherhood and love" rather than of confrontations. He found himself more and more in contradiction with former followers and with current Mexican organizations, especially the left in La Raza Unida Party. Tijerina was still a legend to some militants, but he no longer effectively provided organizational leadership within the movement. In 1972 he undertook one of his many trips to Mexico, this time to see the administration of Luis Echeverria Alvarez. He availed himself of publicity when possible, wrote a rambling autobiography, denounced an alleged international conspiracy, and involved himself in lawsuits; he changed the spelling of his name and stressed that he too was the heir to a land grant. The Alianza became quiescent and lost its influence on the development of Mexican political activity in New Mexico as well as elsewhere.[16] The issue of land remained potent, and land-grant organizing efforts continued in New Mexico, where the community again went through a period of significant electoral political invigoration, first under the leadership of Jerry Apodaca and later that of Toney Anaya.

Chicano Student and Youth Movement

Confrontation politics in the urban areas during the mid-1960s were intensified by the emergence of the "Chicano student movement,"[17] a campus-based phenomenon in California, Texas, New Mexico, Arizona, and the Midwest. Predominantly working class in origin, students in the colleges and universities, at first relatively few in number, organized groups such as the United Mexican American Students, the Mexican American Student Confederation, the Mexican American Student Organization, the Mexican American Youth Organization, and others. These groups struggled to increase educational opportunities for Mexican people and to establish academic programs for the study of the Mexican experience. But their impact went beyond colleges or education because of their strong initial participation in community affairs. Student activism had a wide impact on many activities including community politics, where the older leadership and political practices were often challenged effectively. Ideologically, prior to 1970, student politics exhibited a mixture of contradictory tendencies: a combination of liberal civil rights beliefs, cultural nationalism, and a rudimentary Marxism. A "Third World" tendency attempted to deny the Mexican national thrust and the full development of the Chicano student movement by subordinating it to other minority and white radical movements. The issue was subordination to Asian, Indian, or Black groups—not rejection of cooperation with them, which was continuous. This effort in amalgamation was defeated, as was the attempt by the Socialist Workers Party Young Socialist Alliance to establish hegemony among Chicano student organizations. Repeatedly, the student organizations have had to defend their organizational autonomy.

Beginning in 1969, most student organizations changed their name to El Movimiento Estudiantil Chicano de Aztlan (MECHA). The new name signified the commitment to confront social inequities and to reject assimilation into the dominant society, commitments to be fulfilled through student militant activities both on campus and in the community. From within the student movement, various feminist currents emerged. By the 1970s, however, the militant stance of many MECHA chapters had been weakened, and membership responsibility became little more than what was expected within college social clubs. A few chapters continued the tradition of militant activism while becoming influenced by Marxist ideas or by the activities of more ideological and community-based organizations. Some of the reasons for a problematic evolution included: (1) a loss of organizational direction and purpose, ironically caused by an inability to develop viable goals after achieving initial success in increasing the numbers of Mexican students and establishing Chicano studies programs; (2) an organizational inability to deal with the increasingly heterogeneous class makeup of Mexican students; (3) ideological stagnation; (4) programmatic differences among students; (5) increased institutional repression or manipulation of student political activity; and (6) multiple political organization in the community with a more diverse influence on students. Though periods of stagnation and disorganization occurred, the student movement also moved forward, continuing to evolve while other efforts dissipated. At its best, the work of student activists has been seminal in its influence on much later activity as well as generously courageous in its militancy; at its worst, it has been anarchic and self-indulgent, given to rhetoric and organizational inconsistency. The high tides of student activism were the 1968 school strikes; the blowouts which occurred in many states; the Winter Garden Project (1969); the 1969 Santa Barbara conference, which developed a "Chicano" Plan for Higher Education; the 1969 Denver National Chicano Youth Conference and the 1970 Chicano Moratorium in Los Angeles; support activity in behalf of La Raza Unida Party; the protests against the Bakke case; and activity on behalf of the undocumented worker. Much youth activity focused, of course, on the institutions most immediate to them.[18]

The organization viewed by militant youth as the epitome of militancy was the Brown Berets, which from 1967 through 1972 developed into over twenty chapters, published a newspaper, *La Causa,* and eventually established a successful health clinic.[19] Yet the group never effectively consolidated as a national body. The Berets sought to include both genders and had some excellent women members, while expressing doubts concerning professionals and business persons. They emphasized the right to self-defense against aggression and for self-determination. Their ten-point program addressed issues of housing, culture, justice, employment, and education, and they held, at least as an ideal, a code of ethical conduct and required specific organizational discipline. Along with the Crusade, they were the ones who came closest to articulating an explicit call for self-determination. They were participants in all of the major events between 1968 and 1971, but the two which were unequivocally theirs were the "March Through Aztlan," an effort to vitalize unity and consciousness, and the symbolic occupation and liberation of Santa Catalina Island, which was premised on the claim that the island remained sovereign Mexican land. Though their program was broader, they emphasized in practice school and police issues. Throughout these years, they faced severe harassment and infiltration as well as negative publicity and internal factionalism; and in 1972 their disbandment was announced.

Women participated in the efforts and organizations of the movement across the country, sharing the various tendencies and also, on occasion, the leadership.[20] Women's organizations grew out of community and campus activities. The late sixties witnessed an increasing emphasis on full participation in all aspects of community civic efforts and the realization of activities specific to women. Women's groups included the Chicana Welfare Rights organization of 1968, the Hijas de Cauhuhtemoc group and the Chicana Symposium (UCLA) of 1969, and the Houston Conference Las Mujeres Por La Raza of 1971. Several organizing efforts had developed by 1969, and movement newspapers were increasing their coverage on activities and positions pertinent to women. The initial impetus was for a critique of stereotypes impeding equality. Eventually, the view evolved that women suffered multiple oppression as women, as Mexicans, and as workers.

Across the Southwest, the phenomenon of ad hoc organizations focused on particular issues born of specific local crises or of specific needs ranging, for example, from education reform to problems concerning drugs, undesired urban change, or inequities in War on Poverty programs and welfare rights. In fact, Title II of the Economic Opportunity Act, by stipulating participation by the "client," that is, by the poor, encouraged local group mobilization either by positive outreach or as a negative reaction to the perceived misfunctioning of programs. Self-help organizations developed in many localities, stressing the assertion of one's rights and of one's access to services. More people participated in these activities, which involved direct interface with officials; and the sector most motivated to participate were youth.

The blowouts, student strikes, and walkouts in the public schools were significant in demonstrating the dissatisfaction of Mexicano students with an educational system designed to perpetuate the subordinate status of the Mexican people. Because parents for generations had repeatedly sought positive response from schools and school boards, the prevailing indifference during the sixties was striking. Historically, the public educational system has been one more means of practicing cultural and national aggression against Mexicanos in the United States. Given this relationship, it was virtually inevitable that Mexican students would declare their antagonism. The blowouts or high school student protests occurred across Mexican communities, particularly in Texas and California as well as in New Mexico, Chicago, Denver, Phoenix, and other areas. Massive walkouts involving thousands marked a dramatic leap in the consciousness of Mexican students and the development of new organizational forms through which the youth made history. The blowouts reflected the opposition to cultural and national oppression, and they included demands for classes in Mexican history, bilingual and bicultural education, the hiring of

Mexican teachers, and control of education by the Mexican community.

The Chicano movement was expressed dramatically in Los Angeles
when activists focused community attention on the abysmal conditions
within the city's public school system. After several months of preor-
ganizing activity in March 1968, thousands of Mexican students literally walked out of their classrooms, specifying their grievances and
their proposed solutions in a set of "demands" directed at the Board
of Education which became, in effect, the points of negotiation.[21] The
"Blowouts," as the staged demonstrations were called, involved principally five high schools in the East Los Angeles area; but their impact
reverberated throughout the entire Southwest. With the support of
older Chicano activists as well as one of their teachers, Sal Castro,
the students dramatically drew attention to the racist attitudes held
by many Anglo teachers and to the inferior educational conditions
that plagued East Los Angeles schools. These conditions were epito-
mized by a 50 percent dropout rate for Mexican high school students.
The blowouts precipitated a wave of community outcry and a series
of confrontations between local Mexican residents and the Los Angeles
Board of Education, and eventually, as was to be expected, police
agencies. Students, parents, and community activists demanded "quality education" and bilingual and bicultural school programs. One un-
conscionable response was police harassment and an indictment by
nothing less than the "Grand Jury" for what were, in effect, actions
protected by the U.S. Constitution. During this time, the Chicano
movement gained a level of notice that reached even the Mexican
middle class. To some extent, young Chicanos made a public issue of
the chauvinism and inequality common to institutions that less vocal
members of the community had somehow chosen not to mention; and
they emphasized urban disparities, in particular.

Plan de Santa Barbara

For those committed to equities in education in the midst of an
increasingly militant rhetoric, emphasis was placed on educational
reform in three areas: administrative reforms, K–12; the promulgation
of a bilingual-bicultural curriculum; and access for student, faculty, and
staff in higher education.[22] In total practice, this agenda constituted

a single constellation of efforts aimed at a major issue, namely, quality education. The educational thrust scored successes, but it also involved major failures as the state of education in the seventies and eighties would attest.

In the arena of struggle for higher education for Mexican students and the development of Chicano studies programs, the 1969 Santa Barbara conference and the Plan de Santa Barbara reflected a major attempt to provide conceptual cohesion, to develop common guidelines, and to consolidate past gains and prepare the ground for future ones. Preceded by six months of planning and followed by a year of meetings, the plan was led by a steering committee and involved selected participants. The major thrust of the plan was to stimulate the growth and operation of Chicano studies programs along movement premises and to coordinate politically and organizationally local programs statewide in an effort to further a particular vision of education and one with a particular purpose, both of which the plan provided for the first time. Eventually, programs were established at many campuses, and as such they represented a net gain; but these programs were shaped and directed according to the rules of the university game. Thus, campus action continued concurrently with community action.

Plan de Aztlan

The Chicano Youth Liberation Conference, called by the Crusade and held in Denver, Colorado, in March 1969, was significant in bringing together two thousand Mexican youths from all parts of the United States.[23] But even more significant was its development of a strong nationalist sentiment or an incipient nationalist ideology. In this respect, the Denver conference signaled the break at a national level from the assimilationist "Mexican-American" consciousness and politics of the previous decades. At this conference, Chicanos adopted El Plan Espiritual de Aztlan, a national plan of liberation which spelled out nationalism as its instrument and self-determination as its goal.[24] In the plan's preamble was a call to liberation through solidarity based on culture and nationality. The preamble was followed by demands and adjunctions in major life areas; significantly, these were linked integrally to a specific geographic homeland and to the rights of toilers and the rights of Indian heritage, while the dominant society was identified as composed of oppressors and usurpers. Later the Plan de Aztlan was stripped of what radical element it possessed by stressing its alleged romantic idealism, reducing the concept of Aztlan to a psychological ploy, and limiting advocacy for self-determination to local community control—all of which became possible because of the plan's incomplete analysis which, in turn, allowed its language concerning issues to degenerate into reformism. While politically it was ideologically vague, the Plan Espiritual de Aztlan, with its assertion of autonomy for the Bronze Nation of Aztlan, was to substantiate the initial thrust for much of the subsequent ideological and political developments of "cultural nationalism" among young Mexican people in the United States.

The Moratorium

Following the blowouts, local Chicanos stimulated organization in the communities around a number of other social and political issues. A major issue was U.S. aggression in Vietnam, where Chicano casualties were disproportionate to their number in the stateside population. The brutality and aggressiveness of the war was emphasized in conjunction with the need for establishing solidarity with the Vietnamese struggle for their national liberation. Chicano antiwar activists organized around the Vietnam issues in the aftermath of the Denver 1969 conference for a series of individual and group actions across the country. Perhaps their best-known effort was the 1970 National Chicano Moratorium.[25] On August 29, Chicano antiwar activists staged a large march and rally to protest U.S. intervention in Vietnam and to publicize the disproportionately high rate of Mexican war casualties. Records indicated that approximately thirty thousand people attended the demonstration; more than an antiwar protest, it became a public celebration of the Chicano movement. Though a significant achievement, the moratorium also indicated the inadequacies of the leadership and organization, whose responses were weaker than what was possible, given popular arousal. The moratorium was a culmination of the momentum from the early sixties and signaled two more marked tendencies, a stress on ideology and on internationalism; but it also drew a distinction between the militant and the reformist that could be more clearly understood than before. The moratorium differed in two aspects from other militant minority activity: it stemmed from conscious planning based on clearly perceived goals, and it revealed in its aftermath that the activist sector was stronger than it had ever been before.

Because of its unique historical and cultural context, the moratorium was distinct from other protest action in the country at the time. And although it drew obviously from the youth movement as well as from the United Farm Workers and the Crusade, it differed from other activity because its focus was the government, rather than an institution or a locality, and its ethos was "power." The moratorium was preceded by, consisted of, and was followed by a unique sequence of organizing and protest activity, which led to a harsh militancy unmatched since the strikes of the 1930s and the violence of the 1914–16 period. There were several underlying causes for the East Los Angeles protests of January 1, February, August 29, and September 16, 1970, and of January 9 and 31, 1971. Salient were common issues, some symbols, such as Aztlan, and the blatant actions of state agencies. Protest actions were a response to widely and deeply held grievances and also the result of a long-term pattern of sufferance. Above all, however, these protests were a response to political subordination. There were several convocations and marches, as well as the customary planning meetings, held prior to the major march. These were directed by an ad hoc committee, which engaged in intense discussions, and by an ad hoc executive committee. There were no membership stipulations or agendas; nor was there any structure or even an elected permanent leadership. Thus, the situation was ripe for manipulation and infiltration.

There were several aspects to the circumstances of the organizing process. Foremost was the political reality of Los Angeles city and county governance which was not only negative by omission but by actions that were hostile historically toward Mexican efforts. Another aspect was the organizing energy of Chicanos dating from the 1968 blowouts, an energy visible in the greater number of groups and leaders. Furthermore, the moratorium coincided with the rise of militant youth activity across the country. There was also, as mentioned, the preparatory organizing prior to the large event. In December 1969 a Chicano Anti-Draft conference was held at Denver, where the drive was planned; shortly afterward, two thousand persons attended a rally meeting in Los Angeles on the draft and the war.

Not explicitly associated with moratorium organizing but an indicator of the Los Angeles public temper was the January 1, 1970, East Los Angeles protest which involved youth and older citizens from the immediate area around Whittier Boulevard. Reportedly about one hundred persons, primarily Mexicana, smashed windows and looted stores after a New Year celebration by a crowd of five thousand. During two hours, damage occurred to forty-two storefront windows, non-Mexican owned; and some stores reported looting in the Whittier business district. Sheriffs arrested eleven persons while the actions occurred. On February 28, 1970, five thousand persons marched in the rain for three miles, receiving noticeable support from East Los Angeles residents. In March, at the second annual Chicano Liberation conference held in Denver, a date was selected for the major march in Los Angeles. In addition, marches were planned and staged at Fresno, Riverside, San Francisco, San Diego, Santa Barbara, San Antonio, Austin, Houston, and Chicago. At Los Angeles another force was in the planning stages, namely, police agencies. Though supportive communication with Los Angeles County officials ranged from poor to nil because of their attitude, the Moratorium Committee had kept the police authorities fully informed of its intentions and programs. The committee provided for over two hundred monitors—many of them lawyers or law students as well as clergy—to accompany the marchers and to maintain order. The sheriffs would clear the parade route and direct traffic at cross streets.

On August 29, 1970, approximately twenty-five to thirty thousand persons, mostly Chicano, attended a well-publicized National Chicano Moratorium March. It was supported by many Mexican American organizations across the Southwest; and significantly, representatives from all parts of the Southwest attended. The march stressed resistance against the draft and commitment for social justice within the United States. Major public officials and police administrators denounced the large numbers of "militants" in Los Angeles, declaring they were going to teach them a lesson. The rally was held at Laguna Park, and generally a festive air prevailed. At 2:30 P.M., a disturbance broke out a block away from the park. The police intervened and used the disturbance as an excuse to order the crowd to disperse. They immediately began to move into the crowd, swinging clubs and firing tear-gas canisters. To their surprise, the crowd, particularly the neighborhood youth, responded aggressively, showing little fear. At the peak of the turmoil a dozen fires burned along Whittier Boulevard. About five hundred police were involved in the melee: forty officers were injured and twenty-five police cars put out of action, while three people were killed and four hundred arrested. That same night, four policemen were shot in the Chicano area of the Casablanca district of Riverside.

Born of idealism, the moratorium ended in the terror of police brutality and the reality of blood-stained streets, as well as proactive responses. Unaccustomed to large and militant demonstrations within the Mexican community and unable to tolerate the political expression of the march, local law-enforcement agencies overreacted, going beyond rationality and legality. By nightfall, several demonstrators had been violently attacked by Los Angeles police officers and three people were dead, among them the *Los Angeles Times* columnist Ruben Salazar.[26] An invited speaker, Corky Gonzales, was singled out by the police, arrested, and jailed. With the fervor that sometimes accompanies a crisis, youth in the Mexican community spent the next several months in staging a series of demonstrations throughout Los Angeles.

Belatedly, the Moratorium Committee held a meeting attended by six hundred persons on September 1, 1970, and sought to recover momentum through a proactive stance reaffirming the purpose of the August 29 march and protesting police repression. However, some community leaders preferred to accommodate the police and conservative politicians, insisting on a nonpolitical platform.

Since the nineteenth century the Mexican community in Los Angeles has honored Mexican Independence Day, September 16, with a parade. Because of the August 29, 1970, disturbance there was much discussion concerning whether or not to have a parade in 1970. It was initially cancelled; but a week before the sixteenth and after consultation with the Sheriff's Department, the Mexican Consul General, and the sponsors, it was decided to hold the parade. The site was to be the stadium at the East Los Angeles Community College (ELACC). Although the sheriffs endorsed the idea, the conservative majority of the Board of Trustees of the Los Angeles Community Colleges voted it down. Nevertheless the parade was held, and scheduled to end at Belvedere Park, originally the second choice for the terminus. The more militant marchers headed for ELACC. Taunted by the police, the crowd apparently attacked them with rocks. Fires broke out, and shots were exchanged between the Chicanos and the police. More than one hundred were injured, and three were shot, one of them a deputy. Sixty-four policemen were injured, and approximately seventy people were arrested.

Two more episodes in 1971 reflected the anger of the people and the political purpose underlying the repression. On January 9, 1971, the Los Angeles Police Department moved against a too quickly publicized rally concerning police brutality, held at the Parker Center outside East Los Angeles. Clashes resulted and windows were broken; forty-two of the approximately one thousand persons involved were arrested. The police denounced protesters as "communists" using "Bolshevik tactics." On January 31, 1971, a rally was called for East Los Angeles Park, which is also the location of the East Los Angeles Sheriff's Station. Around five thousand people attended, despite massive public intimidation by the police via the media. The tempo of red-baiting was intense, and internal differences among the organizers were publicly visible. After the rally, the crowd surrounded the Sheriff's Station and put it under siege. Eleven sheriffs were injured and seventeen Chicanos were wounded by police gunfire, with one person killed. The momentum of the moratorium ebbed in a series of staged hearings concentrating on the death of one person and recriminations among activists, as well as red-baiting by the heads of two organizations. In vain, the effort was made to harness Chicano popular arousal and to direct it at city and county governance according to community priorities. Nevertheless, more-structured, specifically targeted efforts followed from the moratorium. In California the movement's option, as it appeared on the surface, was a choice between militant proactive protest, organizational development, or electoral activity.

The Texas La Raza Unida Party

The immediate antecedents of La Raza Unida Party (LRUP) was the Mexican American Youth Organization (MAYO), a student organization in San Antonio and South Texas, whose leadership was, from the first, heavily influenced by José Angel Gutierrez, a well-educated son of a professional family.[27] Gutierrez, Mario Compean, Nacho Perez, and Willie Velasquez—all members of MAYO in the late sixties—conceived a program called the Winter Garden Project, whose purpose was to redirect political, social, and economic resources in a ten-county South Texas area to benefit residents and ultimately to maximize Mexican political representation. This project received support from the Ford Foundation, and later from VISTA and OEO, both of which were federal projects.

The situation in the South Texas barrios was propitious for organizing. It was, and still is, one of the poorest Mexican areas in the country, a place where ethnic and class identities are clearly demarcated. Major precipitants for mobilization were the school practices and the protests around them in 1969 as well as the Mario Compean candidacy for the mayoralty of San Antonio in the same year. MAYO achieved notice and some success, but it also drew the antagonism of the established Democratic leadership, in particular of Congressman Henry B. González. In March 1969, county officials and the governor arbitrarily ousted the VISTA workers and their program at Del Rio. This move was answered by a massive rally of several thousand in protest of these actions and of discrimination in general, especially as it was outlined in the Del Rio Manifesto. By mid-1969 the Ford Foundation had stopped its funding, but MAYO had extended its reach. As a militant student effort, MAYO encountered more severe community conflict than such efforts elsewhere, for there existed in central and south Texas a validated and rooted local political electoral leadership as well as long-standing civil rights organizations and their own leadership. These groups felt that MAYO threatened not only their standing but the gains they had made, which were clearly associated with the entrenched Texan Democratic Party leadership. Thus, rather than a recognition of distinct constituencies, emphases, and means, and all possibly complementary, there occurred a conflict whose consequences were to persist. In January 1970 members of MAYO filed for party status on behalf of "El Partido de la Raza Unida" in Zavala, La Salle, and Dimmit counties. The effort was to focus on school-board and council seats because these were believed to be most immediately accessible to residents.

La Raza Unida's initial and principal target was the electoral effort of the Crystal City local council and school board, which had been targeted earlier by PASSO. LRUP won three school board seats and two on the council. Once again, the Mexicans won a voice on the Crystal City council, a voice that eventually extended to the mayor's office despite the Anglo-controlled economy and politics in this city of twelve thousand.[28] LRUP also won in Cotulla and Carrizo Springs;

in all it had obtained fifteen elected positions, two city council majorities, two school board majorities, and two mayorships. Through elections and massive boycotts of schools (in 1969) and of Anglo-owned businesses, Mexicans had gained access to the formal city machinery but not to the grower- and rancher-dominated economy. This activity was to hamper further efforts, which were now complicated by higher expectations and internal factionalism among the LRUP membership. Negative criticisms accumulated. There were charges that Gutierrez had received money from officials in the Nixon administration to build a health clinic in Crystal City. The fact was that the clinic was necessary and funds for its construction could be applied for. When LRUP also sought support from Mexico's Partido Revolucionario Institucional (PRI) for its schooling, medical, and energy needs, it was criticized, even though these were serious needs among the constituency that needed to be addressed. Nevertheless, events in Crystal City were viewed as a strategy for building a viable national political party of Mexicans, a strategy that grew out of the Crystal City victory and its attendant notoriety.

LRUP was a rising force between 1970 and 1972, winning additional positions in Crystal City, Cotulla, and Carrizo Springs. Registration drives were undertaken in Zavala, Dimmit, La Salle, and Hidalgo counties, and the party's adherents increased. The party convention of October 30, 1971, voted to field state candidates who would oppose the alternate, contrasting strategy to develop greater strength at the south Texas regional level. On June 10, 1972, the first state nominating convention, held in San Antonio, was attended by five hundred delegates from twenty-five counties. Mario Compean was named state chairman, and a slate of candidates was selected, headed by Ramsey Muñiz, a young attorney running for governor; as well as candidates also slated for selected counties. With 215,000 votes, the showing was excellent, and in Zavala County it won the races for sheriff and county attorney, as well as one county commission seat.

At one time, La Raza Unida Party was heralded as *the* political form of the sixties movement.[29] In fact, LRUP was only a partial expression of the movement and one which only partially realized its protean potential. LRUP drew upon the work of PASSO and MAYO, the civil-rights activity of the sixties, the heritage of Mexican–Anglo relations in Texas, and past electoral efforts in Texas. LRUP's membership was drawn from the smaller towns in South Texas and from the San Antonio area, as well as from the lower middle class, and students; some workers and older citizens also participated. In effect, LRUP combined civil rights organizing techniques and Alinsky methods with a heavy component of ethnic regional pride, which it passed off as "nationalism."

With sound reason, the "party" originally sought to mobilize in areas where Mexicans were a majority. Its primary social base was, indeed, South Texas; and to expand beyond this region, as the party attempted to do, was either not entirely and effectively possible or premature for the moment. In any case, statewide and national organizing caused tensions and disarray within the group. Party protestations to the contrary, LRUP was local, electorally focused, and very much dependent on the leadership of José Angel Gutierrez; while liberal, the party was short on analysis, ideas, organizational discipline, and structure. Such shortcomings were not apparent, however, as long as the party was restricted to South Texas and opposed only by archaic Democrats or by "movement" figures whose following was even more limited than LRUP's. Its electoral stress led to viewing the two-party system as *the* source of domination and elevated the question of electoral participation and party loyalty to the level of principle rather than that of a conditional strategy or of tactics.

The National La Raza Unida

The concept of La Raza Unida Party was not limited to the circle around Gutierrez. It had spread since 1967, when the Plan of La Raza Unida was formulated in El Paso, Texas. Third-party participation by Mexicans can be traced back to the Partido del Pueblo and the Partido Liberal Mexicano, as well the more contemporary, existing third parties such as the Partido Constitucional del Pueblo, the Peace and Freedom, and the left "parties." Activists across the country were fascinated by LRUP; many were outgrowing, or graduating from, student organizations while others were leaving the stage of pseudoparamilitary regalia. LRUP organizing committees began to function in the spring of 1970 in Texas and Colorado, and by 1972 in New Mexico and Arizona. At the insistence of Corky Gonzales, a call for a national convention was issued. Representatives from eighteen states and the

District of Columbia responded. Student activists, movement newspapers, and the remnants of the Alianza and the Crusade for Justice
were particularly responsive. The Crusade's leverage on LRUP would
have been far different had the party been launched at the National
Chicano Youth Conference in 1969. In any case, these groups came
together in a convention of three thousand delegates held at the El
Paso del Norte Hotel on September 1, 1972, to "declare" the organization of the National La Raza Unida Party.[30] Two factions con-
tended: the Crystal City group and its allies, and the Crusade and its
allies. In between were the California, New Mexico, and Midwest
contingents that were not clearly identified as being in one camp or
another. Individuals trying to become peacemakers or brokers ended
in being considered questionable by the two contending elements.
From one criterion, the opposing factions could be seen as consisting
of various subgroups: an ideologically left element versus an ideologically liberal element; program-oriented persons versus populist organizers. Anti-Marxism was common and the non-left element
predominated. The timing of the convention was not the most propitious, occurring in the midst of one of the more clearly ideologically
partisan election campaigns, waged between the forces of George
McGovern and those of Richard Nixon.

Corky Gonzales, who had earlier established La Raza Unida Party
in Colorado, was one of the driving forces behind the national convention. Gutierrez and the then popular and influential Ramsey Muñiz
of the Texas LRUP were informed by Gonzales that if they did not
act, he was going to call for a national party convention without them;
this declaration underscored Gonzales's momentum, but Gutierrez and
Muñiz possessed the numbers. Tijerina was invited, but he had a
limited following and only programmatic ideas to offer; and when he
was on the stage, his ineffectiveness became public knowledge. Gonzales went to the convention expecting to be selected as the party
president in time for the national elections, in which LRUP might
play a role.

The results of the four-day convention included the following: La
Raza Unida decided not to endorse any candidate for president in the
regular national elections; Gutierrez was chosen party chairman over
Gonzales; Congreso de Aztlan, which was to represent literally and
figuratively "the nation," was established with Gonzales as presiding
officer; and finally, the basis of a split in the party presented itself in

its opening convention. All sides felt that they were in the right, and so all of them were aggrieved. The ensuing preamble of La Raza Unida, stating its principles and its thirty-one-plank platform, went slightly beyond the Plan de Aztlan. Not unexpectedly, the document supported a guaranteed annual income, national health insurance, no land taxation, bilingual education, parity in federal employment, an increase in admissions to medical schools, parity in jury selections, support for organizing farm workers, and a call for the enforcement of the Treaty of Guadalupe Hidalgo. Somewhat redundant was a declaration of "independence" from the traditional parties. However, the preamble consisted mainly of demands and participation guidelines, many of which were contradicted later by LRUP actions. The uncertainty as to what LRUP was became evident in the preamble of LRUP's statewide Texas program. The Texas program was the basis for subsequent statements issued from the 1972 El Paso conference. These statements were not only confused; they were beneath the circumstances of the moment, and no memorable statement was sounded during this conference.

In the euphoria of the moment, several matters went unnoticed. The victories of the "leaders" were symbolic ones, but the charades revolving around "bodyguards" and the "protocol" of the convention would provide the basis of satirical commentary for some time to come, thus detracting from LRUP's legitimacy. There were, however, more substantive failings. There was no social base to the party other than in the Crystal City LRUP and the Denver Crusade. The principal elements at the convention—the Crusade, the South Texas Raza Unida, and the Alianza—had all reached the plateau of their ascendance, and all were now forces in decline. The convention did not represent even a majority of the conscious adherents of the movement, much less possess an extensive national network. For all its populist rhetoric, LRUP was organizing from the top down. *De facto*, it attempted to develop an umbrella structure over a myriad of followings, rather than to form a single structured party. Petty and inane, direct and indirect comments about Cesar Chavez and the NFWA were spurious, transparent, and short-sighted, and implied, in effect, an exclusion. Thus excluded was the one organization of national stature, NFWA, with its base at the time numbering over thirty thousand workers and scores of organizers, and revealing sizable public support that already made it a force to be reckoned within national and state elections. Considering their sources, the charges against Chavez were transparently hypocritical, for he worked with the Democratic Party and he accepted non-Mexican support. Furthermore, LRUP rhetoric gratuitously alienated the Mexicans in the Democratic Party; and regardless of what LRUP had thought of such an alliance, perhaps over 80 percent of the Mexicans at that time voted with the Democrats, and these people needed to be reached because they represented the immediate bloc of available votes. LRUP's provincial anti-Marxism further alienated the Mexican left who, other than the few in the Socialist Workers Party, viewed the party, in turn, as ridiculous and diversionary. If LRUP was interested in constituent support or in recruitment, these three sectors were obviously potential sources. Furthermore, to move LRUP from electoral politics in Mexican majority areas to minority areas entailed many unresolved questions. Finally, no one took notice of the organization's still patent lack of ideas, analysis, discipline, and structure. The party did not have a cohesive ideological or strategic statement; consequently, it was only capable of making assertions. Apart from failing to consider the distinction between an organization rigorously following an agreed-upon agenda and a pluralistic mass-participant organization, there was no extensive or substantive deliberation as to whether an "electoral-party" mode was the best possibility at the moment. Nor did the conference discuss how to address convincingly the economic motive in voting behavior or how to elicit support on an ethnic basis primarily while seeking to reassure non-ethnics that the party was "above ethnicity," that is, that it was an ideologically progressive party. Moreover, there were no effective measures for obtaining resources, for securing a staff, for implementing a propaganda-outreach instrument, or for establishing a centralized office, or for opening a legal office to deal with the inevitable legal chores. Difficult to understand was the tolerance of Socialist Worker Party members within an ostensibly "nationalist" party. This occurred in New Mexico and California, in particular, and for some Texas leaders the SWP was a preferred ally. After taking into account such criticisms, it must be equally stressed how LRUP's hardworking organizers contributed to political mobilization, improved some conditions for Mexicans in many places, added to the dissemination of the issue of self-determination and also to the growing focus on electoral politics, and generated interest in strengthening relations with forces in Mexico.

After the national convention, the Texas LRUP went on to make a significant and very commendable showing in the 1972 state elections, drawing nearly 215,000 votes (6.5 percent of the total vote) for the governorship and seventeen elected positions; then decline set in and dissent developed in, among other places, Crystal City. In 1974 the total vote for La Raza Unida in Texas dropped to half of its own previous high for governor and other state offices; but in Zavala County it consolidated by winning nearly all of the offices there. LRUP local organizing and electoral efforts in other states never matched those in Texas.

In 1970, as the new party emerged on the scene in Texas, LRUP seemed to some Chicano leaders elsewhere to offer them the possibility of expanding their political voice.[31] Organizing efforts moved into California, where the goal was to register some 66,000 new members by the end of 1971, which would qualify the party for the 1972 primary and general elections. The failure to gain the required number of signatures in California and in Arizona, states with a strong concentration of Mexicans, were major setbacks to the recognition of La Raza Unida as a plausible national electoral party. But in these states certain candidates ran for office by espousing the ideals of La Raza Unida as their platform; and although victories were proclaimed in New Mexico and Colorado, these showings were not electorally significant, in spite of visible numbers of seven thousand votes in Denver and twenty-four thousand at large. La Raza Unida efforts in New Mexico, beginning in 1972, were centered on Bernalillo and San Miguel counties. Involved were youth as well as SWP members. In one county, LRUP garnered over two hundred votes and lost to the traditional party candidates. In 1974 they were more successful with 25 percent of the vote, though they split the community vote, which resulted in an uncommon development: the victory of a white conservative in the race for a normally Mexican-held Board of Education seat. In the 1974 elections the core group set aside its LRUP identity and ran as the "Pueblo Unido." The 8 percent vote total for municipal seats was proclaimed as a victory, even though the liberal Chicanos lost and three conservatives, two Anglos and one Chicano, won. In California events plainly exhibited not only the limitations of La Raza Unida's electoral-party concept but also the limitations of its leadership outside Texas. In Los Angeles the high point was seven thousand votes, and the party experienced difficulty in organizing rallies. Though students were its key adherents, LRUP did not even secure a majority support among students or student organizations in 1973, when many were turning to the left or to conventional forms. Indicative of the panorama was the Colorado LRUP, which left the national organization in 1974. Eventually, by the midseventies, disintegration of LRUP was so clear that even in Crystal City it was splitting into factions. La Raza Unida Party was an idea whose time had come and gone. That the left and elements in the Democratic Party were now in the ascendancy was evident in electoral events in Los Angeles, which revealed the most glaring example of electoral underrepresentation.

Although there were others in the leadership, in addition to still other potential candidates, a notable candidate identified with La Raza Unida in Los Angeles was Raul Ruiz. Ruiz opposed Democratic candidate Richard Alatorre, a broadly supported civil rights activist, and Republican Bill Brophy in the contest for the seat vacated in 1971 by David Roberti in the Forty-eighth Assembly, a multiethnic district. Ruiz managed to garner 7 percent of the vote in losing to Alatorre's 42 percent and Brophy's 47 percent.[32] The Democrat lost, but Alatorre was a Democrat with majority support among Mexicans; and though the Republican who won expressed an abysmal attitude toward Mexican Americans, Ruiz demonstrated that he had even less support than Brophy. It was in this election that the limits of the non-south Texas strategy of La Raza Unida became apparent; to abandon, for the time being, efforts to win seats and to concentrate instead on the role of the "spoiler" was puerile, especially if the goal sought was increased ethnic representation. By aiding in the defeat of the Democratic candidate, La Raza Unida drew attention to problems of underrepresentation and, in effect, made the Democratic Party more responsive to its needs; but in its spoiler role, it also delayed representation for the community and provided a victory for conservative Republicanism, in this case a particularly inept representative. Ruiz continued in the role of political spoiler in 1972 in his race for the Fortieth Assembly, in which he again qualified as an independent by collecting the required two thousand signatures of persons who had not voted in the June primary. He challenged both Republican Robert Aguirre and Democratic incumbent Alex Garcia, a member of the Elections and

Reapportionment Committee. Ruiz concentrated on Garcia's poor attendance record in the Assembly, pointing out that the district was disadvantaged and the area inadequately represented. Nevertheless, Garcia was reelected with 56 percent of the vote; this time, however, Ruiz captured 13 percent—an indication not only that La Raza Unida had some support in the community but also that Garcia was vulnerable. Although Garcia eventually left the assembly seat, he won election to the Senate. The UFW came into the situation, and in a competently run campaign, a reform Chicano Democrat with wide support won the Fortieth Assembly District.

In August 1973, officials of La Raza Unida declared that they would attempt to collect enough signatures to qualify for a spot on the ballot for governor in 1974.[33] They pointed to the divergence in thought between this group and the traditional parties when they charged that all Republican and Democratic contenders had "so far ignored the Chicano community." Of a Chicano Democrat active in the reapportionment fight, a LRUP spokesperson said that he had "taken sides with the parties which have betrayed our people." LRUP could not effectively canvass the state, or even Los Angeles. LRUP did not succeed in its effort.

La Raza Unida emerged again as a newsmaker when a slate of political aspirants representing the party announced their candidacy for city offices in the proposed incorporation of the Los Angeles eastside area in 1974 which had been initiated by the "Ad Hoc Committee to Incorporate East Los Angeles."[34] This had been attempted before, and some believe that an ideal situation for the issue of self-determination existed in a large urban area with an overwhelming Mexican majority. Candidates receiving the highest number of votes would take office if cityhood were approved by the voters. Though it was only one of several participants, La Raza Unida of California's influence as a vehicle in local government was tested, and it failed. In the process, LRUP demonstrated some of the most incompetent electoral efforts ever witnessed in Los Angeles. As a result of this election, the incorporation measure, a goal long sought by community activists, was defeated. The activities of the party declined abruptly.

A major handicap in the development of the La Raza Unida Party in California was the mutual antipathy between the party and Cesar Chavez.[35] The result was an example of unnecessary antipathy between groups that had more commonalities than differences. For all his visibility and connections, Chavez was viewed negatively by La Raza Unida; absurdly, they felt he was negligent in pursuing broader Chicano issues or in demanding political concessions for Chicanos. To LRUP, Chavez was simply an arm of the Anglo political establishment; and allegedly he represented the traditional negotiating posture in politics, one which clashed with La Raza Unida's rhetorical emphasis on Chicano "self-determination." LRUP, however, overlooked UFW strength in California and the fact that they were seeking electoral office in the system for themselves. La Raza Unida was weakened by the inability to incorporate support from a prominent Chicano organization. In contrast, LRUP did cooperate with the Socialist Workers Party, and its name was virtually taken over by SWP adherents in several localities.

There was potential disengagement of the community from, as well as potential realignment with, the traditional party system. The institutional biases of electoral practices had long accounted for the atrophy in participation in national, state, and city government. The few Chicanos who held office often were unable to advance the interests of the community once they were elected. Yet, in terms of immediate results, even La Raza Unida failed Chicanos; to function as a "spoiler" to draw votes away from the usually successful Democratic Party did not advance those interests either. La Raza Unida was unable to extend its grass-roots organization, as the party had done successfully for a while in south Texas. If it had gradually built organizational strength, emphasizing a variety of issues and tactics and an uncompromising ethnic posture, eventually La Raza Unida might have gained a position as a viable force, at least within the community. When the community, deprived of a voice for so long, elected its candidates, they were not from La Raza Unida. By the midseventies a third party option was over. Nevertheless, the momentum for representation continued, and both LRUP adherents and Democrats shared in it, with the impetus for greater representation provided by movement persons.

Representation over Rhetoric

Los Angeles and California have major political importance, but changes within these pertinent political structures—on a state, city, and county level—were slow in coming.[36] The basic issue remained reapportionment, which would enable Chicanos to elect representatives proportionate to their population. Eventually, three assembly persons were elected. In a tradition-bound legislature, the addition of three new Chicano members was a small advance toward a fair representation, bringing five assembly representatives into a total of eighty. Nevertheless, these five Chicanos helped move California's Chicanos one step closer to the political center. Apart from the competence of the candidates, two factors aided in their election victories. First, the United Farm Workers had been extremely active in registering and mobilizing the barrios to defeat the biased Proposition 22, an anti-UFW proposition which would have hindered seriously the farm workers' unionization. Second, the movement was to be credited for the increased political activity of the Chicano community as a whole. Reapportionment remained biased, however.

A proposal authored by state Senator John Harmer (R-Glendale) was described, at a hearing in February 1973, as one "fathered by racism and nurtured by hate and fear." At that time, the plan would have maintained the equal division in state government between the Republican and Democratic parties, but the major point criticized by Chicano representatives was its failure to recreate a Chicano senate district in East Los Angeles that had existed in a previous plan vetoed by the governor at that time, Ronald Reagan. Herman Sillas, in an editorial twelve days later in the Los Angeles Times, described the background of the bill and presented the reasons why he found it unacceptable for East Los Angeles. Sillas likened the reapportionment plan to a butchered side of beef—amateurishly butchered at that—with committee members hacking away until the forty districts emerged protecting the forty incumbent politicians. Chairman Mervin Dymally, who two years earlier had helped draw up the plan ultimately vetoed by Reagan, but which had given East Los Angeles a solid Chicano district, saw his own district redrawn so that his constituency was less than 50 percent black and about 33 percent Chicano. The remaining Chicano areas were divided among several districts, leaving the community with as little as it had possessed prior to the new plan. This plan, however, failed to be adopted. The state Supreme Court, having warned the state government that it would take on the task if the legislature failed to accomplish it in time, finally presented its own reapportionment plan in September 1973. The Supreme Court–

sponsored plan was more attentive to increased minority representation. The new plan could mean possibly two Chicano state senators and four Chicano assemblymen for Los Angeles County.

At the same time that reapportionment of the state senate and assembly districts occupied the efforts of Chicano activists, a similar movement was afoot in the Los Angeles city government.[37] After an attempted lawsuit the previous year, in 1972, the City Council districts had been reapportioned, but somewhat irregularly. A lawsuit was filed early in 1973 against the Los Angeles City Council, charging that the council had "diluted" the potential voting strength of Chicanos in Los Angeles by arbitrarily distributing the Chicano population among the council districts. The fact that suits were filed demonstrated the increasing politicization of the community and a concerted effort for fair apportionment of political districts, but not until ten years later was a council seat gained, and several more years passed before a second seat was secured.

As the events of the sixties and seventies unfolded, a presently unmeasurable element was impacting on political developments, organizations, and leadership.[38] Presumably, police surveillance occurred throughout the Southwest. Targets were determined, strategies devised, and tactics conducted to weaken not only the militancy but also the political organization of all types. The covert activity was concurrent with the more visible and understood overt activity of indictments, arrests, and beatings. Police provocation to commit not only violent acts but more frequently counterproductive actions was a fact, and of course led to the promotion of dissension within or between groups as well as individuals. This did not cease throughout the seventies, though a more benign force did become active.

Cultural Renaissance

As is common to revitalization movements, a resurgence of the arts followed in step with the movement for civil rights.[39] All of the arts in both traditional and innovative forms increased in productivity and in numbers of participants. There was an outpouring of strident poetry, perhaps exceeding other materials in quantity and much of it explicitly political in intent. Theater and music were prominent because of their easier applicability to protest and the graphic arts because of their utility to propagandization. Organizing dance groups and performance art was widespread. Gradually, there came into being a body of more reflective literature. Newspapers were widespread and useful vehicles for stimulating participation. Stable and better financed publishing efforts contributed to the dissemination of information and analysis on a wide variety of topics. Throughout the seventies the medium which reached the widest audiences was film. Energy and optimism were apparent in all of these expressions; while the quality varied greatly, the best was indeed excellent. For the most part the message emphasized pride, condemned discrimination, and demanded equities. This message was easily assimilable by the dominant society and the varied sectors in the community. The emphasis was on ethnic contributions and participation, not insurgency.

The Movement's Insufficiencies

As a minority within the minority, "Chicano movement" leaders of both large and small groups, though they discussed the fact of subordination, did not fully scrutinize the limited solutions posed in the reforms offered to the Chicano community during this time. Commonly, the leadership interpreted the cause of the Chicano's status as "racism," which was not a complete or even coherent explanation. By and large, analysis of the Chicano dilemma emphasized the importance of "race" and "racism" and the liberal means to lessen overt discrimination. The students' emphasis on higher education and the development of Chicano studies exhibited an optimistic belief in the role of the school as a societal institution. Such emphasis was inconsistent with a strong adherence to rhetorical "Chicano nationalism" in the sixties movement and with the projection of Aztlan, which proposed a "nation" that presumably would have the right to independence. But not until the polemics of the midseventies was the national question substantively addressed. "Nationalism" as a rubric was not explained or perhaps understood by more than a few as a political agenda throughout the sixties.

The speeches and writings of Chicano leaders who advocated at least some aspect of collective assertion had three common themes: the need for Chicano identity, for Chicano self-determination, and for independent political and economic action. They viewed the attempts of older organizations to work within the established legal and social order as pointless, and they often proposed the need to work outside the system, which, with a few conspiratorial exceptions, meant working outside institutions while nevertheless directing their efforts at institutions and after receiving resource support from institutions. This sometimes involved, for example, the Alianza movement and its manipulation of theatrical violence, or the Brown Berets' posturing and its potential threat of violence. "Race" analysis, in part, led to an inconsistency between the radical rhetoric preached by the Chicano leaders and the modest reform programs they requested, since it led to proposals emphasizing integration of "ethnics" into the system. In fact, excluding the militant rhetoric, the proposals of Gutierrez, Tijerina, and Gonzales were very similar to those made by civil rights groups of the fifties, who allegedly preached "accommodation" and "assimilation" (groups such as LULAC, the American G.I. Forum, MAPA, PASSO, and so forth).

Chicano leaders of the sixties were impeded by the contradictions between their assertive rhetoric and their conventional reformist demands and programs. For example, the Chicano movement political program was seemingly separatist. However, Gutierrez advocated that LRUP direct its activities toward what were considered traditional forms of electoral political involvement in Texas, like voter-registration drives and campaigning for the election of Chicanos to political offices and school boards. In effect, Gutierrez advocated empowerment through political elections. This stance was not explicitly separatist nor even radical. The "cultural nationalism" of Gonzales, the student organizations, and others amounted, in fact, to an ethnic liberalism both in its basic consistencies and its contradictions. For instance, Gonzales's demands of better housing, education, social services, and greater employment opportunities were addressed to the system. The students' demands for Chicano studies programs and college recruitment programs for Chicanos were addressed to the system. Artists asked for their art to be recognized, integrated, and rewarded. Except for energized and dramatized public protests like demonstrations, strikes, and marches, these petitions took place within familiar and traditional patterns. These programs were of some value, but many Chicano movement leaders failed to realize the limited orientation and inconsistency that these programs offered the Chicano community. In general, the demand for economic strength—whether it was Gutierrez's pressure on Anglo businesses through boycotts, Chavez's securing of grower contracts through strikes and boycotts, or Tijerina's efforts to gain the restitution of Spanish land claims by litigation—was in accord with the establishment of a Chicano middle class effectively competing in the present system. The most militant content in the arts was derived from the heritage of past insurgencies; the Chicano artist was often antiideological, desperate for recognition, and influenced by what was in vogue in the arts generally.

There was both an overemphasis and an underemphasis on leadership, a fact and a problem that was in some cases exalted, in others denied. At first leadership was local. In the sixties some local Chicano leaders received exposure and recognition, but still they were not able to develop a broad following among the Chicano community; that is, Chavez organized farm workers, Gonzales addressed the youth, Gutierrez emphasized Texas, and Tijerina spoke to those in New Mexico who believed in land claims. Small or medium organizations were built on charismatic leaders, or *liderismo;* concurrently, a person assumed control of an organization, and invariably there was a quasi-personality devotion among loyal followers. People followed the leader; the leader became the energy of the group and was viewed as possessing superhuman qualities. The emphasis on charismatic leaders in the Chicano movement had its obvious limits, however. For example, when Tijerina was in prison, the Alianza movement abruptly found itself without a leader and collapsed. A danger of charismatic leadership was its tendency to force activity in the direction of the specific goals, interests, and even the style of a certain leader. For example, the clash between Gonzales's more militant stance at the LRUP conference and Gutierrez's more liberal stance was not addressed. The conflict that erupted within this situation was due to the absence of discussion about what the Chicano community wanted, needed, or was ready to do; nor were these matters discussed in relation to LRUP, only in relation to specific persons. Though there were meetings, there was no integral unity among leaders during this time. This weakness is clearly seen in the condemnation of Chavez because LRUP claimed he was too close to the establishment without even trying to understand his position. Other examples of this failure to understand leadership were seen in Tijerina's pathetic contradictions, the often pointless conflicts between leaders who possessed very similar positions, and more importantly, the failure by leaders as well as their constituencies to examine critically differences between so-called radical leaders and their so-called less radical counterparts. Leadership problems interfered with the function to guide the movement competently and for the interest of the "community," because the "interest" and the "community" were not sufficiently addressed. Leadership was key in building organizations, and leaders were often the principal responsible agents in the demise of organizations. But evidently weaknesses also were overcome by some individuals and organizations.

In stressing self-determination, pride, and even violence, the leadership of the Chicano movement during the period between 1960 and 1970 was moderately successful in making the larger Anglo society acknowledge the discrepancy between the democracy it professed and the reality in the barrios. This leadership undertook the strong action needed to enable the more moderate elements to enter institutions. In reviewing the accomplishments of the sixties, what was achieved were token reforms, representation, and limited mobility. Chicano self-determination was not even attempted, let alone accomplished. The problems confronting the movement were universal almost without fail: the lack of an explicit class constituency; the lack of a radical program to which a constituency was deeply committed; a lack of resources; the lack of structured disciplined organizations; the lack of stable, competent, committed leadership; and the lack of a common critical ideology.

Objectively, the most visible deficiency lay in resources. Resources are indispensable for the activities of a movement in a country like the United States and especially in a community so broadly distributed geographically such as the Mexican. With funding limited, movements such as the Alianza, the Crusade, and LRUP could not carry out their specific goals. For instance, LRUP did not have the resources for extensive campaigns or for adequate media coverage. Movement organizations were inhibited from developing organizational structures within the movement because they had to rely mostly on self-taught volunteers who lacked the organizing power of a full-time, professionally trained, subsidized staff. Persons with leadership responsibilities were faced, in particular, with erratic and poor financial support. Adjustments were made when some Chicano efforts were funded by foundations; government agencies; colleges, universities, or established institutions; and even political parties—and such support tended to redirect the aims of Chicano leadership, even leading to their displacement. There followed the impetus to tailor organizational action and perspectives so as not to harm chances for either continuing or future funding. However, the limits of financial support do not alone explain limited aims. Overall, the apparatus involving electoral support, social status, and legitimacy within existing institutions provided a major reason why many Chicanos avoided endorsing militant organizations or explicitly radical ends. Emphasizing access and reform served to form and reinforce co-opted leaders and a co-opted constituency.

Organization was addressed in various ways, but in many cases not satisfactorily. Among a few, there was the ignorant notion that organization was "elitist." Spontaneity as a problem and tendency was present and more common in particular to the actions of small community groups or to the less politicized students. In nearly all cases, the major efforts entailed planning and providing internal organizational cohesion for their initiation. Many movement efforts were not cohesively organized for effective action over the long term in relation to their membership, leadership, resources, and interim and long-term agendas. Though there were many groups formed during the sixties, most of them lacked organization and internal structure and hence could not provide such for coalition structures. The existence of the Southwest Council aside, no umbrella organization emerged to harness the political activities of the various organizations at that time. But like previous attempts the movement failed in providing a coalition of Chicano political organizations throughout the Southwest; and when these were formed, they were not connected with the "movement." Without this coordination among groups, organizations overlapped in a diversity of goals and orientations; no operational unity existed among Chicano organizations. Organized activity among groups did propagate the enumeration of issues. The members of UFWOC, the Crusade, Alianza, and LRUP might agree on the constellation of issues, but not on methods, aims, or priorities. This opened the way for more single-purpose, specific, and pragmatic groups to eclipse protest and militant groups. These groups promised to be more effective and were so, at least within their limits. They delivered, and they were emphatically pragmatic.

A major deficiency facing organizations and leaders in the 1960s and early 1970s was the lack of an explicitly and widely accepted critique of the dominant society from the point of view of the Mexican experience grounded in explanatory generalizations and proposing a pragmatic future vision, a viable strategy, and a set of tactics. Aspirations, partial critiques, and general statements were produced, but not a single compelling general statement. To compensate for such a lack, at best there were readings and the synthesizing of eclectic materials for the occasion at hand. The implicit common ideology accepted by movement persons was "nationalism," but it was bogus. In effect, what was espoused was culturalism and political access to the dominant system. The potential unity of nationalism was weakened by the impulses toward social status, economic position, and professional attainment which were sought from the system. For those who pursued the exploration of theory for its political utility in contrast to those who wished to engage in "discourse," there was one option; namely, Marxism. However, Marxism invited denunciation, and when this happened the widespread and deeply ingrained phobia against it came into play. Sillier was the denunciation of this or other material because it was "European." Equally debilitating was the rejection of the importance of ideological material per se; the schools had not only disabled generations, but they had ingrained a bias against "intelligence" which was parroted at the same time that the schools were condemned. And sometimes the parrots were the leaders. Whatever the shortcomings, lessons were subsumed while more organized and more conceptualized efforts by those who had experienced the late sixties and early seventies followed.

The Left

From the late sixties through the seventies, as the tendencies of utopian *indigenismo,* cultural nationalism, and Alinskyean civil rights activism declined, more structurally oriented economic critiques of the Mexican reality gained ascendancy. These critiques condensed into a modestly growing Marxist current within the Mexican community, one which contained all of the various Marxist tendencies.

For some, Marxism remained an intellectual fad, a philosophical critique of the society and particularly of its "hegemonic culture." For others, it became the conceptual framework for examining the Mexican experience in a more specific and extensive manner. For still others, Marxism became the ideology combining analysis with a guide to political action and organizational structure. In this cadre of the activist left were members of the generations of the sixties and seventies as well as Marxists from the forties and fifties. Its ideological commonality notwithstanding, its social makeup was varied. A good part of the Mexican left had no specific organizational allegiance, but some of it did and among them a distinction was drawn between those groups stemming from the community and those outside it.

Renewed Marxist organizing among Mexicanos was a manifestation of the increase in general Mexican political activity, but it was also related to a renewal of radical thinking at large. The Marxist groups included the Communist Party, the Socialist Workers Party, the Progressive Labor Party, the Communist Revolutionary Party, the October League, the Communist Labor Party, the Democratic Workers Party, and others.[40] There were also women's groups which synthesized feminist tendencies with Marxism. The majority of the members in these groups were, of course, Anglos of middle-class origins. The tactics of these groups ranged from crudely opportunist agitation to organizing in the workplace and general political education and mobilization. Others devoted themselves to "study." The majority of these groups included only a small number of Mexican members, often students or former students. Their impact on politics consisted of polemics on economic and international issues concerning the community, but otherwise, it was slight. They shared certain characteristics like vitriolic language and factual ignorance. Given their sectarianism and mediocre organizing abilities, none of them were significantly successful in greatly interesting the working-class Mexican; in the Mexican community, they remained small and isolated. However, as they moved into "mass work" their influence would relatively increase. Some of these groups published specific organizational positions on the Mexican in the United States as a national minority with specific national, cultural, and political rights.[41] Others were unclear as to how they viewed the Mexican community.

An example of left-wing work was the effort of the Socialist Workers Party (SWP).[42] With little success but with persistence, they conducted work among Mexican people for at least twenty years. They
were viewed as either disrupting activity or tailing after an issue once
others had done the work of directing the issue; and they were identified by some as the group most empathetic to "Chicano" mobilization.
Overall, opportunistic policies and chauvinistic practices characterized
the SWP among students, farm workers, and La Raza Unida Party;
and they did not offer a clear alternative to reformism, but, in fact,
they contributed to it. Yet there was also an altruistic motivation
involved: the furtherance of radical populist change as well as contributions to the political momentum. Despite the efforts of Mexican
members as far back as 1949, as well as subsequent attempts in the
early 1960s, the SWP inadequately recognized the importance of the
Mexican people and did not analyze the nature of the Chicano civil
rights struggle until 1970.

SWP interest in the Mexican developed primarily with the impacts
of the UFW, the Chicano student and youth movements, and the
Texas La Raza Unida Party. These activities were of compelling interest
initially within three key political arenas for the SWP, as it attempted
to gain political hegemony for its line and its members sought to
capture leadership of the "radical" momentum: (1) the student movement, (2) the antiwar movement, (3) independent political parties,
and, later, (4) the immigrant defense movement. To further SWP
efforts, the *Militant,* an excellently directed newspaper, gave considerable coverage to Chicano actions, organized Chicano conferences,
and published materials from the Chicano movement. The UFW posed
problems to the SWP as a particular and attractive, though idiosyncratic, unionizing effort by workers. Far more experienced than students or ex-students, the UFW leadership was not easily courted or
penetrated, and the latter was the SWP aim. Frustrated, the SWP in
the midsixties questioned the efforts of some members to support actively the NFWA's struggle as reformist, seeking to end all active
support of the farm workers by members of the SWP or its youth arm,
the Young Socialist Alliance (YSA). This discussion reflected factional
divisions within the party as did many of the decisions and policies
of the SWP with respect to the Mexican people and to SWP politics
in general. For the moment, in effect, the SWP criticized the UFW
while supporting unionization. In other areas of activity, SWP efforts

with students or community groups resulted repeatedly in confrontations and in their ouster. They were more successful in antiwar activity at large and in La Raza Unida, in particular. Their chauvinistic attitude was their most easily identified trait.

In examining the external political theory and practice of the SWP and other similar parties, it is important to distinguish between propaganda directed at the rank and file and sympathizers, on the one hand, and on the other, the actual organizational actions and priorities of the political leadership of the organization. Rank-and-file members, particularly if they were members of the YSA, the youth group, often would have a somewhat specific and more altruistic understanding of a particular political policy or position that they were advocating for the Chicano movement. The actual internal political basis, intent, or reasons for the adoption of the position by the leadership may have included considerations removed from the current mobilization or issues—for example, factionalism over international decisions or differences within the general Trotskyist movement nationally and internationally. Many rank-and-file members of the YSA and, to a lesser extent, the SWP objectively believed that the SWP program for Chicano rights and SWP practice in the movement advanced the liberation of the Mexican people. In many cases, they were uninformed that the actual machinations of the SWP leadership did not focus on this as their priority and often were insensitive to the priorities of the community or as to why they were rejected. SWP recognized the "movement" because they viewed it as a growing arena of political struggle for recruiting Mexican youth and for pushing the adoption of its "transitional program," particularly by La Raza Unida Party. SWP used its Mexican members and its own participation in the "movement" to gain greater legitimacy within the left and in its struggles against the Communist Party, the Progressive Labor Party, and others within the antiwar movement during the early seventies. This participation was also useful in flushing out the internal opposition within the SWP and to sharpen debate internally.

The role of the SWP and the YSA within, or in relation to, the Mexican movement was not unique; rather, it was basically a repeat performance of SWP attempts to gain hegemony in the Black movement, which had finally rejected them. Evaluating the positions and activities of any multinational organization within the Mexican movement will show generally the same characteristics and usually similar failures and rejections that occur within other struggles. For example, SWP attempts to stimulate an independent Black political party with their transitional program, that is, the Michigan Freedom Now Party of the early sixties, demonstrated the same type of opportunism and sectarianism displayed by the SWP and the YSA in relation to La Raza Unida Party. In any case, on several occasions the SWP was pointedly asked not to participate. The SWP would create problems in relation to the farm workers' struggle, the student movement, Chicano studies, the moratorium, electoral efforts, and, worst of all, in relation to mobilization for immigrant rights. In the eighties, however, the SWP played a much more positive role in the mobilization on behalf of nonintervention in Central America. As a left organization, the SWP was targeted by police agencies and there were statements to the effect that it had been heavily infiltrated over the years. This surely affected its tactics, which was probably also the case for other organizations, including those SWP competed with.

During the seventies the most salient progressive organization functioning in the Mexican community was Centro de Acción Social Autónoma-Hermandad General de Trabajadores (CASA-HGT).[43] Over time, its base included workers, some professionals, and some students. Stressing class and nationality for a time, the organization indicated the developing national and class consciousness among activists within the Mexican people in the United States. Among other concepts, CASA proceeded from the conceptualization that Mexican workers, regardless of which side of the border they are born on, experience the same exploitation under capitalism and that the possibility for radical social change in the United States is linked to an international process. In community political mobilization, they stressed working-class interests and unity based on nationality and on selected progressive issues. They believed in effective international solidarity and in working with organized and spontaneous community mobilizations; they sought the militant union leadership, rank-and-file membership, and also politically conscious but unorganized individuals. Their effective labor organizing and their ties with other Latino organizations, such as those in the Puerto Rican community, were promising. CASA devoted special attention to trans-border labor, economic, and political developments and established precedent-setting relations with groups in Mexico.

The key to CASA's political efforts was their disciplined membership, as well as their direct and integral ties to the community of which they were a part and in which they worked; and not least, CASA's sensitivity in political deployment, to tactics and propaganda, and to Mexican culture and the relationship with Mexico. Within a few years, CASA achieved a significant record of success. They pushed forward ideological and organizational development by providing militant leadership in a wide set of activities nationally and in Los Angeles, a most important Mexican community. The newspaper *Sin Fronteras* was clearly the best militant print organ of the movement. CASA identified two key questions—those concerning national consciousness and the undocumented worker—to further the militant direction that was to be realized through organizing the Mexican worker and selected political activity.

The demise of CASA must be examined through its mixed origins and a series of splits dating from 1972. The origins of CASA derive from late 1968, when it began as an organization devoted to modest services for undocumented persons and built on a "membership" determined by the payment of a small fee in return for a "card." Though CASA had accumulated resources, there was little structure or accountability; but there were any number of internal conflicts, along with the invariable denunciations, particularly those concerning financial matters. Conscious of its own limits as well as the weaknesses of previous organizations, it was forcibly reorganized and its membership restructured between 1974 and 1975. Its previous leaders were displaced; they had been drawn from MAPA and from organizations active in the sixties in Los Angeles, such as Católicos por la Raza and the UFW. In the process leading to reorganization, particularly important was the incorporation of members with extensive experience in Mexico as well as the cohort around Prensa Sembradora. Reorganization was a continual process. Within CASA, there were major unsolved issues of factional leadership centering on internal democratic practices and the structure and priorities of the organization, and erupting on a matter of personal ethics. Ostensibly a well-structured organization, CASA was undermined by a clique of relatives, who were challenged by two factions, one that sought to emphasize worker organizing and another that emphasized organizational strengthening and ideological ascertainment. After a period of intense internal debate and major changes in leadership and in internal modes of participation, CASA members chose to disband as a national organization, although local groups continued to function and former members remained active in community issues. Indisputably, CASA contributed to radical mobilization and discourse in the seventies, and its legacy informed the work of other organizations in the eighties.

Another organization influential at yet another level was the August Twenty-ninth Movement, whose roots and efforts lay partially in the Chicano community and partially elsewhere, drawing its founding members from student organizations and movement newspapers.[44] Though multiethnic, to call attention to itself, it emphasized the so-called "Chicano question," that is, the proclamation of the right to self-determination while, in effect, remaining antinationalist. It became less a Chicano group and more a multiethnic one, stressing a Marxism idiosyncratically interpreted through the writings of Mao Tse-tung and at a time that Mao's work left less of an impact than previously. Like other left groups, this one stressed propaganda and the distribution of materials. It interjected itself into a number of situations rather than creating mobilization on the basis of an issue. In some cases, August Twenty-ninth members were so clumsy that their efforts became counterproductive to their own ends; for example, in their interventions in Chilili, New Mexico, or in specific MECHA chapters, or in some labor disputes. Other efforts were more effective, such as the anti-Bakke campaign and the Farah strike. Without much public notice, the group went through some sharp internal purges, coalesced with other groups, and reformed itself and these as the League of Revolutionary Struggle, a much more effectively organized and directed group ostensibly focusing on student and labor organizing issues and more prone to support cautiously a range of issues involving civil rights equities and electoral campaigns. They continued to prefer covert rather than overt work, infiltration rather than direct mobilization, and to conduct both a public and a closed discourse.

Rather than sharply stated ideological organizing, and instead of a single highly structured organization with a disciplined membership, more prevalent among militant civil rights activists of the seventies was the formation of multiethnic coalitions embracing a variety of groups and their issues, including peace, ecology, nonintervention, animal rights, gays and lesbians, and so forth. Their actions were directed at government and businesses and often dovetailed into efforts by liberal Democrats. Throughout the sixties and seventies, militant civil rights activity, rather than becoming encompassed gradually by a dominant membership organization, remained as it had begun, as a coalition of groups and individuals temporarily united on a specific issue for a specific effort.

4

Conservatism: New Players and Strategies from the 1970s to the 1980s

The Electorate

Voting is the most direct political act available to most citizens as well as the most frequently practiced political activity among Mexicans. Pluralities can determine elections, and pluralities are affected by the difference between the potential, the qualified, and the actual vote.[1] Bloc votes count more, but Mexicans are not yet a fully consistent and effective bloc vote although they do act as one upon occasion. Of the approximately 3.8 million persons of Mexican origin who were of voting age in the eighties, 1 million, or 24 percent of the total, were reported as having voted in the 1978 congressional elections. Approximately slightly more than half of the eligible voters have been registered, and about 60 percent of these actually vote. Allegedly, the most telling weakness is the less than maximum potential voting, while the explanations given are either cultural or structural in nature. Clearly, past discriminatory practices have hindered voting. However, voting has been conducted generation after generation, and in some instances it has been relatively high. What has varied have been local conditions, requirements, candidacies, and motivation. Registration can be lower, but like voter turnout, it also has been higher than other groups. A citizen must derive satisfaction and have an expectation of gain from the act of voting.

Though there are exceptions, Mexicans are more likely to vote for a Mexican candidate and for a candidate who effectively appeals for their vote. Quantity and quality of voting reflect the diversity of

155

the community, but voting takes place incrementally and reveals general patterns; some instances of high-population concentrations exhibit higher voting participation. The combination of dispersal across the republic with regional concentration is a potential advantage. Speculatively, unbalanced partisan affiliation may or may not be an advantage, but since World War II it has exhibited a strong persistence which is not easily subject to change by an organizational or leadership call. For Mexicans as for others in any given election, the franchise involves, at most, a plurality among those residing and eligible in the community, and it is subject to manipulation, constraints, and probably, on occasion, fraud. However, Mexican voter registration in 1980 was 25 percent higher than in 1976; and voter turnout in 1980 was 20 percent higher than in 1976. Both registration and voting increased in the eighties. From one vantage point, the youth of the population and the large numbers of non-U.S. citizens subtracted from the political strength of the total, but they demonstrated future potential electoral strength. Two million Mexicans who were eligible to vote were not registered. Interest in political affairs and participation in politics were the major thrusts of the 1980s; both elected officeholders and those participating in the Democratic and Republican parties were on the increase. Seven out of ten identified as Democrats, and were thus likely to vote that way. Approximately one-third had a strong interest in politics, while one-third had some interest and one-third little interest; somewhat the same distribution also occurred on the political spectrum between liberals, moderates, and conservatives. Those on the left seemed small in contrast to the other groupings. However, a significant percentage of approximately 25 percent reported themselves as independent, and the age group with the lowest voter participation was the one between eighteen and twenty-five. Political participation tended to be higher according to a person's level of education, income, and employment status.

Mexican concentration remains most significant electorally in California, Texas, New Mexico, Arizona, and Illinois, three of which are important electoral states. While non-Mexican Latinos are strong in New York and Florida, concentration in key states is what makes the vote potentially crucial; in numbers, the Mexican is only 4 percent of the total U.S. population and between 2 and 3 percent of the electorate. To increase leverage in states beyond the Southwest and in total numbers would compel closer cooperation among the Latino groups. In 1980 there were approximately 3.4 million Latinos registered. By 1984 this had increased to 3.8 million, or 12 percent, and significantly only 2 million voted. In 1986, 4.2 million were registered, and 5 million were projected in 1988. To date, the social, historical, and economic realities of Latino groups have been reflected in distinct political attitudes, participation, and agendas; and these differences are reflected in priorities in domestic and foreign relations. Latinos were 4.5 percent of the total U.S. population in 1970, 6.5 percent in 1980, and by the year 2000 they may be 10 percent. The past electoral profile indicates that without constant effort the electoral base could decline, for there are no permanent plateaus in registrants or in voters.

Electoral Politics

Though occasionally punctuated by decline, the growing momentum in recent community politics was due to electoral activity. After the high point in 1960, the vote dropped in most places during the election of 1964. Insufficient voter registration and voter turnout significantly reduced the impact of Mexican American voters in the 1968 elections, with the exception of Texas.[2] A significant influence upon low Mexican voter turnouts in November was the assassination at the end of the California primary of Senator Robert Kennedy, the favored candidate among a large majority of Mexican Democratic voters who had turned out for him in significant numbers during the primaries. Though the electoral primaries of 1968 were overshadowed by the developing impact of the movement, there was dramatic infighting between the Mexican adherents of Robert Kennedy, Eugene McCarthy, and Hubert Humphrey. Some of the established leaders from organizations or holding elected office were active or covert supporters of Humphrey, a fact that many would later prefer to ignore, especially after the events of the convention in Chicago. There, congressmen, *mapistas*, and others watched complacently as the police beat student demonstrators.

While Hubert Humphrey was to receive over 87 percent of the Mexican American vote in the general election, and Richard Nixon 11 percent, the actual number of votes cast was more than one-sixth less than among Mexicans in the 1960 presidential election. The

Mexican American voters in the state of Texas were a significant exception. In Texas, due to lawsuits, which were often the result of MALDEF litigation, and the Voting Rights Act, the poll tax formerly used to exclude Mexican Americans was eliminated. At the same time, AFL–CIO unions and Mexican American organizations registered many thousands of new voters. As a result, Hubert Humphrey received 300,000 Mexican American votes in Texas, allowing him to carry the state by a total of only 39,000 votes. Richard Nixon thus lost Texas's twenty-five electoral votes; in New Mexico, however, he received 40 percent of the vote, partly the result of an effort by Nixon aides to develop a strategy to court conservative Latinos, upper income Mexicans, and other Latino potential Republicans. They looked especially to the conservative Cuban exile community as well as to all other potentially conservative bloc voters. In any case, during the 1968 elections there were independents or dissident Democrats running for office in several parts of the Southwest. They did not do noticeably well. Though absolute numbers dropped, Democrats received votes of 70 and 80 percent.

As before, alternative political parties in various states, such as the California Peace and Freedom Party and New Mexico's Peoples Constitutionalist Party, which received 2 percent of the vote, had little impact upon mainstream Mexican Americans; there was, however, a numerically small but soon to become symbolically significant surge of support for alternative politics among some Mexican American college students. It was hardly to be expected that Mexican American Democratic voters would be attracted by left political groups when they expressed modest support even for Democratic Party protest candidates such as Eugene McCarthy; but in 1970 this changed slightly due to the emergence of La Raza Unida in some Texas local elections, even though "movement" candidates in Colorado and New Mexico did relatively poorly and in California the Peace and Freedom Party received less than 2 percent of the vote. One exception was Oscar Acosta, who ran as an independent for sheriff in Los Angeles and received 100,000 votes. On the other hand, in the Arizona gubernatorial race Democratic candidate Raul Castro lost by seven thousand votes.

Progressive politics gathered strength when, in 1972, George McGovern, who had focused primarily upon anti-Vietnam sentiment and a radical economic plan, made significant appeals to Mexican

Americans which resulted in highly visible and effective support from the United Farm Workers and other progressives.[3] The McGovern campaign was significantly different in its ethos, internal operation, and constituent accessibility as well as in its relatively unambiguous progressivism on issues ranging from disarmament to the arts. It was also different because rather than placing once again among the also rans, the left wing of the Democratic Party had actually won the 1972 nomination. The primary featured an intense contest between McGovern progressives and moderates and conservatives supporting Humphrey or Edmund Muskie. The established leadership provided lukewarm and again ineffective support in the general elections for the progressive candidacy of McGovern, who was also sniped at, if not attacked, by adherents of La Raza Unida. Political operatives read the polls and knew Richard Nixon was not only very likely to win but to win by a landslide. McGovern received nearly 60 percent of the Mexican vote, and this vote as well as the Black vote were the only traditional constituencies of the Democratic coalition that remained in the Democratic column. Nixon received nearly 30 percent of the national Latino vote, noticeably increasing his vote from 1968 and again gaining nearly 40 percent in New Mexico. For congressional seats, the Democrats continued to receive 85 percent of the vote.

Throughout the late sixties and early seventies many inhibitors to voting were addressed as well as districting practices that proved negative in their effect on Mexican officeholding.[4] Between the seventies and the eighties, the context of electoral politics became larger and more complex as the result of an interplay of relative changes: the national increase and distribution of Mexicans; the increase in momentum and leadership provided by the "movement"; the relative increase in the middle class and its resources; the changes in the United States social and legal structure; and the relative liberalization of the dominant society. These aspects were partially reflected in the numbers of elected and appointed officials of Mexican descent. Specific figures underscore these phenomena in electoral politics. Nationally, in 1976, there were over three thousand Spanish-surname elected officials, counting school-board members.[5] A majority of these were of Mexican descent, and included the special assistant to the president, one senator, several congressmen, two governors, one speaker of the legislature, one state legislature majority leader, and over seventy state legislators. Among the women there were one Mexican county commissioner in Chicago, a secretary of state, several state senators, several state legislators, and a deputy mayor in Los Angeles. Both men and women held an increased number of offices at many levels, but their total did not exceed 1 percent of all elected officials. Somewhat more telling, Mexicans were to be found in groups of the political spectrum from the right to the left, in the two major parties, and in a third party, La Raza Unida. Significantly, a Mexican progressive sector was growing within the Democratic Party.

This reality and its historical precedents denied certain common observations; electoral politics was not a new step for a community laden with positive promises. It was simplistic to say that there was no Mexican representation, participation, or progress in electoral politics per se; nor were there positive benefits to be derived from electoral politics per se, or positive benefits to be derived from electoral politics for the community. Nonetheless, full Mexicano political rights continued to be denied, and the community was continually and grossly underrepresented. What political results were obtained from electoral participation were critically modest from the perspective of ethnic and class interests. Mexican representation in New Mexico had been the strongest and most continuous in the nation, but the socioeconomic and educational status of the population was among the lowest in the United States.

Electoral activity was, and is, expressed in a variety of partisanships. Drawing special notoriety were two such electoral partisanships, one from the left and the other from the right: La Raza Unida Party, an independent effort; and the Latinos in the Republican Party during the Nixon years. Mexicans in the Republican Party date from the nineteenth century; what was new was the priority given to the Latino "vote" by the party and the impact this activity had beyond New Mexico.[6] Prior to 1968, Republican strategists considered it important to diminish the Mexican Democratic vote, and thus they gave special attention to it. According to their strategy, they preferred to obtain a part of this vote themselves but what was most important was to cut into the Democratic vote. This effort worked slightly in 1968, and for the presidency Republicans received 11 percent of the Mexican vote. This priority was again stressed in 1970 for the 1972 election, which Nixon won by a landslide, gaining 25 percent of the Mexican vote. However, in early 1970 victory in 1972 had seemed problematic.

Another decision was to restructure the Inter-Agency Committee on Mexican American Affairs, making it broader in scope and designating a new entity, the Cabinet Committee on Opportunities for the Spanish Speaking People.

To attempt to ensure the success of this Republican strategy, money was to be spent on increasing the vote and was also to be gathered from the Mexican community. Efforts were made to accentuate differences between Mexican organizations, and Mexican appointments were given high visibility: Ramona Banuelos as treasurer of the United States; Philip Sanchez as head of the Office of Economic Opportunity; Hilary Sandoval as administrator of the Small Business Administration; Carlos Villareal as an Urban Mass Transportation appointee; Martin Castillo, initially, and, later, Henry Ramirez as chairman and Hank Quevedo as director of the Cabinet Committee on Opportunities for Spanish-Speaking People. Appointments also went to the late Ignacio López, Ben Fernandez, Raymond Telles, Fernando Oaxaca, and others; all of whom were highly successful professionals and conservative Catholics in the private sector, but among them were those who had been immigrant migrant workers and others who came from families dating back six generations. Most of these appointments were phased out after 1972, when perhaps they were no longer needed electorally. Even so, the Nixon administration established an unprecedented record in Mexican appointments; and it also made available some money to the Mexican community, especially for programs developing Mexican small businesses, for consulting firms, and allegedly for political groups. This money intensified infighting from 1968 to 1972. Through heavy pressure, the administration also took money out as campaign contributions; and as a result, Mexicans had the dubious honor of being mentioned during the Watergate "affair."

Usually, Mexican participation in the Republican Party has been part of the conservative sector of the community, coming from upper and middle income sectors, professionals, highly educated and often, but not always, notably assimilated persons. The incremental growth of voting strength has continued to reach over 20 percent, and often in district and state elections and in presidential elections the turnout is higher, reaching roughly 30 percent as in 1980, 1984, and 1988. They have also spent increasing sums. The most visible Republican participants at the national level were Henry Ramirez, head of the Cabinet Committee during the Nixon administration; Fernando Baca, special assistant to President Gerald Ford; and Ramona Banuelos and Katherine Ortega, who were appointed as treasurers of the United States, with the latter also serving as a Republican Convention Keynote Speaker in 1984. President Ronald Reagan named as his closest Chicano appointees Nestor D. Sanchez from New Mexico, a former CIA operative who claims to be descended from "conquistadores," and Cathi Villalpando from Texas, whose qualifications included a total absence of experience and a total commitment to conservatism. The most outspoken Republican appointee was Linda Chavez, who responded in negative terms to nearly every single government policy intended to support Latinos. The leadership of this party fortified its activities by the organization of the Republican National Hispanic Assembly, long headed by Fernando Oaxaca, and by stressing its few elected officials, such as Manuel Lujan (R-New Mexico). A weakness. was the party's lack of candidates. A campaign that drew notoriety was also the closest one waged, the candidacy in 1988 of Linda Chavez for the Senate seat in Maryland. More astute efforts by Republicans included analyzing the purported conservative value potential among Mexicans and supporting selected redistricting which included the probability of indirectly favoring Republican candidates in the future by drawing upon a concentration of Anglo voters. In any case, the Republican vote also returned to pre–New Deal distribution of the vote between the two major parties.

The Democratic Party

The Democratic Party has been the most amorphous and varied in composition of the groups involving Mexicans in electoral politics.[7] What is remarkable is not the loyalty of the Mexican to the Democrats, which in some cases has been more, in others less, than other ethnic groups; but the gross disregard of the party for the Mexican voters and their leadership. Some slight change has taken place within the party with regard to Mexican participation and issues; nonetheless, the party on the whole has exploited and manipulated the Mexican vote; and it is still restrictionist toward Mexicans. Major economic interests and dominating elite factions govern Democratic Party politics, and it is a pillar of the U.S. electoral system. On the other hand, the Democratic Party is the "liberal alternative" of the two major parties.

Hundreds of thousands of Mexicans vote for its candidates and policies; and it is the party which, albeit limited, offers the most participation and the most programs to Mexicans. The party is composed of an array of interests from the right-center to the left-center, thus covering a space which overlaps with the Republican Party and one which would belong to a left-wing labor party. Legitimacy and momentum is provided by the left wing of the party, but it is governed by the center. Mexican progressives in the party argue the following matters: to abandon electoral politics is to leave a battleground open to the opposition; and reforms which raise the standard of living, even if limited, are important, and furthermore, without a strong liberal wing in the Democratic Party the tendency toward conservativism would be stronger in the United States as a whole. Certainly within the Democratic Party there are always contending factions and ideas, a continual pull between the moderates and conservatives and the liberals and progressives. Among Mexicans within the party, there is contention continually between the more progressive and more pro-Raza element and the more moderate or conservative proassimilation forces. Within the party, Mexican activists are generally left centrists. What, then, is the change in the Mexican's position within the Democratic Party? The change is indeed one of degree.

Between approximately two and three million Spanish-surname voters registered in the 1960s and 1970s, perhaps reaching four million in the late eighties; the majority of these registered voters were of Mexican descent and a majority voted Democratic.[8] Mexican votes for the Democratic Party hit a high of 90 percent and, on occasion, dropped to 60 to 70 percent. In national elections in 1980, 1984, and 1988, Mexicans voted approximately 70 percent of the time for the Democratic ticket. Overall, Mexican participation, voter registration, and voting figures varied considerably, depending upon candidates and issues, and further indicating a selective political judgment. The high loyalty to the Democratic Party, deserved or not, was a reflection of the class and ethnic position of the majority of Mexicans, not of an unreflective attachment to traditional voting patterns. Class and ethnic position influenced a vote for the more liberal candidate of the two major parties. In areas of Texas, some who momentarily saw a viable alternative in LRUP and had faith in its leadership may have deserted the Democratic Party, voting for dissident candidates within the party. Like the United States electorate as a whole, the Mexican vote was increasingly prone to independence, selection, and conscious nonparticipation in specific campaigns.

Changes within the party structure date from 1972.[9] While the numbers of elected officials increased, the large majority of Mexican officials were members of the Democratic Party, and their state and national visibility as well as their national coordination was increasing. Contributing to all this, for a while in the seventies, was the strong and efficient coordinating role of the Office of Spanish-Speaking Affairs in the Democratic National Committee, under the leadership of José Aragon, one of the ablest professionals in the country at the time. This coordination worked to strengthen communication, registration, unity of action, and the training of campaign technicians among Mexican Democrats. The Carter administration provided a significant momentum to Chicano participation in national politics, particularly through appointments at various levels.

Developments interrelated with the increase in participation and visibility were the organization of a Latino Caucus within the Democratic National Committee (DNC), which was made up of national committee members,[10] the majority of whom were Mexicans; and the organization of a Latino Caucus by convention delegates at national party conventions, a phenomenon which began in 1968, reached a peak in the 1972 convention, and then occurred again in 1976. In 1968 a total of 95 Latino delegates and alternates attended; in contrast, in 1972, 232 delegates and alternates were chosen. In 1984 there were 271 Latino delegates and 92 alternates, and in 1988 approximately the same. Both caucuses indicated the incremental development of pan-Latino cooperation, and they exerted modest pressure on national candidates, the party platform, and the general party machinery. The DNC Caucus was, however, more important because it was recognized and structured. The activist and progressive qualities of the office and caucuses was dependent upon the character of the individuals involved. Local and state partisan organizations increased in number and membership, and became more effective electoral organs than the older and nonpartisan ones.

Throughout the seventies and eighties, running parallel to these efforts although possessing more potential influence, was the organizing by Mexican Democratic officials at state and local levels. Such groups came into being in the seventies partly because, given the numbers, it was now possible to attempt such an organization and because the individual elected officials needed an instrument to exert leverage in local, state, and national primaries and general elections and on state and national administrations. Such phenomena were visible at the state level in Texas, California, and elsewhere, wherever Mexican members formed Chicano legislative caucuses. Some commonality of aims existed among these Democratic elements: people understandably were interested in strengthening their own political position, and there was agreement in general, but not on specifics, to support the issues of bilingual education, NFWA, manpower training programs, and special programs in housing, business development, health, education, and other areas.

In campaigns, Mexicans generally experience much frustration; for each success, there are scores of defeats.[11] Nonetheless, community education, organizational experience, and political maturation accrue from electoral campaigns. Mexican electoral activists have stronger leverage and a greater accessibility to party participation in primaries, in very close races, or in races where markedly liberal candidates oppose more conservative ones. Such was visible in Mexican participation and militancy in national campaigns beginning with John F. Kennedy's in 1959–60, and running through Lyndon B. Johnson's in 1964, Robert F. Kennedy's in 1968, Hubert Humphrey's in 1968, George McGovern's in 1972, and Jimmy Carter's in 1976 and 1980, Walter Mondale's in 1984, and Michael Dukakis's in 1988. The character of individual participation at all levels as well as the advocacy and acceptance of "Chicano" or Latino platforms has varied widely, depending on the temper of national politics, the national candidate, and the degree of Mexican cohesion in the campaigns. With each campaign, the structural participation improved but not the overall public recognition given to the Mexican, which ebbs and rises.

The progressive versus liberal versus moderate to conservative contention is visible in these national campaigns. Assemblyman Richard Alatorre of California chaired the Convention Credentials Committee in 1984 and, in the same year, state Senator Polly Baca Barragan of Colorado was vice-chair of the Democratic National Committee. In 1984 the majority of party officials as well as the majority of delegates supported Walter Mondale. The Jesse Jackson primary effort and its supportive vehicle, the Rainbow Coalition, made an impact on the Latino and Chicano communities incrementally, but more in the Midwest and in California than elsewhere. The Rainbow Coalition has been an effort built around a charismatic individual, with economic and social sensitivity and a progressive agenda but not with an effective, efficient, or stable multiethnic, progressive coalition. Voting for Jackson by Chicanos increased in 1988, but it could have been stronger. There were particular reasons for the Chicano response; the plus was Jackson himself and his agenda, while the negative was pragmatics, the decision of elected leaders and organizations to go with a "winner." The Dukakis campaign was, however, a disappointment.

Outside the formal or quasiformal party structure, developments impacted on electoral and community politics as a whole.[12] The Southwest Voter Registration Education Project (SVREP), founded in 1974 by Willie Velasquez of San Antonio, a former member of MAYO and of LRUP, focused on securing resources and support for registration campaigns during national and local elections. It is the clearest example of the belief in voter registration and voting as *the* priority, and one in which numbers are the measure. Establishing a network of volunteers with a small staff, SVREP has contributed significantly to the increase of registered voters across the country and thus to the election of Mexicans and the greater electoral recognition that the community has received. SVREP has conducted studies on figures, views, and issues, and published these reports. After an association with Joaquin Avila of MALDEF, a noted attorney and an expert on electoral matters, SVREP has co-filed lawsuits to enforce the Voting Rights Act, and it has intervened to encourage local districts to restructure themselves. Its activities have occurred across the Southwest and Midwest, with the most salient successes occurring in Texas. Governed by a visible and respected board, SVREP has continually suffered from a lack of resources. Voter registration is appreciated, but its funding is uneven. Not lacking resources, the National Association of Latino Elected Officials (NALEO) was formed in 1975.[13] Developed from an association of Democrats, it embraced elected and appointed officials from both parties and provided issue analysis and dissemination, training, information exchange, and advocacy at the national levels. It has also sought to increase funds for political analysis and research; and over the years its stature has grown.

Trade Unions

A strong auxiliary to political efforts in nearly all communities are the unions which have Mexican membership.[14] Presently, there are greater numbers of Mexican union organizers than previously, and officials and leaders from the rank of shop steward on up number several thousand perhaps. Mexican representation to local, state, and international labor conventions has increased, as has labor's presence in community affairs. Indicative of the increase in the number of Mexican and Latino union officials was the organization of the Labor Council for Latin American Advancement in 1973, directed by Paul Montemayor. A national organization, the Labor Council was organized, in part, through the efforts of Latinos themselves and partly by decision of the AFL–CIO leadership; it was promoted by a desire to foment and yet direct and perhaps contain the increasing participation of Latinos within the AFL–CIO structure. The Labor Council's purpose is to mobilize Latino trade unionists and their respective communities in support of labor issues and Democratic Party candidates. If the Labor Council addressed itself to the problems of Latino workers inside and outside the unions, thus being permitted a latitude of action beyond the usual parameters of the national AFL–CIO leadership, such an act would occasionally test the AFL–CIO's own often conservative ends. The AFL–CIO has been conservative within national politics, often willing to favor one group of workers over others; and it has been charged with being a conduit for State Department and CIA strategies. Local Latino or Mexican American labor councils are found in cities such as Los Angeles and Detroit. To date, Mexican labor leadership is most visible during national and state elections. In the unions, Mexicans are growing in their numerical importance among auto workers, mine workers, railroad workers, cannery workers, teamsters, longshoremen, garment workers, construction workers, steel workers, and, of course, agricultural workers, where they are a majority. It must be understood that many unions are discriminatory and politically conservative and the leadership petrified and, on occasion, corrupt. Nonetheless, Mexican presence in the unions is significant for political developments. Unions have been active forces with resources in local, state, and national elections.

Throughout the seventies national lobbies expanded. The National Council of La Raza was founded for the initial purpose of facilitating local organization and mobilization while providing access to informational and developmental resources as well as furnishing advocacy at the national level.[15] While growing to some one hundred affiliated groups and claiming an outreach to hundreds of thousands

of people, it soon came to stress economic development projects and
its association with the corporate sector. Based in Washington, D.C.,
El Congreso, the National Congress of Hispanic American Citizens,
directed by Manuel Fierro, served as a lobby for the concerns of the
Spanish-speaking peoples at the national level.[16] The multitude of
"nonpartisan" middle-class professional associations also began having
an effect on electoral politics.[17]

Concurrently significant in politics has been the formation of informal or quasiformal affinity groups of influence brokers and fund-
raising individuals and hangers-on who are key or try to be key in
electoral politics. They are not of high political visibility, and they
usually group around an individual or a circle of individuals. The
cement is self-interest and personal advancement, and it involves the
pooling of resources, influence, and contacts for maximum effect.
Though still limited, fund-raising capability has increased significantly
among Mexicans; and for its maximum possibility, two elements are
needed: potential resources and the skill to utilize these resources.
Each year more money is raised, though success continues to be uneven.

In Congress, seniority, public status, access to campaign resources,
and the willingness to trade votes are important.[18] Activists have high
expectations from congressional representatives, and federal officeholding is the area that receives the most attention from activist
organizations. Representational progress has been slow, but reasonable
expectations might include two or three senators and two dozen con-
gresspersons. Ten congressional seats and one senate seat have been
the maximum thus far. Democrat Senator Joseph M. Montoya, elected
in 1970, was the federal officeholder with the most extensive experience. He was a supporter of civil rights and social legislation, and
the Bilingual Education Act, but he was also a strong advocate of
defense and of an aggressive foreign policy. Prior to the sixties, federal
officeholding was a feature of New Mexico primarily. But in the sixties
congressional representatives were elected from Texas and California.
Henry B. González of Texas, chairman of the House Committee on
Banking, Finance, and Urban Affairs, and Edward R. Roybal of California, chair of the House Select Committee on Aging, have been
among the most known and respected congressmen, and both are
traditional "New Deal" Democrats, liberals, supportive of social and
economic legislation while strong on defense. Another Democrat who

has been more influential is E. "Kika" de la Garza of Texas, the chairman of the House Agricultural Committee and a more conservative politician. Much more conservative, however, has been Republican Manuel Lujan of New Mexico, elected in 1968. Because of the notorious paucity of elected Latino Republican officials, he has enjoyed prominence in the party and popularity among business persons. In the seventies and eighties more aggressive spokespersons were elected—each one a Democrat—including Bill Richardson in New Mexico, Salomon Ortiz and Albert Bustamente in Texas, and Marty Martinez and Estevan Torres in California. All of those in Congress represent districts with significant numbers of Mexican wage-earning voters, but these districts also have distinct constituencies even among those in the same state. In the seventies the Hispanic Congressional Caucus was formed. As a loose coalition, the group has profile and informational benefits for the members, their local electorate, and the larger national constituency, but it is rare when they all hold the identical position on a bill for identical reasons; moreover, their number is not of major significance in a house of over four hundred members. As individual senior members of Congress, Roybal, Gonzalez, and De La Garza have potential power, but they do not always achieve effective visible success in behalf of Mexicans.

State politics has evidenced the most visible success. Three persons have been elected to governors' posts, and the number of legislators has increased.[19] Jerry Apodaca was elected governor of New Mexico in 1974, and in the same year Raul Castro became governor of Arizona; while Toney Anaya was elected as New Mexico governor in 1982. Although New Mexico continued as the strongest area of participation, gains were recorded in all states. Increased local efforts promoting voter registration and participation have accounted mainly for this upsurge, which is also the result of cumulative effects from the 1965, 1970, and 1975 Voting Rights acts. In New Mexico, Jerry Apodaca, a moderate Democrat, and the unprecedented five elective statewide positions benefited from an invigoration of politics throughout the state and the ability to draw votes from the growing urbanization of Albuquerque and Santa Fe. Toney Anaya, a liberal Democrat, emphasized education and improved services while cultivating ties outside New Mexico. Anaya, though young, had an impressive record of prior experience both in Washington and in New Mexico. He was an aggressive leader, despite the serious limitations of shortfalls in the budget and majority opposition in both houses of the legislature. Anaya advocated development and educational reform and succeeded in significantly increasing the numbers of women and minorities in appointed positions. Both Apodaca and Anaya were attractive and charismatic individuals who were well informed on state issues and able to develop support beyond their Mexican base; and both were pressured into, but also interested in, assuming national stature. Anaya's extensive out-of-state work became a liability among state voters; however, his position as governor was difficult from the first for state financial and political reasons. Still, as a one-term governor his influence was inevitably on the decline as his tenure proceeded, but his popularity among all constituencies dropped precipitously, seriously impairing his chances for holding a future elective office. After one losing effort, Raul Castro of Arizona, born in Sonora, Mexico, and a moderate Democrat, succeeded in being elected to govern one of the most conservative states by building on a coalition of Mexicans, Navajos, businessmen, and some agricultural interests. He left office before completing his term to become ambassador to Argentina; previously, he had served in El Salvador and Bolivia.

Legislative representation has increased significantly from what it was in the sixties, with the exception of New Mexico which has usually had at least one-third Mexican representation (thirty-four) and remains the state with the highest percentage proportionally of Mexican voters. The change perceptible in New Mexico is in the type of officeholder, from the older, traditional, and locally rooted *políticos*, part of sensitive and extensive kinship and friendship networks, to more educated, urban based, and independent officeholders. California's representation included three state senators and four representatives, among them some highly visible individuals such as Art Torres, Richard Alatorre, and Gloria Molina; the conservative Ruben Anaya; the vociferous Joe Montoya; the respected Peter Chacon; and the moderate Charles Calderon. Colorado and Arizona have had seven and twelve representatives, respectively, in the legislatures as well as minority or majority speakers in one or another of the houses of Congress. There were several prominent legislators: Polly Baca Barragan, Reuben Valdez from Colorado, and Alfredo Gutierrez from Arizona. Texas has had four in the Senate and twenty-one in the House—among them, Judith Zaffirini in the Senate, and Irma Rangel and Lina Guerrero in the House. California and Texas should have higher absolute numbers.

The authority and hence the potential of legislative representatives vary as do their compensation and resources. The more successful area of legislative activity has been in incremental reforms to the educational systems, and in some economic legislation concerning the improvement of wages and protections. With an occasional exception, major state legislative initiatives have been frustrated.

Local offices are of the most immediate importance, but there are hundreds of officeholders at the local levels; and even in New Mexico the numbers have increased from previous highs.[20] Local issues are proverbially dominant in political discourses. Major achievements have been mayorships such as those of Federico Peña in Denver, Colorado, and of Henry Cisneros in San Antonio, Texas; as well as in a half-dozen small- to medium-size cities. There were common characteristics· in political ideology, personal style, and means for achieving office. Peña and Cisneros have achieved prominence at a national level. Both benefited from the repeated efforts at mobilization in Denver and San Antonio, and both succeeded in forming coalitions that joined their ethnic base with progrowth business interests and middle-class white liberals. Both of them are well-educated, articulate, and attractive politicians who are also more conservative than liberal. In many localities, Mexicans were elected to council positions, and in some places they secured a majority. San Antonio has been the most visible of these. In Los Angeles, in the eighties one and then two Chicanos were elected at last to the City Council, and one was a woman, Gloria Molina. Women were also elected to city councils in Denver (Debbie Ortega) and in San Antonio (Maria Berriozabal).

One of the most compelling actions in Chicano electoral politics of the 1980s was the strong Latino participation in the city politics of Chicago, which had its organizational and leadership roots in the 1960s and 1970s.[21] A threshold experience was the MALDEF suit of 1982, intended to end the gross gerrymandering which in Chicago as elsewhere was motivated by the Democratic Party. Jesús García (of the Twenty-second) and Juan Solis (of the Twenty-fifth) were elected aldermen. Chicanos became a recognized but modest force which was pinned by the internal struggles among the larger Black forces, the traditional white Democrats, and the periodic progressive insurgencies. Several other Chicanos secured alderman seats in the area; there was a Chicano Cook County Commissioner and elections and appointments to various boards. A growing trend of empowerment was strengthened by the energetic support provided to Harold Washington's mayoralty campaigns and the campaigning by Chicano leaders such as Toney Anaya and others. Chicano participation in the political life of the Midwest and Northwest was increasing notably and was a distinct novel event in the landscape of Mexican political participation. By the 1980s there were several hundred Latino elected and appointed officials in the Midwest.

Among the indicators of the exclusion of Mexicans from policy-making and government positions has been the near absence at all levels of significant appointed positions prior to the seventies.[22] Though these positions are operationally much more feasible to achieve than access to electoral office, there are scores of positions from the federal to the local levels which have never been granted to a Mexican. Since the seventies, appointed officials have increased in number and in the significance of the office. The most important offices are judgeships and executive positions, followed by the major policy boards and commissions. Partisan service, legitimacy, and expertise or personal ties come into play as well as public relations and electoral considerations. Appointments are also made to dilute protest or to facilitate negative change in a particular program. In his last months in office, President Reagan appointed Lauro Cavazos from Texas as secretary of education, the first such cabinet-level appointment for a Latino. President George Bush continued Cavazos's appointment, and also named Manuel Lujan of New Mexico as secretary of the interior.

Mexican electoral politics was a part of the complex of the complete political spectrum within the community, of its social and economic matrix as well as the national and international scene. Neither the cliches of mainstream political scientists nor those of some movement spokespersons of the late sixties have survived. The electorate constituency has grown and its full potential is not realized, but it remains critical and skeptical. Mexican politics takes place and has impact at the local, state, and national levels. Primaries have been the quickening times. New and old, crude and sophisticated politics coexist, as do mainstream and radical politics. Traditional organizations continue as new ones develop. Money, resources, and professional political capability sift "winners" from "losers," and support networks crisscross state lines. Business persons, the unions, the bureaucrats, and the professional elements have grown in their importance. Contemporary political networks indicate the presence of

"Mexican American" establishments and the strengthening of a middle-class leadership. The middle-class activists and their establishments strengthen themselves by maximizing resources and coordination, but they have no extensive popular base other than the working sector. The middle class is not likely to become large enough to serve as its own electoral base. They are brokers and tenuous ones at that, and sometimes the brokers get brokered. Hence their dependency on support from Anglo or other patrons, business persons and union representatives, membership organizations, pressure groups of all kinds, and their own skeptical and temperamental grass-roots constituents.

Electoral figures have demonstrated clearly the electoral political underrepresentation of the Mexican, but they also indicate the positive potential of the future.[23] Electoral figures and potential are not only optimistic in relation to immediate electoral politics; there is also much room for growth. The 1970 U.S. Census counted 6,293,000 people of Mexican origin, while the 1980 census recorded a 50 percent increase. All experts agree that the census undercounts the Mexican population, with estimates varying from 10 to 25 percent, and even as high as 50 percent. At one point, there were six million Latinos eligible to register; yet only two million were registered, with 65 percent going unregistered. Consistently, registration has been only partially tapped. Mexicans have a 40 percent lower registration and 49 percent lower voter turnout than the U.S. population as a whole. In Texas of the midseventies, after all of the civil rights activity and electoral work of LRUP, only 19.3 percent of the eligible Mexican population was registered. According to the 1980 census, Mexicans comprised 17 percent of the population in the southwestern states and only 10 percent of the elected state legislators, 7 percent of the elected county officials, and 6 percent of the elected municipal officials. In Los Angeles, the community with the largest Mexican population in the United States, not one Mexican was an elected county representative in 1985. In California, a "liberal" state, out of 15,650 federal, state, and county officials less than 2 percent were Mexican. There are approximately one hundred congressional districts, with 5 percent or more Latino populations, and twenty-five congressional districts with 25 percent or more Latino population, all of which may indicate that in one-fifth of the congressional districts the Mexican Latino community could exert pressure on congressional voting and double its congressional representation.

The above figures indicate undercounting, injustice, and the often proclaimed yet unfulfilled political potential of the Mexican. The five southwestern states had eighty-eight presidential electoral votes in 1972; this number has increased since then, and it is likely to increase again after 1990.[24] In an optimum scenario, Mexican votes potentially outnumbered by three to one the winning plurality in these states for the 1972 elections. If effective mass electoral pan-Latino cooperation develops, Illinois and New York, as well as Florida, could be added to the strength of the five southwestern states. Possibly, Latinos could influence nearly two hundred electoral votes. Optimum scenarios are the exception, however. Viewed by some skeptically and by others as a breakthrough, the 1965 Voting Rights Act was expanded in 1975 to include Mexicans and to secure for them protection from discrimination at the polls; in effect, promoting proactive concern for their voting rights and participation.[25] The provisions of the act are operational when Mexicans comprise more than 5 percent of the population and less than 50 percent are registered in Texas, Colorado, Arizona, and California. This seemingly liberal legislation may have nonliberal consequences as yet unforeseen. Enthusiasm is cooled by the fact that at roughly the same time this act was signed, persecution of undocumented Mexican workers increased, and although the Immigration Reform and Control Act (IRCA) of 1986 provided for regularization of immigrant status and eventual naturalization for over a million Latinos, more were excluded than included. Also darkening hopes is the fact that Latinos do not yet comprise even 5 percent of the voters nationwide, while other state combinations and voter patterns, rather than Latino-biased optimum scenarios, determine elections. In the vortex of activity are the continuing organizing efforts among middle-class sectors, the highs and lows of the economy, and the relationship with Mexico.

The Middle Class Organizes

The success, albeit limited, of the "movement" in increasing schooling and employment opportunities and focusing government attention on Mexicano problems had softened the initial resistance and pejorative attitudes of the established Mexican community leadership, which realized that its own interests could be served best by working in the movement tide.[26] Exemplary of this change in attitude and position were MAPA, the G.I. Forum, Democratic Party activists, and LU-LAC. Old and new left-wing organizations also decided to join and lend their support. Almost as affected but less noticed has been the continued presence and influence of *asociaciones patrioticas* and *mutualistas* in the community. Organizational politics were strengthened by an increase in the numerical size of the Mexican middle class as well as by mobilization in behalf of equity demands in general. In large measure, the increasing number of Mexican professionals and bureaucrats can be directly attributed to the impetus and opportunities provided by the movement. Demands for jobs, appointments, slots, and promotions led predictably to this phenomenon. The saliency of the middle class in certain areas is to be expected not only because of its skills, but also because the larger society's leadership will enhance its counterpart within the minority community once it must give this community recognition.

By the beginning of the 1960s, traditional middle-class organizations such as LULAC, the CSO, and the American G.I. Forum were either stagnating or in decline.[27] Their position in the Mexican community was still important, but they were more negotiation- and accommodation-oriented as opposed to confrontation and change-oriented. The events of the sixties revived them by creating resources and greater civic participation. The rise of student activism based on confrontational tactics in the community called into question middle-class leadership and organization, but it also contributed to the mobilization of the middle classes. Initially, the differences were primarily between the students and the middle-class elements and were based on tactics rather than issues. Only later, after their original hostility had dissipated and the climate was more auspicious, did the middle-class groupings begin to participate and organize. For the most part, this action was geared to satisfying its class interests. By then, it had to face much severe criticism which was based both on principle and on tactics drawn primarily from Marxist or nationalist organizations and individuals. As specific beneficiaries of government grants, LULAC and the G.I. Forum grew noticeably, reaching memberships of over 100,000 and with each conducting a range of continuous programs, services, and activities while their elected leaderships received national stature. Other institutional sectors came around; namely, the national and

state government, teachers, union leaderships, the Catholic and Protestant churches, and the Democratic and Republican state organizations. Curious allies of the middle-class leadership were, in a few
instances, some of the ex-felon inmate and/or ex-addict groups who,
for a while, had been culturalistic in their rhetoric and participants
in "movement" organizing.

Consciously or unconsciously, the entrance of middle-class groups
was based on class interests and resulted in channeling the energies
of the "Chicano movement" into gradualist and reformist change that
was not unduly unsettling to the status quo. Since the early seventies,
literally scores of special interests and professional organizations have
come into existence in nearly every aspect of community activity,
advancing their specific interests which are usually economic. Invariably, there has occurred a jostling for benefits and visibility, and they
have been drawn into the pressure politics of competing sectors among
the elite.

Some government coordinating agencies facilitated employment
for the middle class. At the national government level, the Inter-
Agency Committee for Mexican American Affairs was established and
later became the Cabinet Committee on Spanish-Speaking Affairs.[28]
This committee was intended to address itself first to the needs of
Mexicans, and later to all Spanish-speaking peoples on a national
level. During its existence, it was geared to the bureaucratic advancement of the Mexican and other Spanish-speaking middle classes. Similar agencies and commissions were also established at the state and
local levels.

Established nationally in 1973, and with over ninety chapters
across the republic, the Incorporated Mexican American Government
Employees (IMAGE) lobbied for equal employment opportunities and
counterdiscrimination for Latinos at the federal, state, and local levels.[29]
In particular, they have addressed congressional representatives and
senior federal appointees. Their position is simple: more opportunities
for employment means improved services, all of which benefits the
community. These efforts have achieved some reforms, but they have
hardly ever identified, much less addressed themselves, to the root of
the problem; instead, all actions were, and are, directed toward the
symptoms.

Much of the business of politics is business, and an interactive
relation exists between the political and the entrepreneurial; access

to capital or contracts is basic to business, and money is basic to politics. In any case, a major recognized need was the enhancement of business and economic development; and buttressing this was the argument that social problems are, at bottom, problems of insufficient local economic development. "Chicano" businesses were in demand.[30] In 1969, the Office of Minority Business Enterprise (OMBE) came to play a major role in local minority politics and entrepreneurship; it was a major catalyst for more overt civic participation by business-related persons. The National Economic Development Association (NEDA), whose avowed purpose when it was formed was to further "free enterprise," provided managerial and financial assistance as well as access to business opportunities and capital to entrepreneurs, all through twenty-five offices across the country and a budget of several million dollars. Headed by an eighteen-member board, it incorporated and based itself in Los Angeles. There were several state, local, and national chambers of commerce. The Latin American Manufacturers Association (LAMA) worked to secure government contracts and subcontracts for its members through lobbying and technical assistance. The federal regulations which have made the establishment of the Minority Enterprise Small Business Investment Corporation (MESBIC) possible have been a power generator for entrepreneurs. Accountants, engineers, health professionals, police officers, teachers, and attorneys have formed groups that all, to some extent, interact with political officeholders and organizations. National organizations such as LULAC and the National Council have special business enhancement activities. Important to business people, apart from OMBE and NEDA, are the Economic Development Administration, the Small Business Administration, the Office of Economic Opportunity, and, where they exist, similar state offices. These are all public and regulated, but insider information and access is advantageous to the business person. Banking and investment possibilities are, of course, attractive to those with funds.

Middle-class women's groups appeared with great vigor.[31] Among them were the Comisión Femenil Mexicana Nacional established in 1970, the Chicana Forum begun in 1976, and the Mexican American Women's National Association started in 1976, with the last the most candid of these organizations. Their principal aim is to promote the

careers of their members and of women in their educational and economic sector. They lobby for appointments and grants from foundations and corporations. The most representative has been the National
Network of Hispanic Women (1977), consciously a "network" of "leaders" from the professions, private business, education, and the corporations. The national LULAC women (Mujeres en Acción) may
have the largest membership of any of these women's organizations.
Intercambios Femeniles, a women's magazine, faithfully mirrors the values and positions of these types of organizations. Though the overall
women's civil rights effort has had impact, Latino women have not
benefited as much as white women. One major and potential institutional conflict remains latent: the common pro-choice position of
women's groups leads to some polemics with the church.

The church is one institution that provides an interactive and
continuous bridge between sectors. The churches are multifaceted in
their activities, from the religious to the political. The Protestant
churches, especially the Episcopalian, Methodist, Baptist, and Presbyterian, were of special significance in mobilizing resources and support for urban problems.[32] In contrast to the Catholic church, Protestant
clergy often were more socially sensitive and more politically skillful.
Many of them were part of the leadership establishment in the community and were linked to them by kinship. Efforts by the Protestant
churches, especially by the Presbyterians, were directed at farm workers
as well as urbanites. The migrant ministry was established as a vehicle
to provide traveling crews of farm workers with individuals who could
attempt to solve problems as they arose while also seeking to bring
Mexicans within the Protestant fold and to enhance its constituents.
Protestant churches directed their energies toward support and social
services while also lobbying for reforms within the political system.

Similar, but for a period lesser, efforts were carried out by the
Catholic church, which had taken the Mexican Catholic allegiance
for granted.[33] After years of neglecting the social ills of the Mexican
community, and after facing confrontations, the Catholic church was
influenced by Pope John XXIII and the Vatican Council, resulting in
the reinvigoration of the Bishop's Committee for the Spanish-Speaking, which had been established in the 1940s. Founded in 1948, the
Secretariat for Hispanic Affairs has been increasingly active since the
midseventies. The group essentially functions for Mexicans at the
national political level as a lobby and support group. Their efforts on

behalf of the NFWA and of migrant labor generally have been important in ameliorating the farm worker's social and economic situation. Mexican and Latino Catholics are an increasingly important constituency for the United States church. Important in moving the church toward a more attentive position were the militant demonstrations of the Católicos por la Raza against the church policies and hierarchy; the demonstrators were indicted and tried, and received unusually harsh sentences. Stemming from the impetus at San Antonio and Bishop (later Archbishop) Patrick Fores, the Mexican religious organized their own national organization, PADRES, and agitated for pro-Latino change within the church as well as expressing reform-advocacy tendencies. Out of this group came the several elected Mexican bishops of the seventies and eighties, including the Archbishop of New Mexico, Robert Sanchez; in the mideighties, the bishops numbered eighteen, approximately divided between liberals and moderates among the nearly three hundred bishops in the United States. Among their main activities, apart from strengthening their presence and numbers in the church, have been giving support to the NFWA and providing some lobbying for the improvement of social and educational conditions in the Mexican communities, as well as ending discriminating practices by government law enforcement agencies, and contributing a major effort in behalf of immigrant rights in the late eighties. PADRES has addressed the significance of culture and community unity from the perspective that considers these factors as related to the strength of religious beliefs and to the church as an institution. It has held several national and regional *encuentros*, convocations of religious and lay persons, in an attempt to agree on agendas of action. Groups of nuns and lay persons have also been formed. A few radical theological groups have emerged to discourse on Mexican issues. Their energies have been directed more toward a continuing dialogue and theoretical discussion on the potential elements of the unity of Christianity and Marxism, while stressing Christian humanism which emphasizes social solidarity and mutually supportive action for quality of life as well as spirituality expressed in daily life. The more ideological took up the dialogue of liberation theology. Clearly, the number of religious active in progressive and social causes had increased, although as an institution the church maintains a conservative bent. Nevertheless, the 1984 pastoral statement, "Catholic Social Teaching and the United States Economy," was a farsighted, conscientious statement because of its commitment to economic and social justice as well as to international peace.

Church-affiliated organizations such as United Neighborhood Organization (UNO) begun in 1975 and Communities Organized for Public Services (COPS) (established in 1974), located in California and Texas, respectively, were in the late seventies and eighties the community entities closest to being mass organizations.[34] To some extent, they were reproduced in other areas, such as in the El Paso Interreligious Sponsoring Organization (EPISO) and Valley Interfaith. Given the weakness of democratic participation in the United States and the tendency for a self-serving leadership to control organizations, organizing the local residents is a radical occurrence. These efforts have been explicitly reformist and incremental in their position and Alinskyean in their methods. They have consistently and ostensibly eschewed ideology and partisanship per se. Since the forties, the basic precepts of an approach to the organizing of low-income persons, influenced by the training methods of Saul Alinsky and associated with the Industrial Areas Foundation, have been widely known and practiced in Chicano community organizing. In truth, the basic methods ascribed to Alinsky are *do's* and *don't's* common to a particular kind of organizing: (1) full-time organizers, trained but dependent on local support; (2) identification of a set of issues by informal polling, and the selection of the one with the most agitational potential and the lowest risks; (3) tactical fluidity; (4) the building of a local committee and eventually a coalition, and from this some recognized review commission on the issue; and (5) nonpartisan, nonideological discourse and, if need be, aggressive action to keep this so. Churches, the Industrial Areas Foundation, and Alinsky have maintained a partnership for years, dating back at least to CSO in the forties. In the eighties, these COPS–UNO chapters grew extensively and secured measurable gains in local as well as statewide reforms. They definitely enhanced the empowerment of local residents and balanced the influence of other forces. They also enhanced the influence of the church. In effect, they were reformist centrists with the potential of moving to the right or to the left. Similar organizations were established in several areas in the Southwest. In the fall of 1986, a major event was held, called "Celebración '86" by Archbishop Roger Mahony of Los Angeles. A gathering of fifty thousand persons convened at Dodger Stadium to commit themselves both religiously as well as in social action to support the rights of immigrants and the homeless; and to improve education, end violence, and gain economic and representational rights embraced in a "Plan for Hispanic Ministry." For a majority of Mexicans, there remains a link between collective identity and the church, and it remains a strong unifying force.

The organizations viewed as the lead ones for the community—MALDEF, the National Council of La Raza, LULAC, and the G.I. Forum—have shifted from moderate reformist postures and energetic advocacy to more conservative stands.[35] All have tailored their postures to secure indispensable funding for their activities, and in particular funds from the corporate sector. The volunteer membership of social service organizations, as opposed to board-centered ones, have been more consistent over time, although their decentralized structure results in chapter disparities and their internal politics reflect intense debate. They, in fact, exhibit regional diversity and local variation, as well as unevenness in organization and leadership; at the national level, they are strong and growing. Locally among national organizations, LULAC celebrated its fiftieth anniversary in 1979, having gone through the most marked shifts in political emphasis from moderate to activist to centrist with a range of leaders and also becoming a pan-Latino organization, effectively including Puerto Ricans, Cubans, and others in its 110,000 membership and its five hundred councils in forty-five states with some chapters abroad. Half of its membership are women, and there are several youth councils. The major areas of strength continue to be California and Texas, and its membership includes both wage earners and professionals as well as urban and rural groups. The persistence of LULAC and the G.I. Forum are explainable by several reasons: they are vehicles for persons who wish to contribute and to be active in a conscious and predetermined framework; the mix of professional and nonprofessionals provides the constituency and expertise strengths; clearly stated constitutions, bylaws, and membership responsibilities make for understood group expectations, as well as for organizational democracy and fluidity in priorities and tactics; and local councils, regular meetings, and communications and national conventions enhance coherence.

Though there were a number of major organizations and attempts made in coordinating them, there was no major progress toward creating an overall umbrella organization.[36] Attempts initiated in the late sixties and the early seventies did not adequately fill this need; though

they differed, tentative steps included the efforts made by Edward
Roybal in Washington and by Armando Navarro through the National
Chicano Forum, in Salt Lake City, Utah. In the late 1970s and 1980s
a concern was expressed for greater cohesiveness in advocacy by senior
elected officials and representatives of the major organizations as well
as by activists from scores of local organizations. Hence, efforts to this
end were led by Pablo Sedillo of the National Hispanic Leadership
Conference, Henry Cisneros of the Hispanic Agenda, and Armando
Navarro of Impacto 2000. In response a selected number agreed to
convene to consider a basic list of issues and resolutions to these issues
as well as to explore international relations.

The International

Through the seventies and eighties, internationally related activity
increased in relation to issues and interfaces of various kinds. Explicitly
organized and selected delegations visited Israel, Germany, Spain,
Cuba, and elsewhere abroad. These delegations included elected officials, organizational leaders, artists, business persons, and academics.
Some of the leadership was emphatic in insisting that international
visibility was an important resource; and as one might expect, Mexico-
related activity was the most widespread.

In the 1970s the relationship with the Mexican communities
across the border assumed more dynamic and important dimensions.[37]
During the presidency of Luis Echeverria Alvarez (from 1970 to 1976)
and subsequent regimes, systematic attempts have been made by Mexicans and Chicanos for closer ties and cooperative programs and aims
involving a diversity of interested parties. The immediate origins of
this most recent rapprochement dates from the late sixties and early
seventies. On one hand, the progressive sectors in the Chicano community and in Mexico sought each other out, and among Echeverria's
positions was a proactive international policy. Members of the Mexican
population in the United States sought officials in the administration.
A number of high-level officers and advisors to President Echeverria
had direct knowledge of the Chicano community and its social and
economic links to Mexico. In trips to the United States, specific
meetings were arranged between President Echeverria and prominent
Chicano leaders and Chicano educational spokespersons. A dialogue

was initiated on a mutually advantageous policy for both Mexican communities, one based upon educational, economic, and cultural considerations, as well as on implicitly mutual political benefits. Although never clearly defined nor articulated, the policy between Chicanos and Mexico did involve certain purposes, a dialogue for mutual reconnaissance and exploration of possible areas of cooperation, implicit strategies, mutual support for specific aims, and a variety of sectors. Relations were of two broad types: those conducted with and by official agencies, and those involving others.

Public relations were erratic and affected by the as-yet-undefined operational mode and its limits. They were also affected by the changes on both sides of the border. With the oil discoveries during the José López Portillo regime (from 1976 to 1982), the Mexican state enjoyed for a brief period an economic bonanza that resulted in optimistic developmental expectations and a discussion of a new relationship with the United States, one that would stress interdependence instead of dependence. During the López Portillo regime, Mexico continued relations with Chicanos, although less visibly so than during the Echeverria administration. When it seemed that Mexico was in a stronger bargaining position vis-à-vis the United States, Chicanos were moving forward politically, and both could have more aggressively formulated the design of a partnership, the priority given officially to Chicano–Mexico relations decreased. Next, delimited by fiscal and international vulnerability, the administration of Miguel de La Madrid (from 1982 to 1988) did not fully implement its well-informed position (articulated during the presidential campaign) toward the Chicano community; nevertheless the sentiment continued for discussion, support, and ties through cultural and educational programs and the monitoring of the developing Chicano political and economic possibilities. Opposition groups devoted more attention to ties across the border, also noting the potential for an audience for themselves across the border. As electoral activity intensified in Mexico, so did its spillover effects in the Mexican American communities. But importantly, interaction did continue and the articulation became more specific.

Status and Problems

With the 1980s, a new political and cultural phase began for the Mexican community.[38] By the late 1970s, the Chicano movement had diffused. The intensity of the decade had exhausted some activists, and activism itself had become a consciously delimited activity. Mexican political players were no longer an easily identifiable two or three sectors within the community, nor did they share the same ethnic fervor or radical perspective as the Chicanos who had first created the context and opportunity for empowerment. Rather, they had become a complex amalgam of interests, backgrounds, and goals. A growing number of professional politicians surfaced from a variety of Mexican communities, each of them espousing the concerns of a unique political constituency. By the 1970s, many young Mexicans had explored the tolerance of the establishment, and in every way possible, they pursued what the system offered. In that turnabout, young Chicanos motivated a large percentage of their community to exhibit a stronger public presentation. In effect, they demanded that society at large receive a new message about what it was to be Mexican. They also generated support for educational, political, and economic advancement. Public officials began addressing issues of concern to Mexicans in a more considered manner. Finally, and perhaps most important, the Chicano movement forced certain concessions from the Anglo mainstream; and some of these concessions—partial bilingual education, underfunded Chicano studies programs, and unenthusiastic affirmative action employment practices—created a setting from which a viable Mexican middle class could rise to local prominence. The 1960s laid the groundwork for a series of economic advancements, but in the 1970s, a viable middle class emerged within the community. Yet the short-term occupational gains of the seventies were undeniably dwarfed by the economic setbacks of the early 1980s. Like other United States constituencies, however, the Mexican spent the late eighties in totaling the score card, and the score was short. Today, Mexicans continue to feel the damaging effects of drastic federal budget cuts and less government support for affirmative action and bilingual education. Culturally, the past twenty years have been a time of revitalization within the community, self-evident in the energies directed into the arts, media, and religious institutions, as well as a period of increased efforts at integration.

But in the whip of that cultural whirlwind, the community remains tempered by a uniquely Mexican concern for cultural continuity and political affirmation, while it is ambivalent as to how pluralistic the allegedly diverse system is. In the seventies the dominant society made

two overarching responses; one was the promulgation of the term
Hispanic and its supportive conceptualization. The term *Hispanic* was
a transparent ploy, undercutting the ethnic revitalization movement.
It quickly became the preferred term by bureaucrats, academics, business, and media. Another was the promulgation of the fear of this
insurgency which centered on immigration and language, and a renewed emphasis on assimilation and denial of Mexican rights qua
Mexicans—a noticeable phenomenon in Texas and California, in particular. In terms of language, however, two significant trends have
strengthened over the past two decades. On the one hand, a sizable
segment of the community speaks Spanish primarily. On the other
hand, the part of the local community which is English-only has
increased. In fact, many second, third, and fourth generation Mexican
Americans are unable to speak Spanish, although they continue to
understand it. Their linguistic limitation is primarily due to the sat-
uration of English-language media combined with a lack of formal
Spanish-language maintenance.

The Reagan era was a period of selfish emphasis, jingoism and
chauvinism, and a lack of access. The number of persons in a poverty
status increased. The Reagan administration was not only inaccessible;
it was generally negative toward the basic social and economic needs
of the community, and it undertook specific negative actions concerning immigration and labor. Both antiworker and antiunion policies
impacted on the Chicano community. But also affected were middle-
class organizations: their funding suffered, and their activities were
adjusted accordingly.

In the eighties, the Mexican people in the United States and in
Mexico continued a range of general commonalities based on shared
economic, social, political, cultural, and geopolitical realities. They
also shared the current crises facing progressive sectors and workers
in both the United States and Mexico. The eighties resulted in additional hardships and challenges for the Mexican-origin population
in the United States. Not only has the Chicano community been beset
by traditional problems, attitudes, and policies, as well as indirectly
by the vulnerable situation of the Mexican state in the throes of its
profound economic and physical crisis; recently emerging political and
societal trends in the United States have made the social struggle more
problematic and difficult for the Mexican people in the United States.
Concurrently, though, the Chicano had begun to fulfill a political

potential within the United States. Chicano organizations, civic groups, and recently elected officials have intensified their efforts and agendas for civil rights, socioeconomic reforms, and political equality with real though limited success. One positive area of impact has been on public bureaucracies. Public agencies have improved their services to the community as a result of continuous pressure, and the numbers of Mexicans working in public service agencies have increased. From a nearly wholly negative dynamic between government offices and the Mexican community, at long last attention was provided to services on behalf of Mexicans. Repeated demands for positions have made possible what was once a rarity; namely, Mexican public service personnel.

Throughout the eighties, the work and life-experience for the majority in the Chicano community has been one of hardship, sacrifice, and few rewards. Various manifestations of social life exemplify this human condition. On the whole, housing has been poor, as segregation and poor economic situations forced many Mexican families to reside in dilapidated and unhealthy housing in urban and rural areas. Social services persistently have been undersupplied and are not readily available. Education for Mexican Americans has not been well funded or staffed. There has been no integral formal schooling in Spanish, and the use of Spanish has been prohibited for school children; Mexican culture in U.S. schooling has been ridiculed. Poor educational services seriously have placed children and youth at a severe disadvantage. The U.S. legal system has operated contrary to Chicano interests. The courts, juries, and the police have long records of victimizing the Mexican people and have applied a harsher standard of justice to them. In effect, police have had many communities under siege through search-and-seizure practices, heavy patrolling of Chicano neighborhoods, and other overt repression. Through a series of tactics like poll taxes, language competency exams, gerrymandering, and intimidation, the Mexican has been hampered from participating fully in the political process.

On the job market, the Mexican worker has confronted a whole series of injustices which undermined his ability to secure meaningful well-being. Discrimination and lack of advancement on the job has been the rule. Mexicans were relegated to the worst jobs, received lower pay, were generally underclassified for the work they did, found promotion difficult, and were among the first to be fired and the last to be hired. Social security, unemployment, and other workers benefits have been minimal and difficult to acquire. Often, the right to organize unions has been curtailed. Antiunion laws—the so-called right-to-work laws—have been in effect currently in many states where Mexicans are concentrated, in Texas, New Mexico, and Arizona, for example. Within the unions, discrimination does exist; and few Mexicans have held important positions, while Mexican workers have not received an equal voice in union policies because of the machinations of the bureaucracy and because the Spanish language is rejected. Worse, many unions have been uninterested in organizing Mexican workers. Mexican women were even more exploited in their daily lives than males; for in addition to racism and class discrimination, they encountered sexism. On the job, they have been grossly underpaid and subemployed. And it is the job situation for the majority of the community which is key.

5

Current Perspectives: Empowerment

Late Twentieth-Century Dilemmas:
Issues of Culture, Class, and Economics

In spite of much adversity, the Mexican community has consistently sought a more socially just existence. The political history of the Chicano includes a continuous effort for social justice in regard to its political, economic, and cultural rights—a struggle waged with uneven success. Encompassing a reformist agenda for social change, the "Movimiento" transcended class lines, generations, regions, and gender. Chicano activism emerged as a challenge to the assumptions, politics, and principles of the established political and social order. The emphasis of *Chicanismo* was upon community autonomy, individual self-worth, cultural pride, and political and economic equity. The Chicano movement encompassed issues of education, civil rights, health, poverty, labor, access to professions, institutionalized racism, political participation, the arts, urban ecology, land rights, and many others. Optimum visionary goals pertinent to these issues were not realized, yet incremental gains of the Chicano community may be dated from the effects of this movement.

As the 1980s unfolded, the Chicano community in the United States was at a historical juncture. Much had been accomplished, new problems had arisen, and past injustices still lingered, as did obstacles to progress. After two decades since the start of the Movimiento, these years of sustained conflict and struggle had yielded some positive results. A cultural and artistic flowering was a predominant feature of

the late 1960s, the 1970s, and the early 1980s. There has been increased access by Chicanos to all levels of education. Chicano studies
and bilingual–bicultural programs are now established in over fifty
colleges; and studies in academic fields are now conducted by Mexican
scholars on behalf of their community. Chicano writers, scholars,
artists, and filmmakers have received national and international recognition. In absolute figures, the total income of the community has
increased as have limited economic opportunities for the professional
and business sectors. The Chicano movement underscored the Mexican-origin population's pride in its history and its role within the
dominant society. For many, the Movimiento provided hope for the
future. At present, demographic growth and political and economic
potentiality offer bases for both optimism and frustration. And during
the 1980s, the Mexican community in the United States exhibited
both persisting and changing realities.

The Society

As before, the community continues in a quite heterogeneous
fashion politically, socially, economically, and culturally.[1] In the eighties
it is estimated that between 8 and 10 million persons of Mexican
origin reside in the United States, excluding a half-million to 2 million
undocumented Mexican workers. In March 1979, the United States
census estimated 7.3 million people of Mexican origin, a low estimate;
allowing for a 10 percent undercount, the figure would be 8 million.
The census in 1980 estimated 8.7 million, but allowing for an undercount the figure would be 10 million. The majority of persons of
Spanish surname origin ("Hispanics"), about 7 million in number,
lived in the five southwestern states (Arizona, California, New Mexico, Colorado, and Texas), and most of these persons, 86 percent,
were of Mexican origin. About 4.5 million persons in the state of
California were of Spanish-surname origin, followed by 2.7 million in
Texas, 410,000 in Arizona, 389,000 in New Mexico, and 260,000 in
Colorado. Over a million and a half persons of Mexican descent reside
in the midwestern cities of Chicago and Detroit, and their surrounding
areas. The Mexican community continued to be a fast-growing ethnic
minority in the United States. There was a 60 percent population
increase comparing the 1970 census figures to those in 1980. In fact,

demographers project that in the 1990s Latinos would become the largest numerical minority in the country and that Mexicans are the largest subgroup of Latinos in the United States. The Spanish surname–origin population remains a young population, while the general population in the United States will soon reach a higher age level. The average age of Latinos is twenty-two years, eight years younger than the national average. One out of eight persons of Spanish-surname origin was under five years of age, compared with about one of every fourteen non-Spanish surname. Mexican American median age is 19.3 years, obviously an important political and economic consideration for the future.

As a group in the Mexican American population, women have a social and economic profile which has clearly been disadvantageous with regard to their income, education, mobility, services, political participation, and so forth. Thus, the issue of women's rights became a major one, and women's groups were among the most visible and militant. The average Latina in the eighties was entering her peak child-bearing years, from nineteen to twenty-nine. This indicates an unprecedented population growth for Latinos during the next ten to twenty years. With the Latino population doubling every twenty-five to twenty-seven years, by the year 2005 Latino men and women may number 24 million. Partly because women in general usually marry at younger ages than do men, there were proportionally more single Spanish surname–origin men than women in March 1979: about 35 percent of the men of Spanish surname origin who were twenty-four years old and over were single, compared with only 27 percent of Spanish-origin women. Divorced- and single-women heads of households have continued to increase.

Significant differences exist between Mexicans and even within generations in the same family. The majority of the Mexican immigrant population has been characterized by low educational levels and few skills. Yet in many cases the first generation after immigration among Mexicans has been relatively successful socioeconomically in contrast to their forefathers, even though the parent group has an average fourth-grade education; children do triple that figure, however, and achieve improved occupations as well. Overall, among the children of immigrants the numbers of persons in the middle and upper income levels slowly increase, and however modest the gains have been, some distance separates these persons from others whose numbers are greater and who have very low incomes. However, there is a relative decline in status inheritance from the first generation to the second generation, which does not do as well as the first. Yet in educational achievement, a traditional indicator of probability of success, the Mexican community overall lags significantly behind the dominant society. The Mexican American has, as a median, ten years of schooling, while the Anglo has thirteen years. In 1979 only about 35 percent of Mexicans twenty-five years or older had completed high school, as compared to 69 percent of Anglo Americans. Only 3 percent of Chicanos completed four years of college or more in 1978. The highest proportion of Mexican college enrollments is at the community college level. At the university level, enrollments have not advanced dramatically; however, those with professional or advanced degrees are quite apart educationally from those with little education, and among those with some education there is the difference between those wholly educated in the United States and those educated in Mexico or in both places. However, Mexican students are improving their educational skills, and their interests are increasingly diversifying as more students enter the sciences, communications, art, professional schools, and the social sciences rather than the humanities. One of the most remarkable traits of Mexicans in the United States is the retention of Spanish as a significant means of communication and identification. Nearly 90 percent of the Mexican-origin population speak or understand some Spanish, a notable feat given the fact that only recently has the use of Spanish been allowed in some schools; but language competencies are significant variations in the population to which many are very sensitive. Significantly, Spanish-language media have increased. Both legal and undocumented immigration adds significantly to the Mexican American population. The immigrant has lower skills and educational levels than the Mexican American, and is most often monolingual in Spanish.

The Economy

On the socioeconomic ladder, the Mexican community still lags far behind the dominant society.[2] Marked differences still exist between Latinos and non-Spanish origin populations in occupational characteristics. Of the non-Spanish origin civilian labor-force, 17 percent were employed as professional and technical workers, while 6 percent of employed Mexicans were in that occupational group. The percentage of Mexican-origin population working as managers and administrators was also only 6 percent. The largest concentration of employment for Chicanos was the 61 percent in blue-collar work and 13 percent in service work. Variations also exist between genders. About 7 percent of the men were employed as managers in March 1979; yet only 4 percent of the women were in those professional positions. In clerical positions 32 percent of employed Mexican women were found, and only 6 percent of Mexican men. About 6 percent of the Mexican American labor force is in agriculture, but there is a variation in the type of employment held.

Income for Chicanos continues to be considerably lower than for the non-Latino population. In 1979 the median income reported by Mexicans was approximately 70 percent of that of Anglos. In particular, a significantly smaller proportion of Mexican men were in the upper part of the income distribution as compared with men not of Hispanic origin: only 13 percent of Mexicans showed an income above fifteen thousand dollars a year, whereas 32 percent of Anglo Americans had an annual income over fifteen thousand dollars. In all occupational situations, from manual work to professional, the Mexican earns less than his Anglo counterpart. Among Mexicans, income differentials by sex were evident. Mexican men had nearly twice the income of women. Variations on income depend also on geographic distribution and educational attainment among Latinos. Because the Southwest has weaker unionization provisions and suffers lower pay scales and a lower standard of living than the rest of the country, Mexican income is lower in relation to other groups. An inverse to geographic patterns is the relationship to industrial centers where pay is better, specifically the Midwest where pay scales are much better than in the Southwest or Northeast, and Mexicans in industrial employment earn more than other wage earners in the population. Educational attainment is directly related to income. The median income in 1978 of Latino men twenty-five years old and over, who had completed four years of high school, was about 12,600 dollars; by contrast, the median for Latino men of the same age, with only eight years of school completed, was substantially lower at 9,000 dollars. How much needs to be done in this area is evident by the fact that in 1978 about 20 percent of all Mexican families in the United States were still living below the poverty line; and this percentage has changed for the worse since that time.

The dispersion of Mexican concentrations in city barrios has been increasing from the 1960s to the present. This dispersion suggests the creations of new barrios with their own local systems for self-sustenance and group identity. Two issues continue to be of concern economically: housing and business development. Housing is the single most important economic need and investment. To strengthen the resources of the common unity is, in part, to strengthen its indigenous economy and its local business development. A current phenomenon among the Mexican community is the strong interest in business and the growth of a consumer market, amounting to the quite significant figure of over fifty billion dollars yearly. There are over 100,000 Mexican-owned businesses, but only 44 percent of these gross over one million dollars in sales. Significantly, profits and investments have increased despite the recession.

Current Dilemmas

During the eighties, the ten million Mexicans and Mexican Americans demographically constitute a complex social island in the midst of the United States. They experienced a crisis objectively and subjectively in step with the experience of other peoples, but not as severe or as clear. This crisis resulted from persisting and objective disadvantages, and ironically, from political amelioration as well as changes in the group's relations with other minority groups. Mexican Americans are undergoing a crisis of consciousness concerning their identity and an exhaustion of some values and goals upheld by past activism. Though it is not yet fully understood or appreciated, the crisis has been visible in a variety of areas.

The spatial, land-demographic position of the Mexican American community has changed in relation to U.S. society as a whole as well as in its relation to other minority groups; it has become *both* concentrated and dispersed. Since 1848, when they ceased to be citizens of the Mexican state, Mexicans in the United States have been relatively small numerically and delimited to the area along the border with the mother country. Today the community registers from eight to ten million—a population larger than that of some countries and which continues to be strong particularly in the five southwestern states of California, New Mexico, Arizona, Colorado, and Texas. However, today the population is also found in all fifty states; and in some local areas where they are particularly numerous their sense of identity varies. Moreover, in 1980 the Mexican was only one group among a growing Latin American population in the United States, a population which now comprises all Latin American nationalities. The "Mexico de afuera" became part of the phenomenon of "America Latina de afuera." For better or worse, this phenomenon impacts to what extent Mexicans can pursue strictly Mexican interests. Ironically, the political coming together of "La Raza Cósmica" is occurring in the United States, but the immediate result in public discourse has been to diminish adamant Mexican or Chicano assertion.

The Mexican community has evolved both in numbers and in complexity. However, the gains have registered as *absolute* only in reference to its own conditions in past decades. Thus, its position *relative* to the Anglo community has not improved and, in fact, it may have worsened, especially since 1976. Only large solutions involving massive federal and state intervention offer a significant probability of improvement. However, state intervention along the lines of the "war on poverty" programs is not probable now nor in the immediate future. Certainly, relative gains are visible in the modest improvements for the middle class—for the most part, college-educated professionals and small business persons—and the increment in wealth for the wealthy entrepreneurs. These gains are important not only economically but politically as well. Interestingly, these majority sectors have been significant proponents for social and cultural equity on behalf of all Mexicans, a characteristic they share with their Black counterparts. However, because of political self-protection, the advantaged move in step with the reigning conservatism and the distance that separates them from the working poor of their own community potentially could increase. Thus, the alienation may impact negatively on what has heretofore been an important strength of the entire Chicano community, its cross-class coalition on behalf of civil rights and economic equity.

During the 1980s it was evident to anyone observing the U.S. media, as well as the actions of the White House and of other political and business entities, that "Hispanics," of whom Mexicans constitute the majority, were receiving unprecedented national visibility. However, this visibility was not the result of massive actions on their part but of needs and decisions determined outside the community and often blatantly manipulated vis-à-vis other discontented constituencies within the United States. It was not a visibility commensurate with explicit power. Undoubtedly, the real electoral numbers and economic resources of the Mexican American community have meant significant gains in political officeholding, involving governorships and mayorships and other offices; yet these gains are vulnerable to the hostile reactions of majority public opinion as well as to legal alterations in how officials are elected. Furthermore, these gains, with the exception of executive positions such as mayorships and governorships, are in *legislative* bodies where the efficiency of Mexican American officeholders is checkmated by their minority status; when they campaign for office they must seek votes from all citizens, not only Chicanos. Thus, political realities of minority status remain critical even as tangible gains are being made.

The United States is dominated by a conservative liberal ideology which permeates its political and institutional life. For the past two decades the Mexican American has drawn inspiration from the rhetoric or mystique of the "Chicano Movement" of the sixties, in spite of its ill-defined nature subject to a multitude of interpretations; nonetheless, at its core it was insurgent, populistic, radical, and nationalistic. Obviously, this political mystique was an anomaly within the body politic of a country such as the United States, which stresses amalgamation and accommodation in politics and culture. The rhetoric and tactics of this mystique have been visibly exhausted for some twenty years; the transition hoped for by radical optimists was a growing political trend in the direction of a systematic socialism. As is pathetically obvious, an overt and even minimally strong socialist left in the United States is virtually nonexistent. The ever continuous and growing political activism of the Mexican American faced with the determination to be effective vis-à-vis community needs has meant, in practice, adaptation to the dominant reality. The left in the Chicano community has not fared any better than the left elsewhere, although, as elsewhere, the potential for the growth of left-wing activity continues. Yet without a strong indigenous left, conservative tendencies increase their radius. Ambiguity, hostility, and insufficient resolve have characterized an arena which remains proverbially challenging and contradictory.

Mexican Immigration

For the Chicano community, Mexican immigration to the United States has been among its paramount issues.[3] As an issue, it combines at least three themes: intraethnic solidarity, civil rights, and workers rights. The partial successes have been important, but the outcome always carries, at best, some or, at worst, many negative consequences. Immigration from Mexico has not only added objectively to the Chicano community, but, both objectively and subjectively, it has also reinforced culture, tradition, and language. These contributions escape easy short- or long-term analyses of results. The fact is that a significant number of present-day Chicanos are direct descendants of mid- and late twentieth-century Mexican immigrants. For the past decade, Mexican immigration has been at the forefront of the Chicano struggle because of cultural, labor, and political ramifications for the Mexican American community. The issue has heightened Chicano–Mexicano relationships in general.

The severe economic crisis affecting Mexico has resulted in more Mexican workers being forced to seek opportunities for employment in the United States. At the same time that immigration has increased, so has repression and efforts by the U.S. Immigration and Naturalization Service to control the flow of Mexican labor to the United States. During the years of the Reagan administration, strategies and tactics for detection and apprehension intensified toward Mexican migrant workers. These actions were responding to a national policy which reflected the protectionist; xenophobic, and racist attitudes of the administration and of sectors of the dominant society.

Historically, Chicanos have responded aggressively against such policies and attitudes. Chicanos have been one of the single most consistent pressure groups in defense of human rights for immigrants, particularly from 1972, the year Peter Rodino introduced a discriminatory bill, to October 1986, when the Simpson-Mazzolli Immigration Reform and Control Act (IRCA) was passed. Almost without exception, Chicano contemporary organizations and individual leaders—

including MALDEF, LULAC, NCLR, and their elected officials—
have lobbied strongly against the exploitation of Mexican workers in
the United States.

Although the debate on, and policy implementation of, Mexican
immigration law has ebbed and flowed in the United States, the
immigration question has continued its momentum among the Chicano community. In spite of concentrated efforts, demonstrations,
organized pressure, and scholarly works, the net positive results have
been rather mixed. There is greater consciousness on the issue, and
many legal decisions have granted some protections. Also, a significant
minority among undocumented workers have regularized their status.
Given the political climate and the antiimmigrant public opinion
among many sectors of U.S. society, the continuance of repressive
measures is inevitable; the result will be further repression and discrimination directed against Mexican workers in the United States,
both the native born and immigrants. Issues surrounding immigration,
then, are issues of labor, culture, and international relations; and one
juncture is the border.

The Border

Historically, the border region has been the core area for the
Mexican American community; and its demographic, cultural, and
political importance remains.[4] The borderlands are a region of increasing importance for three objective reasons: the consequences of
an international boundary in a contracting world; the consequences
of contiguous, uneven, but accelerating economic development over
a large geographic area; and the consequences of an expanding bilingual and bicultural population for two highly defensive societies. These
consequences stem from national and international economic and
social phenomena interacting with multiplying force. Visibly formal
structures are impacted here as elsewhere by change, but both culture
and politics on the border have a particularly historical tradition. The
borderlands are an *arena* for two major national systems facing each
other and responding to international changes; but both interface with
local cultures and political systems, resulting in a continuing interaction of change and retardation, economic amalgamation and cultural
interpenetration, synthesis and national conflict. Consequently, the

border retains its historical character of syncretic adaptation and power contention even as it undergoes change and enters the future. Moreover, Mexicans who reside in the region work in the fields, factories, and offices, thus creating the culture and economy of the land.

The United States–Mexico border region is significant because it intersects two national jurisdictions. Thus, the "national" and "regional" qualities of the area join in varied combinations with important contending results. Extending for nearly two thousand miles horizontally from West to East, its vertical limits to the North and South vacillate and merge in contact with forces from either interior. These national forces meet each other, but they also meet the heterogeneity of the border region. Particular cultural, economic, and political subregions along the length of the border both compound and reflect this general heterogeneity in a fluctuation encompassing linguistics, ecology, health, economy, education, history, and politics. The border is an international zone, a part of two republics, but it is also a series of localities. Hence, the international, national, and local aspects often pose dilemmas for resolution. These disparities are joined by a common boundary drawn through the formalities of war, and which denotes formal political systems while only tenuously demarcating contrasting cultures and national histories. The undeniability of *La Línea* makes for a sharing of concerns, needs, and social features that are premised on the contemporary phase of the political economy. The boundary separates and segregates formal jurisdictions, but human survival negates a total division. There is a continuing flow of people, information, labor, capital, and trade across the boundary, and these are indeed international matters.

The International

From the sixties through the eighties, international issues impacted more visibly on the Chicano community, but they did so within the constraints and limits of awareness and mobilization common to the U.S. electorates. Though not limited to these, Latin America, Mexico, and the border were of particular note. Each succeeding administration from Kennedy to Reagan fueled this interest and participation, either negatively or positively. This process was uneven and disparate in its composition as well as in its ends; and it was affected by specific considerations, among them the incomplete awareness by the community and its political players of international information, and the greater diversity of issues and points of view in this arena as well as those of other distinct Latino communities which were interested and involved in Latin American issues. This involvement complicated both advocacy and deployment on foreign affairs.

The Chicano community had a far more complicated situation vis-à-vis Latin American issues because Latin America was a much more complicated situation. If the Irish American attitude toward Northern Ireland, the Jewish position in relation to the State of Israel, or Blacks' position in relation to apartheid *seemed* clear, the Chicano posture was more mixed. The importance of Latin America might be agreed upon, but cultural affinity was not the determining element in searching for a consensus. In fact, there was no consensus and little effort to build one; partisan and ideological considerations as well as views on the preferred future for Latin America were varied in expression among Chicanos and other Latinos.

In February 1980, a significant step was attempted when the Hispanic Council on Foreign Relations was incorporated. Wittingly or not, it sought to be ineffectively representative in various ways; it was bipartisan and multi-Latino, and eventually it was chaired by the Republican entrepreneur Fernando Oaxaca. A conclusion from its extant experience was the difficulty of arriving at a policy consensus beyond stressing the importance of the region and the need for more Latino representation in policy and in diplomacy. Unreflectively, the emphasis has been, first, on quantitative access, that is, appointments, and second, on addressing Latin American "problems." Preferable would be a qualitative assessment as to what a Latino position should be and then deciding on the Latino role, addressing both issues to the United States and its functionaries, banks, and corporations. Generally, oblique attention was given to the United States' historical and contemporary relationships to Latin America. When this happened, the compelling reason was negative, at least in relation to the conventional Latin American view, and the negative was endorsed. To distinguish between an incumbent position, given general realities, and personal intrinsic positions vis-à-vis a specific remedy was to walk on coals; for example, the significance of nonintervention contrasted with the particularist demand for intervention.

United States–Latin American Policy

Chicano spokesmen have sought to influence positively Latin American policy, but to date, they must condone it or oppose it in reality, for they are in no position to change it substantively. The "international game" of the United States is not subject to altruism, but to the military and economic dictates of the elite.[5] Historically, U.S. foreign policy toward Latin America has been formulated by select circles within the dominant society. Few persons of Hispanic ancestry have held positions of importance either in the State Department or other agencies in charge of United States–Latin American policy. As the Chicano struggle established contacts with other progressive movements and leaders in the Third World, an important international dimension was included in the political stance of Chicano spokespersons. Naturally, the main concern was and continues to be United States–Mexican relations. More directly, as Chicanos increased their participation and prominence in the Democratic Party, a standard demand of operatives and elected officials was the right of Latinos to participate in Latin American policy. After Chicanos strongly voiced the demand to be included in Latin American–United States policy, President Carter responded by naming various Chicanos to high administrative positions in the Latin American area. Appointed were Ralph Guzman in the State Department; Julian Nava, Mari Lucy Jaramillo, and Raul Castro as ambassadors to Mexico, Honduras, and Argentina, respectively; and Estevan Torres as U.S. Ambassador to UNESCO.

The situation changed under President Ronald Reagan. There were no Chicanos in similar diplomatic positions, though there were other Latinos and Cuban-Americans who received Reagan appointments. Rather than participating in policymaking, many Chicanos were part of the growing opposition to the Reagan administration's Central American policy. Progressive Chicanos, in struggling to overcome similar conditions of oppression and imposition from the outside, have condemned U.S. intervention and the support of exploitative regimes in Central America. Many participated in organizations focused on Central America. Progressive Chicano organizations and individuals intensified efforts of solidarity for the Salvadorean liberation movement and the Nicaraguan Sandinista government. However, the efforts did not produce a widespread response, and a message about national strategy and tactics in Central America and specifically targeted to the community had not been developed by 1988. For the most part, the elected Chicano leadership did not take an active position in favor of radical change in Central America. In the immediate future, the Chicano community could very well become one of the central opposition groups against U.S. intervention in Latin America and abroad; but undoubtedly this issue will be debated more on ideological and pragmatic grounds than from an ethnic stance. To date, the Hispanic Congressional Caucus and other elected officials have not been highly visible on international issues, and in most cases they have expressed sentiments and voted not in sympathy with the popular movements in Central America. Individual leaders will have to devote more time and study to international issues than previously, because international issues do affect the community, even though knowledge of the local issues is invariably paramount.

Limits and Realities of Chicano–Mexicano Relations

Among political issues, none have been of such long-standing concern or so uneven in expectation as the relations between the Mexican communities—the Chicano and the Mexicano. These relations have a long history and a spectrum of players.[6] Though bifurcated by a legal and political border of over two thousand miles, the two communities have nonetheless shared common traditions, religion, and culture as well as enduring oppression, economic exploitation, and racial discrimination. While mutual ties and a similar historical process exists between the two communities, the limits of real understanding becomes apparent when it is considered how each group has often viewed the other.

The explanations for occasions of alienation rather than of camaraderie are themselves complexly historical. Obviously, questions of generations, class differences, and heterogeneity of both Mexican communities made for differences within the general similarities. Moreover, various concrete realities have traditionally worked against the development of closer relations between Chicanos and Mexicanos. On the one hand, many in the Chicano community have had no opportunity to know Mexico and its culture critically. Until the late 1960s, Chicanos in the educational system of the United States were systematically denied the use of their native language, Spanish. Through a combination of ridicule, reprimand, and punishment, many parents, in trying to protect their children and seek what was best for them encouraged the use of English over the use of Spanish. Thus, the means of communication has been substantially weakened. Equally weak is a common fund of mutual knowledge. Mexican culture and history were also completely omitted from formal studies from kindergarten through twelfth grade in U.S. schools. Particularly pernicious has been a phenomenon known as the "Spanish Myth." The "Spanish Myth" in the United States became institutionalized—all that was of significant worth from the Mexican heritage was "Spanish"; all that was negative was Mexican. Negative stereotyping of Mexicans was and is predominant in U.S. literature, the arts, and the media in general. Repeatedly, Chicanos were denied access to higher education which could have exposed them to a formal study of Mexico, because it is only in universities that they have had access to a few classes in Mexican history, literature, and art. Few Chicanos were economically able to travel throughout Mexico, visit extensively, and thus know its development and complexity. And when Chicanos did travel in Mexico, they encountered ridicule and even discrimination because of the lack of Spanish skills and knowledge of Mexico; thus, ironically they were also penalized in the homeland for being Mexican, that is, Mexicanos from the United States, and domination had deprived them of solidarity with their trans-border kin.

In Mexico, there is also a lack of knowledge not only of Chicanos and Chicano politics but of the ways and byways of the domestic United States, though they know firsthand the international United States. Conditions, attitudes, and general public opinion were not conducive to enhancing relations with the Chicano community. As more people left Mexico and settled in the United States, the resentment among Mexicans in Mexico increased. These feelings were compounded by the fact that when Mexican tourists traveled to the United States and encountered postimmigrant Chicanos, their stereotype was reinforced because the majority of Chicanos did not speak their kind of Spanish nor act entirely in the manner expected; instead, they were out of step with contemporary culture. Thus, in the twentieth century the term *pocho*, used by Mexicans to denote Chicanos, came into use. Their negative interpretation became the predominant view of Chicanos by Mexicans in Mexico. As the years went by, stereotypes of Chicanos became fixed. Most Mexicans alleged that Chicanos consciously and willingly negated their Mexican heritage and Spanish language; it was believed that Chicanos had a conde-scending attitude toward Mexico and Mexicanos. Later, class biases were incorporated into the stereotypes—most Chicanos were thought to be descendants of popular classes, since it was believed that only the unskilled, the illiterates, and the poor migrated to the United States. Yet interaction has continued at all levels, particularly socially and economically and particularly at the border. But Mexico has gone through dramatic changes in the post-1960s, and its civic society is as complex as its politics.

Much like other decolonization movements, the Chicano social struggle sought to regain its radical legacy, history, language, and culture. Since the struggle was against oppressive and discriminatory sectors of the United States, a rejection of the dominant society and a romanticized search for Mexican ties and bonds was an explainable process. Uncritically, activist Chicanos not only hoped and sought to recapture a denied past, but expected the Mexican state, progressive organizations, and the people in Mexico to champion their cause and to provide moral and material support for the Chicano movement. Although this endeavor was often illusory, limited success occurred, and concrete gains were made. A few Mexicans sought out the Chicano community as a possible constituency and pressure group in the United States, and as a vehicle for making Mexico more positively visible. It was perceived that Chicanos would advocate the interests of Mexico as a whole, if not specific Mexican interests. It was felt that the continued demographic growth of the Chicano would provide a basis for political and economic relations and with positive gains in the immediate future that would coincide with Mexican foreign policy interests. Certainly, the immigration issue was a tangible common interest between political activists from both communities, and com-mercial possibilities were important to the business sectors. But if the proceedings suggest a rapprochement, the matter was not so simple. Some Chicanos assumed an aggressive posture vis-à-vis Mexican af-fairs, and some Mexicans assumed that Chicanos should be their un-questioning supporters at the same time. For its own ends, the right wing in the United States developed a marked interest in Mexico, and this interest historically has been negative.

One feature of Mexico that Chicanos faced was the extensive

pressure and presence of government in all aspects of life and in all spaces of the civic terrain. Obviously, since Chicanos in education and culture pursue enrichment programs and since government agencies have resources and jurisdiction, interaction involving the state is the most visible but also the most vulnerable; in any case, interaction is not limited to state agencies. Important gains, however, have been accomplished in specific levels and through individual efforts. Such has been the case in the areas of labor relations between certain unions and labor organizers, and particularly in the fields of culture and education. Through scholarly programs, Chicanos received attention from the Mexican media and publishers; and, in turn, Mexico was more sensitively interpreted to constituencies in the United States. Chicano arts was the focus of some enthusiasm, and even the movie industry filmed a number of commercial and documentary films on Chicano themes. But the most immediate and important result was strengthening public consciousness on the rights of undocumented workers, a process which subsequently led to effectuating the policy importance of immigration and the responsibility of different publics toward immigrants.

The vitalization of culture is obviously linked to its probability of persistence, and Mexico has been seen as an important reservoir of cultural strength; and although gains have been made, alienation recedes slowly before solidarity. It is in the realm of culture and education where Chicano–Mexican relations have had most success and will continue to do so. Education enhancement programs, modest as they may be, have provided a number of Chicano and Mexicano intellectuals with the opportunity to interact. The continued support for this interaction is one of the most positive trans-border aspects; another is the recognition of the flowering of Chicano culture and scholarly activity by Mexican organizations and individuals. In the seventies and eighties, there has been a noticeable effort by Mexican institutions, agencies, and organizations to promote Chicano interaction. More protean consequences, however, are not in "studies" or "sensitivity," but in the terrain of economics and politics; and the negative variable for Mexico or Latin America is the United States.

6

Conclusion: Resolution of the Moment

Vitality and incremental influence characterize the political history of the Hispanic community. This history is both positive and negative, and expresses a tradition not always fully known or appreciated by all of the contemporary participants, Chicano and non-Chicano alike. Political efforts continue to vary in expression in accordance with the temper of the time and the response of the majority society's institutions; for example, petitions can lead to mass protests, which may be disrupted quickly. Organizations express a given consciousness and are salient manifestations of specific activity; they continue to reveal persistence and innovation, yet they are only a part of a larger political landscape. Domination is reflected in the persistence of issues across time and space and the specific conscious efforts to address these issues as well as the frustration of such efforts.

To be Mexican in the United States is still to be against the hegemonic grain, whether right or left. The unifying element is ethnic consciousness, which interacts with class in the sense that the dynamics of community politics addresses both ethnic and class consciousness. The pressures, requirements, and dependencies of leadership have increased, and the spectrum of leadership has also diversified; but the distinctions between autochthonous and designated leadership remain, and so do their weaknesses.

Political activity among Chicanos has waxed and waned during periods of economic dislocation and adjustment and in facing hostile circumstances. A latent or overt anti-Mexican ideology is always being propagated by certain circles. Concomitantly, there are the recurring practices of deportation, anti-Mexican legislation, continued exploitation on the job, the deployment of the ever-present police power against Mexicans, and the continual scapegoating and pursuit of undocumented workers—all attacks on the Mexican community. Within this social milieu, Mexican American mobilization activity in the United States is both galvanized and seen as suspect. Politically, U.S. government representatives view transnational Mexican linkages as questionable. Nevertheless, limited to the existing system, the elements are present politically for a future more positive than the past; but they are in fact problematic because they pose questions, not unqualified affirmations.

As the eighties came to a close, a number of important developments were representative of incremental trends. Demographically and economically striking was the increase in numbers as well as the economic significance of the population to levels not previously experienced. Stemming from this, but also distinct, was the greater targeted attention directed to the community. The community was bombarded not only with appeals and arguments that both strengthened and weakened; it was also given a widely circulated image. Levels of education were indeed growing; and the growth of the college-educated population was striking, as was the increase in professionals in unprecedented numbers. The political participation of women increased dramatically the players, resources, and efforts in civic life. A greater organizational sophistication was evident, as well as the proclaimed necessity to participate in community civic life. There have been also mounting differences, apart from continuing disparities between immigrants recently arrived and the longer-term residents. Disparities between regions were accounted for by the character and tempo of the economy, as were the more ominous differences between those with a high income and education and those who become more, not less, impoverished and undereducated. Leaders nearly always come from the middle class and are increasingly homogeneous in educational background, moderate in posture and personal style, and cautious about overemphasizing ethnicity. College and professional degrees are the rule, as are an orthodox family context, a conforming appearance, and facility in articulation. Generally unorthodox, nonconforming leadership is marginalized. To date, in the late 1980s as in the past, the dominant current has been centrist liberalism affected by oscillating moderate, conservative, or progressive impacts. Radical challenge remains the exception. The indispensable requirements for political success have not changed: organization, resources, numbers, skills, and leadership.

Whether embodied by men or women, there remain six pillars to civic life and, in particular, blocks in the political edifice. Each alleges sustaining general as well as particular interests. For a variety of reasons, preeminent in civic activity are elected officials; they are the gatekeepers and monitors in the Mexican community more than in other sectors of the larger society. Professionals, particularly attorneys, have enjoyed a prominence throughout the seventies and eighties. The presence of business persons has already been felt and will grow because of their resources and their ability to become the patrons of others as well as because of their unquestioned legitimacy in the larger society. While churches also possess this reputation, they also have access to numbers, outreach, and an integral community-level organizational network, and they have the will necessary to use these assets. Though only 20 percent of the workers are organized, unions have resources and some numbers, but here a decline rather than an increase in effectiveness is most likely. Next to neighborhood, work remains the most salient organizational magnet; and work organization remains the largest reservoir of strength. Last are the civic organizations which have an organizational membership and structure and can make a telling commitment. They continue to persist and grow, rather than decline, through the eighties.

The demographic growth and economic significance of the Mexican community in the United States will continue; but "hype" must be taken for what it is even though the hype represents notice. However, numbers and purchasing power, or even production power, do not, in themselves, cultivate, much less assure, political power. Growth should strengthen the community's working-class character; however economic, industrial, and occupational changes are varied and also growing is a subordinate nonworking sector which is incrementally impoverished. At this time, economic and educational gains for the community are impacting upon its class composition. The national or cultural character of the community has been undergoing change, while the continuing presence of a Mexican culture veils the significant loss of culture. Worsening crises may sharpen Chicano political consciousness, accentuating the change in its political direction from liberal to progressive; however, conservative trends in the United States will continue to have an impact upon the community. A conservative trend is indeed strong and drawing upon the petty capitalist tradition found in Mexico and the continual enhancement of capitalist values and aspirations in the United States. Demographic experts project that by 1990 and 2000, Latinos will be the largest minority group in the United States and Mexicans will continue to be the largest Latino subgroup. Numbers, of course, do not give cohesion or identity in themselves. However, in the Southwest numbers will particularly increase, but so will the numbers of other groups. Though the community pursues or rather raises its own ends, these ends are in practice integrated with those of others.

Implicitly, the common aspiration of all social efforts in the community is survival. The emphasis visible in political activity is equality. As yet the net effect, to the extent that it has been successful, is greater integration. Most visibly manipulated is ethnicity; cohesive demands that are also ethnic qua ethnicity have not been adamantly and consistently raised, much less obtained. But whether the ends sought are the attainment of equality in the current system or major change in the system itself, there are needs to be attended to in the effort to ensure greater political influence which, to date, has been secured most commonly through protest mobilization, the ballot, the sales receipt, the court order, and the union card. The ballot has unique singularity in the United States because there are few other general avenues open to the average citizen for direct participation.

There are proverbially five aspects to political power: numbers, resources, organization, skills, and leadership. There are twelve major problems in the effort to maximize Mexican political power in the United States: (1) the utilization of numbers; (2) effective organizations; (3) Mexican working-class and civic consciousness; (4) trade union organizing; (5) Spanish language inclusion and promotion; (6) inclusion of, and rights for, the undocumented worker population; (7) increased occupational, income, and educational status; (8) increased political resources and skills; (9) increased voter registration; (10) increased quality leadership; (11) pan-Latino cooperation in the United States; and (12) an international presence. All of these are deployable for electoral and organizational mobilization within a political system

and with latitude, however dominated that system may be by a min-
iscule number of people who comprise the governing elite, particularly
at the national level. The system offers a choice of labels and partners,
Republican or Democrat, with allowances made for liberals, moderates, and conservatives; the interaction between these are such that
they comprise a single system, and only within this system does
politics take place. The range of options in which to address issues
and the access to policy remain narrow. It is this constricted stage of
political and/or ideological options that serves to funnel and filter
dissent; repression of alternative politics is achieved through *forced
consent* buttressed by the state's formidable intelligence and enforcement capabilities, which are always looming even when they are not
being used directly. There is a real and present danger for those wanting
for whatever reasons(s) to test these limits, for fear is a guaranteed
political asset used by the system.

The persisting historical Chicano demands have been for civil,
cultural, economic, juridical, and political rights. These are encompassed, and variously expressed in contemporary times, by the issues
of equity in all areas of life: bilingualism, political participation, quality
education, the rights of undocumented workers, employment, rights
on the job, job training, economic development, rights of Mexican
women, police and political practices, housing, social services, health
services, census counting, urban development, and foreign policy issues. Underlying these issues, explicitly or implicitly, is the desirability
of and methods for social change. Past and contemporary progressive
political platforms express, in part or in its entirety, this emphasis on
positive social change, and coherent political programs in the future
must deal with these platforms. To date, what has been granted are
incremental concessions in the areas of voting, employment, schooling, and immigration rights. Minimum objectives have been pursued
and minimum objectives have been achieved. Though there has been
a great stress on voting qua voting as a measure of political achievement
and influence, the act of voting does not promise the achievement of
full equities, much less direct and full democracy.

In the past twenty years, several avenues for change have been
pursued. Mexican electoral political participation in the United States
historically has been multifaceted. Participation in traditional political
parties has led to reforms in the area of civil rights and to the election
and appointment of Mexicans to office at the national, state, and local

levels. These elected officials basically represent the rise to and con-solidation of power, albeit limited to the Mexican American middle and upper classes. Some real benefits obviously do accrue to the general community, and, among elected officials, there are forthright and progressive individuals. Through appointments, jobs, and small in-dividual efforts of problem resolution at the local level, elected and appointed officials have been able to continue in power. Most represent districts with mixed racial and cultural constituencies, therefore di-minishing their accountability to their Mexican American constitu-ents; and they are subject to lobbying pressures from different sources. Although many are liberal, few will want or be able to challenge the dominant system as a whole. Politicians are committed to resolving problems within the system, and reform has its limits.

Mexicans have formed and joined radical groups. These groups have represented the varying and competing ideological positions of the left in the United States. Third-party political movements or radical advocacy groups such as La Raza Unida and CASA have strengthened reformist gains and raised the level of political discussion, but they have not been effective in realizing their optimum oganiza-tional goals. Once again the United States system has assimilated seemingly independent efforts, although there were successes at the local level and aspirations were raised by victories. Eventually they lost strength, and Mexican Americans within the conventional parties gained strength. In the final analysis, any autonomous effort by Mex-icans in the United States that was restricted to a focus on electoral politics or on single issues would be seen as exclusivistic and be con-sidered problematic. Neither white radical nor liberal groups have as yet served Mexicans well. Traditionally, leftists and liberals in the United States have suffered from an inability to overcome their Anglo chauvinism, usually denying the validity of Mexican national con-sciousness, activity, and priorities in determining their political prin-ciples and practices. Anglo leftists have too often forgotten that to deny the historical rights of a people is to undermine democratic rights, and that it is for the people in question to vindicate their rights in all forms of organized struggle—political, ideological, and economic. The role of the Mexican working class has yet to be fully recognized as integral to any radical political process in the United States. There are particular horizons to Mexican political activities, limits drawn by the failure of the left to attract mass support or for a labor party to rise; thus, political participation takes place within eclectic amalgamations focused on advocacy or on electioneering. Coalitions across ethnic lines have been problematic and premised on an issue basis; once the given issue is advanced, a coalition tends to deteriorate.

A number of liabilities continue to characterize the Mexican political position. One is the lack of a center for a broadly distributed community; its most compacted areas of demographic concentration, northern New Mexico and south Texas, cannot offer this role. There are no unifying overarching institutions; neither the Catholic church nor the trade unions could play this role because of their delimited character, and in any case they exclude many. There is no core set of beliefs or aims beyond assurances or aspirations of survival and equity or the abolishment of discrimination; but discrimination is not shared by all, and some have secured economic equities. There is an unevenness to political influence and the ability to exert it. There is invariably a sector which will have more and a sector which will have less; in most cases, legitimacy is determined outside the community, and it is the dominant society which determines what and who is politically legitimate vis-à-vis Mexicans and within the Mexican community. A criteria for all this is adherence or loyalty before legitimacy is awarded. In any case, politics are conflictual both within and outside the group, and these increase as consciousness and mobilization heighten.

Historically, there has been a political momentum and mystique in the Mexican community; but what is needed is not ad-hoc activity but agreement on programs, tactical guidelines, and generally recognized national political vehicles—in sum, program and organization. There is no need to dwell on the potential political strength of the Mexican community in general. The strength is there. However, the general Mexican working class, that is, the mass of the community, is severely underorganized despite the multitude of existing organizations, and it often has been divided in many ways, which dilutes political strength. Nevertheless, the Mexican community may be a key group, to some degree cohesive, and in specific situations it may hold the balance of power between contending forces in U.S. political issues in specific major states or localities, and thus possess influence nationally. For a disadvantaged community in electoral or mobilization politics, this means mass politics, and the mass remains the working sector.

Historical facts amply document that there has been no lack of organizing, ideas, and leadership which have been and are expressed in the national and class resistance of Mexicans in the United States. Mexicans possess a rich organizational heritage. The record does show, however, that Mexican organizations must deal with features of U.S. society that impede the progress of the community as well as organizing efforts on its behalf. Mexican unity and resistance are the key to gains to be derived from the various forms of struggle for social justice. To achieve equity, a necessary condition is the continuing development of both single-membership advocacy and confrontational groups as well as strong "operational unity" coalitions, which can be vehicles for the national community on specific issues. Crucial to this development is the need for generalized national political consciousness, agreed-upon priorities, and principled leadership. Basic is a mass electorate joined to disciplined core organizations, and leaderships with integrity and commitment which can be assured of authority and respect by a wide spectrum of organizations and individuals. It is a waste of time to spend effort only in rhetorically denouncing the system or in blaming Mexicans themselves for political frustrations. Granted that politicians, institutions, and the economy are exploitative and divisive, what remains to be done is to recognize and deal with the heterogeneity within the Mexican community, understanding that workers compose its majority. Mexicans must come to terms with the political process and social reality, and then deal with them as they are.

Notes

Chapter 1

1. In the preface to F. Chris Garcia, ed., *La Causa Política: A Chicano Politics Reader* (South Bend, Ind.: University of Notre Dame Press, 1974), p. vii, the lack of writings on Mexican American politics is decried, pointing out that there is as yet no textbook on the subject. Carlos Muñoz, "The State of Art in the Study of Chicano Politics" in Isidro D. Ortiz, ed., *Chicanos and the Social Sciences: A Decade of Research and Development 1970–1980* (Santa Barbara: Center for Chicano Studies, University of California, Santa Barbara, 1983), also observes the paucity of literature. Both, however, underscore the increasing interest in the subject. A recent book of readings is F. Chris Garcia, ed., *Latinos and the Political System* (Notre Dame: University of Notre Dame Press, 1988). For an introduction to how Mexican American politics may be reviewed, see F. Chris Garcia and Rudolfo de la Garza, *The Chicano Political Experience: Three Perspectives* (North Scituate, Ma.: Duxbury Press, 1977). For a systems approach to politics generally, see David Easton, *A Systems Analysis of Political Life* (New York: John C. Wiley and Sons, 1965). A pithy readable statement often alluded to is Harold D. Lasswell, *Politics: Who Gets What, When, How* (New York: McGraw-Hill, 1936).

This present work is part of ongoing research on politics, labor, and culture. For polemical advocacy of the author's view, see Juan Gómez-Quiñones, "On Culture," *Revista Chicano-Riqueña*, vol. 5 (Summer 1977). The term *domination* is used approximate to the usage by Amilcar Cabral, Roberto Fernandez Retamar, and Antonio Gramsci; that is, as a general condition based on force and manipulated consent involving repression, oppression, and suppression of cultural, social, economic, and political life of the people. Among English readers, an early use and definition may be found in the work

215

of Max Weber; while Herbert Marcuse has contributed to its wider usage. See for the former, *From Max Weber: Essays in Sociology,* eds. H. H. Gerth and C. Wright Mills (New York: Oxford, 1958) and for the latter, *An Essay on Liberation* (Boston: Beacon Press, 1969).

2. Among the many definitional statements on ethnic groups are the following. According to R. A. Schermerhorn, an ethnic group may be considered as "a collectivity within a larger society [with] real or putative common ancestry, memories of a shared historical past, and a cultural focus on one or more symbolic elements defined as the epitome of their peoplehood." In F. Barth's words, "Ethnic groups are largely biologically self-perpetuating, share fundamental cultural values, realized in overt unity in cultural forms, make up a field of communication and interaction, and has [have] a membership which identifies itself, and is identified by others, as constituting a category distinguishable from other categories of the same order." Milton Gordon defines ethnicity as "peoplehood," either primordially given or optionally cultivated. See: Richard A. Schermerhorn, *Comparative Ethnic Relations: A Framework for Theory and Research* (New York: Random House), 1970 and Frederick Barth, *Ethnic Groups and Boundaries* (Boston: Little, Brown and Company, 1969). A basic statement on ethnicity in the United States is Milton M. Gordon, *Assimilation in American Life: The Role of Race, Religion, and National Origins* (Oxford: Oxford University Press, 1964); this work is often a point of departure for those studying "integration" and "assimilation" of Mexican Americans. A recent examination is Joe R. Feagin, *Racial and Ethnic Relations* (Englewood Cliffs, N.J.: Prentice-Hall, Inc., 1978). In contrast to the conventional views, there is Ronald Takaki, *From Different Shores: Perspectives on Race and Ethnicity in America* (Oxford: Oxford University Press, 1987). A conventional concern for traditional sociologists, and now for historical sociologists, in viewing "immigrants" is the attempt to discern their rate of integration into the dominant society, as well as their rate of loss of culture as they "advance." An article published twenty years ago, in 1968, did not find this a simple linear process for Mexicans; see Joan Moore, "Social Class, Assimilation, and Acculturation" in June Helm, ed., *Spanish Speaking People in the United States* (Seattle: American Ethnological Society, 1968). An attempt at a comprehensive statement on ethnic groups in the United States is Stephen Thernstrom, ed., *Harvard Encyclopedia of American Ethnic Groups* (Cambridge: Harvard University Press, 1980). Though informative and containing some useful summary articles, and despite an ostensible display of the objective apparatus, this book offers more ideology than social science.

3. For an injunction to a more encompassing and critical political history, see Benjamin J. Schwartz, "A Brief Defense of Political and Intellectual History . . . with Particular Reference to Non-Western Cultures," in Felix

Gilbert and Stephen R. Graubard, eds. *Historical Studies Today* (New York: W. W. Norton and Company, 1972). For an assessment of paradigm and methodology, see E. J. Hobsbawm, "From Social History to the History of Society," in ibid. A major contemporary influence on critical approaches to contemporary society is Antonio Gramsci. A convenient collection is Gramsci, *Selections from the Prison Notebooks* (New York: International Publishers, 1971). For a brief summary of the political aspects of his concept of hegemony, see Roger Simon, "Gramsci's Concept of Hegemony," *Marxism Today* (March 1977). For a critique of Gramsci, see Perry Anderson, "The Antinomies of Antonio Gramsci," *New Left Review*, no. 100 (1977). For a defense, see Carlos Pereyra, "Estado y Sociedad Civil," *Cuadernos Políticos*, numero 21 (Julio–Septiembre 1979). Gramsci's writings, "State and Civil Society," "Problems of Marxism," and "The Philosophy of Praxis" (*Selections from the Prison Notebooks*, New York: International Publishers, 1971) often draw more attention than his others. For the working historian, more interesting is *Il Risorgimento* (Torino: Einaudi, 1954). Gramsci's insights may inform and enlighten the practice of activists related to organization and tactics, but conceptual and methodological application to the social sciences and humanities is still being tested. In 1977, through a combined undergraduate seminar, I and a group of students tested the applicability of Gramscian insights to the Chicano experience and found much of this thought "national," that is, valid primarily for examining the Italian experience.

4. For a discussion of cultural, ethno, and hegemonic constructs to problems in United States history, see T. J. Jackson Lears, "The Concept of Cultural Hegemony: Problems and Possibilities," *American Historical Review*, vol. 90 (June 1985). A comprehensive statement by Chicano Studies political scientists on the field, its literature paradigms, and its methods and priorities has not been available.

5. For an introductory discussion of the politics of interest groups, see Robert A. Dahl, *A Preface to Democratic Theory* (Chicago: University of Chicago Press, 1956); and Edgar Litt, *Ethnic Politics in America* (Glenview, Il.: Scott, Foresman and Co., 1970). For ethnic questions and politics, see: Cynthia H. Enloe, *Ethnic Conflict and Political Development* (Boston: University Press of America, 1973); Andrew M. Greeley, *Why Can't They Be Like Us? Facts and Fallacies about Ethnic Group Differences and Group Conflict in America* (Old Bethpage, N.Y.: American Jewish Committee, 1969); and Nathan Glazer and Daniel Moynihan, eds., *Ethnicity: Theory and Experience* (Cambridge, Mass.: Howard, 1976). See also Michael Novak, *The Rise of the Unmeltable Ethnics: Politics and Culture in the Seventies* (New York: Macmillan, 1972). For statistical examination of the ethnic in United States political history, see: Robert P. Swierenga, "Ethnocultural Political Analysis: A New Approach to American Ethnic Studies," *Journal of American Studies*,

vol. 5 (1971); Paul Kleppner, "Beyond the 'New Political History': A Review Essay," *Historical Methods Newsletter*, vol. 6 (1972); Samuel T. McSeveney, "Ethnic Groups, Ethnic Conflicts, and Recent Quantitative Research in American Political History," *International Migration Review*, vol. 7 (1972).

6. On socialization in general, see Gabriel Almond and Sidney Verba, *The Civic Culture* (Boston: Little, Brown and Company, 1965), and Ithiel de Sola Pool, "Plural Society in the Southwest: A Comparative Perspective," in Edward Spicer and Raymond Thompson, eds., *Plural Society in the Southwest* (New York: Interbook, 1972). On ethnic socialization and its relations to political behavior, see Robert Kelley, "Ideology and Political Culture from Jefferson to Nixon," *American Historical Review*, vol. 82 (June 1977). For three points of view in a discussion of ethics, see George Novak, ed., *Their Morals and Ours* (New York: Merit Publishers, 1969). For normative evaluation of contemporary state and society, see Arnaldo Cordova, *Sociedad y estado en el mundo moderno* (México, D.F.: Grijalbo, 1976); on responsibility, see Leszek Kolakowski, *Toward a Marxist Humanism* (New York: Grove Press, 1969), pp. 188–210. For a discussion of the aesthetics of freedom and the general community, see Herbert Marcuse, "Kant" in *Studies in Critical Philosophy* (Boston: Beacon, 1972). The idea of community as a normative criterion/ideal is, of course, at the core of Mexica political thought; for them, community was social and economic, which anchored their normative imperative. However, in Western thought as transmitted by Iberians, the discussion dates from the Romans, particularly the Stoic philosophers, and was reintroduced by Giambattista Vico during the Renaissance. And Vico, in turn, has been a focus of critical political thought; see Arnaldo Cordova, *Sociedad y estado*. Ethics, choice, judgment, responsibility, and social reference have been taken up by one twentieth-century Mexican philosopher, Antonio Caso; see, for example, his *La existencia como económica, doctrinas y ideas* (México, D.F.: Botos, 1919), and *El peligro del hombre* (México, D.F.: Stylo, 1942). See J. Gómez-Quiñones, "Antonio Caso: A Rejection of the Idea of Progress," in *Investigaciones Contemporaneas sobre Historia de México: Memorias de la Tercera Reunion* (México, D.F.: Universidad Nacional de México; University of Texas Press, 1969).

7. For overall views of this history and its historiography, see Juan Gómez-Quiñones, "Toward a Perspective on Chicano History," *Aztlan*, vol. 2 (Fall 1971). For a contrast, see Arthur F. Corwin, "Mexican-American History: An Assessment," *Pacific Historical Review*, vol. 43 (August 1973).

8. For available studies with an overview of post–World War II politics, see: Ralph C. Guzman, *The Political Socialization of the Mexican American People* (New York: Arno Press, 1976); and Maurilio Vigil, *Chicano Politics* (Washington, D.C.: University Press of America, 1978); F. Chris Garcia and Rudolph O. de la Garza, *The Chicano Political Experience: Three Perspectives*

(North Scituate, Mass.: Duxbury Press, 1977); and Christine Sierra, "Chicano Political Development: Historical Considerations" in Eugene E. Garcia, et al., eds., *Chicano Studies: A Multidisciplinary Approach* (New York and London: Teachers College, Columbia University, 1984).

9. For contrasting interpretations in texts on the history, see Carey McWilliams, *North from Mexico, The Spanish-Speaking People of the United States* (New York: Greenwood Press, 1968); Rodolfo Acuna, *Occupied America, A History of Chicanos* (2d ed., New York: Harper and Row, 1981); and Julian Samora and Patricia Vandel Simon, *A History of the Mexican American People* (Notre Dame: University of Notre Dame Press, 1977).

10. For the debate on the homeland, identity, and nomenclature, see Sylvia Rodriguez, "The Hispano Homeland Debate" (unpublished paper, October 1986); Carlos H. Arce, "A Reconsideration of Chicano Culture and Identity," *Daedalus*, vol. 110 (Spring 1981); see also Erich Rosenthal, "Acculturation without Assimilation?" *American Journal of Sociology*, vol. 65 (November 1960), pp. 257–88.

11. For two district examination of classes, see Antonio Rios-Bustamante, "Las clases sociales mexicanas en Estados Unidos," *Historia y Sociedad* no. 20 (1978), and Mario Barera, "Chicano Class Structure" in Garcia, *Chicano Studies*. For general class, ethnic, and political relationships, see Michael Parenti, "Ethnic Politics and Ethnic Identification," *American Political Science Review*, vol. 61 (September 1967). For a discussion of classes among major colored minorities, see the thoughtful essay by Joan W. Moore, "Minorities in the American Class System," *Daedalus*, vol. 110 (Spring 1982). For a general discussion of class and politics in United States political history, see Edward Pessen, "Social Structure and Politics in American History," *American Historical Review*, vol. 87 (October 1982).

12. On forms expressed over time in political activity see Rodolfo Acuna, *Occupied America*, passim. For pertinent discussion in broad terms, see Biagio de Giovanni, "Lenin, Gramsci y la base teorica del pluralismo," *Dialectica*, vol. 4 (December 1974); and Antonio Gramsci, "State and Civil Society," in *Selections*, pp. 206–76.

13. There are few materials on twentieth-century leadership, but see Ralph C. Guzman, *Political Socialization*, pp. 157–84; Frances Jerome Woods, *Mexican Ethnic Leadership in San Antonio, Texas* (New York: Arno Press, 1976), pp. 37–89; and Julian Samora and James B. Watson, "Subordinate Leadership in a Bi-cultural Community," *American Sociological Review*, vol. 19 (1954). And for a general, if condescending, discussion on the subject, see the introduction to John Higham, ed., *Ethnic Leadership* (Baltimore: Johns Hopkins University Press, 1978).

14. On organizations, see Miguel David Tirado, "Mexican American Political Organization as 'The Key to Chicano Political Power,'" *Aztlan*, vol.

1 (Spring 1970); and Maurilio Vigil, "Ethnic Organizations among the Mexican-Americans of New Mexico: A Political Perspective" (Ph.D. diss., University of New Mexico, 1975). Establishing the structure of governance may be seen as an exercise of social civic organization, and obviously this was done both in the colonial and in the Mexican periods.

15. On episodic ideology, see Octavio I. Romano-V., "The Historical and Intellectual Presence of Mexican-Americans," El Grito, vol. 2 (Winter 1969); and for a general discussion, see Robert Lane, Political Ideology (New York: Free Press, 1962). Formally, ideology may be seen as consisting of a problem, an explanation, a strategy, and a vision or goal. Another way is to see it as a philosophy of history, a view of the present and a planned way for advancing a desired future.

16. See Juan Gómez-Quiñones and Luis L. Arroyo, "On the State of Chicano History: Observations on Its Development, Interpretations, and Theory, 1970–1974," Western Historical Quarterly, vol. 7 (April 1976).

17. For general discussion of formation, see Juan Gómez-Quiñones and Antonio Rios-Bustamante, "La Comunidad al Norte del Rio Bravo," in David R. Maciel, ed., La otra cara de México: El pueblo chicano (México, D.F.: Ediciones El Caballito, 1977).

18. For reviews of the paucity of literature and richness of activity, see Carlos Muñoz, "Toward a Chicano Perspective of Political Analysis," Aztlan, vol. 1 (Fall 1970); and Leo Grebler, et al., The Mexican American People (New York: Free Press, 1970), p. 7.

19. For several essays on this subject, see Carlos Vasquez and Manuel Garcia y Griego, eds., Mexican–U.S. Relations: Conflict and Convergence (Los Angeles: Chicano Studies Research Center, University of California, Los Angeles, 1983).

20. On stereotypes and perceptions of Mexicans, see Octavio I. Romano-V., "The Anthropology and Sociology of the Mexican Americans: The Distortion of Mexican American History," El Grito, vol. 2 (Fall 1968); Francisco Armando Rios, "The Mexican in Fact, Fiction, and Folklore," El Grito, vol. 2 (Summer 1969); and Cecil Robinson, With the Years of Strangers: The Mexican in American Literature (Tucson: University of Arizona Press, 1963). For blaming the victim syndrome, see William Ryan, Blaming the Victim (New York: Pantheon, 1971).

21. On pluralist approaches, see Garcia, La Causa Política; Robert A. Dahl, A Preface to Democratic Theory (Chicago: University of Chicago Press, 1956), Who Governs (New Haven: Yale University Press, 1961), and Pluralist Democracy in the United States (Chicago: Rand, McNally and Co., 1957). For a sharp and thoughtful critique, see Fred A. Cervantes, "Chicanos within

the Political Economy: Some Questions Concerning Pluralist Ideology, Representation and the Economy," *Aztlan*, vol. 7 (Fall 1976); and also Muñoz, "Toward a Chicano Perspective."

22. On the course of the literature as a processual effort, see Carlos Muñoz, "Quest for Paradigm," in National Association for Chicano Studies, eds., *History, Culture, and Society: Chicano Studies in the 1980's* (Ypsilanti, Mich.: Bilingual Press/Editorial Bilingue, 1983). He does not fully consider the elements of a paradigm as continually evolving apart from the internal colonial model debate.

23. On early work see Guzman, *Political Socialization;* Samora, *La Raza: Forgotten Americans* (Notre Dame: University of Notre Dame Press, 1966); Grebler, et al., *Mexican American People;* and Ernesto Galarza, *Spiders in the House and Workers in the Field* (Notre Dame: University of Notre Dame Press, 1970). For the most part, the political practice was liberal within the Democratic Party.

24. See Mario Barrera, et al., "The Barrio as an Internal Colony," in Harlon Hahn, ed., *Urban Affairs Annual Review*, vol. 6 (1972); Guillermo V. Flores and Ronald Bailey, "Internal Colonialism and Racial Minorities in the U.S.: An Overview" in Frank Bonilla, et al., *Structures of Dependency* (Stanford: 1973); and Joan Moore, "Colonialism: The Case of the Mexican-American," *Social Problems*, vol. 17 (Spring 1970), pp. 463–72. Though their focus is on the utility and application of the model, these works have distinctive emphases. Barrera, in "Barrio as an Internal Colony," "The essence, then of being an internal colony means existing in a condition of powerlessness." Furthermore, they state, "Of all of the mechanisms of domination, the racist mobilization of bias may be the most pervasive and most subtle in its effects." For an elegant critique of the internal colonial model, see Fred A. Cervantes, "Chicanos as a Post Colonial Minority: Some Questions Concerning the Adequacy of the Paradigm of International Colonialism," in Reynaldo Flores Macias, ed., *Perspectivas en Chicano Studies* (Los Angeles: Chicano Studies Center, University of California, Los Angeles, 1977). To be congruent with the model's view of mobilization, however, the internal colonial authors would then need to identify and endorse national liberation, which they do not do. Presumably, this intellectual tendency would be associated in practice with independent unionism or with ethnic exclusive politics; but it was not. Its practice was, at most, visible in a few Chicano Studies programs, though the authors were committed to "Ethnic" studies.

25. Some examples are Francisco H. Vasquez, "European Ideas in Mexico: An Analysis of Mexican Philosophical Discourse" (Ph.D. diss., Claremont Graduate School, 1977); Rymd. Rocco, "Chicano Studies and Critical Political Theory" in Eugene E. Garcia, et al., *Chicano Studies: A Multidisciplinary Approach;* and José M. López, "An Alternative to Cultural Nationalism"

(unpublished manuscript, n.d.). Early in the development of Chicano Studies, Elihu Carranza raised such concerns. See *Pensamientos on los Chicanos* (Berkeley: California Book Co., 1969) and *Chicanismo: Philosophical Fragments* (Dubuque, Iowa: Kendal Hunt, 1978). For some of the advisements influential on the language of political science "critical theorists," see Max Horkheimer, *Critical Theory* (New York: Herder and Herder, 1972), particularly the section on conventional and innovative paradigms, pp. 188–243; and Trent Schroyer, *The Critique of Domination* (New York: Horkheimer and Braziller, 1973). Called for since 1970, a sustained analysis of any basis on Chicano politics that would follow the outlines of language critical-theory exponents is not yet available nor do they account for the counterhegemonic elements present currently. Not Marxist, though they claim Hegel and Marx, the Frankfurt school is the inspiration, particularly Jurgen Habermas, with the notable influence of Max Weber. For the language critical-theory exponents, "consciousness" is to be gained by study and discussion and as a means to "unity." The "practice" is campus dialogue. To the cynical, this idealist appeal or ascription to "unity," a normative expectation for cohesion, independent of class interests and an ethnic political goal, is socially abstract or potentially one more manipulation to further veiled interests, or at worse an argument for no politics. Those alienated from the Mexican community, but academically radical in their views, may be attracted to this formulation. Such subjective idealism would be distant to many community activists. For activists as incisive analysts and ideologues, see Richard Flacks, "Notes on the Crisis of Sociology," *Social Policy,* vol. 2 (March–April 1972).

26. For a developing interest in this type of study, see issues of the *Social Science Quarterly* published during 1973 and 1984, and the publications of the Southwest Voter Registration Project. For a review of 1970s literature, see Carlos Muñoz, "The State of the Art in the Study of Chicano Politics" in Isidro D. Ortiz, et al., *Chicanos and the Social Sciences: A Decade of Research and Development (1970–1980)* (Santa Barbara: Center for Chicano Studies, University of California, Santa Barbara, 1983).

27. Mario Barrera, "The Historical Evolution of Chicano Ethnic Goals: A Bibliographic Essay," *Sage Race Relations Abstracts,* vol. 10 (February 1985). Overviews of organizations are often accompanied by some piety about alleged middle-class deficiencies which are denounced pro forma even as they are embraced.

28. Carlos Muñoz, "Chicano Politics: The Current Conjuncture," in Mike Davis, et al., eds., *The Year Left 2, An American Socialist Yearbook* (London: Verso, 1987). There are several steps to the race–class argument, but the conundrum reached is culturalism or assimilation, a political radicalism or ultra-left participation.

29. Examples would be Cervantes, "Chicanos within the Political Economy" and "Chicanos as a Post-Colonial Minority," and the evolution of the work of Richard Santillan, from "The Concept of Chicano Political Self-Determination within a Capitalist Society: A Case Study of the Incorporation of East Los Angeles, 1974" (unpublished manuscript, n.d.), to "Styles and Strategies," in Garcia, ed., *Latinos and the Political System*. For a review of Marxist work, see Estevan T. Flores, "The Mexican Origin People in the United States and Marxist Thought in Chicano Studies" in Bertell Ollman and Edward Vernoff, eds., *The Left Academy: Marxist Scholarship on American Campuses* (New York: Praeger, 1986). For the refinement of political economy and political sociology turned history, see David Montejano, *Anglos and Mexicans in the Making of Texas* (Austin: University of Texas Press, 1987).

30. See Richard P. Appelbaum, *Theories of Social Change* (Chicago: Markham, 1970), pp. 65–98; and Nathan Rotenstreich, *Theory and Practice* (The Hague: Martinus Nijhoff, 1977), chapter 1; see also John Horton, "Order and Conflict Theories of Social Problems as Competing Ideologies," *The American Journal of Sociology*, vol. 71 (May 1966); and Jurgen Habermas, *Knowledge and Human Interests* (Boston: Beacon Press, 1971).

31. For a critique of pluralism as the prevailing orthodoxy, see Kenneth Prewit and Alan Stone, *The Ruling Elites: Theory, Power and American Democracy* (New York: Harper and Row, 1973), pp. 114–28; and Robert Presthus, *Men at the Top* (New York: Oxford University Press, 1964), pp. 10–24. For examples of pluralism's application, see William D. Antonio and William Form, *Influentials in Two Border Cities* (Notre Dame: University of Notre Dame Press, 1965), passim; Edward Banfield, *Big City Politics* (New York: Random House, 1965), p. 76.

32. For critical analysis of government, see Theodore Lowi, *American Government: Incomplete Conquest* (Hinsdale, Ill.: Dryden Press, 1976); Darryl Baskin, "American Pluralism: Theory, Practice, and Ideology," *Journal of Politics*, vol. 32 (February 1970), pp. 71–85; and Michael Parenti, "Power and Pluralism: A View from the Bottom," *Journal of Politics*, vol. 32 (August 1970), pp. 501–30.

33. For a critical interpretation of United States history, see Howard Zinn, *A People's History of the United States* (New York: Harper and Row, 1981); Thomas R. Dye and L. Harmon Zeigler, *The Irony of Democracy* (North Scituate, Mass.: Duxbury Press, 1975); and G. William Domhoff, *Who Rules America?* (Englewood Cliffs: Prentice-Hall, 1967) and *Higher Circles: The Governing Class in America* (New York: Vintage Books, 1971). For a standard celebratory view of United States development, see David M. Potter, *People of Plenty: Economic Abundance and the American Character* (Chicago: University of Chicago, 1954); and Robert G. McCloskey, "American Political Thought and the Study of Politics," *American Political Science Review*, vol.

51 (March 1957). Indeed, the Spanish and English were competitors and their forms, organization, ideology, and leadership for expansion were distinct, as were the results.

34. For views of what an adequate explanatory paradigm may entail, see comments by Barrera, "The Study of Politics and the Chicano"; Muñoz, "Toward a Chicano Perspective"; Garcia and de la Garza, *Chicano Political Experience;* Gómez-Quiñones, "Toward a Perspective on Chicano History"; and Gómez-Quiñones and Arroyo, "On the State of Chicano History."

35. See Robert J. Welin, "Marxist Political Analysis," in Andrew Effrat, ed., *Perspectives in Political Sociology* (New York: Bobbs-Merrill, 1973); Paul Walton, "From Surplus Value to Surplus Theories: Marx, Marcuse and MacIntyre," *Social Research,* vol. 37 (Winter 1970); and Jerry Cohen, "Critical Theory: The Philosophy of Marcuse," *New Left Review,* no. 57 (September–October 1969). For manipulative socialization, see Peter Bachrach and Morton Baratz, *Power and Poverty* (New York: Oxford University Press, 1970). For an exciting, eclectic, and fervid critique of revisionist historiography, set against the pervasiveness of dominant popular and academic thought, see John Patrick Diggins, "Comrades and Citizens: New Mythologies in American Historiography," *American Historical Review,* vol. 90 (June 1985).

Chapter 2

1. For understanding the political relations of the period from the 1940s to the 1960s, the writings by participants Ernesto Galarza, George Sanchez, Ralph Guzman, and to a lesser extent, Daniel Valdes are particularly helpful to be cited; and for humorous insight into barrio life and politics, there are the short stories of Mario Suarez. Despite limitations, works by Ralph Guzman and Daniel Valdes are valuable because they are works on politics by individuals with academic training and considerable direct experience in politics. For contrast as to what was said about political circumstances in three articles appearing ten years apart in nationally distributed publications, see: Enrique Prado, "Sinarquism in the United States," *New Republic,* vol. 109, no. 4 (July 26, 1943); G. W. Sherman, "A People Come of Age," *The Nation,* vol. 176, no. 13 (March 18, 1953); and "Revolt of the Mexicans," *Time,* vol. 81, no. 15 (April 12, 1963). For a sharply contrasting view to the one presented here, see Manuel P. Servin, "The Post World War II Mexican Americans, 1925–1965: A Non-Achieving Minority," in Manuel P. Servin, ed., *The Mexican Americans: An Awakening Minority* (Beverly Hills: Glencoe Press, 1970). For analysis of the politics of the pre–World War II period, see Juan Gómez-Quiñones, "The New Century and the New Challenges, 1900–1941" (unpublished manuscript, 1988).

2. For empirical data to interpret the quality of life, see Elizabeth Broadbent, "The Distribution of Mexican Population in the U.S." (Ph.D. diss., University of Chicago, 1941); Leo Grebler, et al., *The Mexican-American People: The Nation's Second Largest Minority* (New York: Free Press, 1976), pp. 206–18; W. Rey Crawford, "The Latin American in Wartime United States," *Annals of the American Academy of Political and Social Science*, vol. 223 (September 1942); U.S. Bureau of the Census, *United States Census, 1960: Persons of Spanish Surname*, p. 12; *United States Census 1960: Nonwhite Population by Race*, p. 9. For a graphic review of living conditions, see Pauline Kibbie, *Latin Americans in Texas* (Albuquerque: University of New Mexico Press, 1946), pp. 81–236; and Robert Coles and Harry Huge, "Thorns on the Yellow Rose of Texas," *New Republic* (April 19, 1969). There was also continuing interest in the "study" of physical characteristics of minorities, which, for Mexicans, were seen as changing; see Marcus S. Goldstein, *Demographic and Bodily Changes in Descendants of Mexican Immigrants* (Austin: University of Texas, Institute of Latin American Studies, 1943).

3. For classes, see A. Rios-Bustamante, "Las clases sociales mexicanas en Estados Unidos," *Historia y Sociedad*, no. 20 (1978); Mario Barrera, "Chicano Class Structure" in Eugene E. Garcia, et al., eds., *Chicano Studies: A Multidisciplinary Approach* (New York and London: Teachers College, Columbia University, 1984); and Fernando Peñalosa, "A Socioeconomic Class Typology of Mexican Americans," *Sociological Inquiry*, vol. 26 (Winter 1966). For an outsider's comments on classes based on observation, see William Madsen, *The Mexican Americans of South Texas* (New York: Holt, Rinehart and Winston, 1964), pp. 24–43; Nancy L. González, *The Spanish Americans of New Mexico* (Albuquerque: University of New Mexico Press, 1969), pp. 75–83; and Ruth Tuck, *Not with the Fist: Mexican-Americans in a Southwest City* (New York: Harcourt, Brace and Company, 1946), pp. 131–44.

4. For views on what community writers felt were the elements of change and needs, see Ernesto Galarza, "The Mexican American: A National Concern," *Common Ground*, vol. 9 (Summer 1949); Ralph Guzman, *Roots without Rights* (Los Angeles: American Civil Rights Union, Los Angeles Chapter, 1958); and the remarks of Carlos Casteneda, "Arquitecios de Nuestros Propios Destinos" [Column], *La Prensa* (May 16, 1952); and Joan W. Moore and Ralph Concern, "The Mexican-American: New Wind from the Southwest," *The Nation* (May 30, 1966).

5. A graphic articulation of equities denied and now claimed, as well as the best available direct account of Mexican American participation in the United States armed forces in World War II, remains the work by army veteran Raul Morin, *Among the Valiant: Mexican-Americans in World War II and Korea* (Alhambra, Calif.: Borden Publishing Company, 1963); and Ruth

D. Tuck, *Not with the Fist*. For references to Mexican armed forces participation, see John H. Burma, *Spanish-Speaking Groups in the United States* (Detroit: Blaine Ethridge Books, 1974). See also United States Department of Defense, *Hispanics in American's Defense* (Washington, D.C.: United States Department of Defense, 1981). For discussions of the widely commented attitudinal and ideological effects of the war on Mexican Americans, see: Albert M. Camarillo, "The G.I. Generation," *Aztlan*, vol. 2 (Fall 1971); Carl Allsup, *The American G.I. Forum: A History of a Mexican-American Organization* (Austin: Center for Mexican American Studies, University of Texas, 1982); Mario T. Garcia, "Americans All: The Mexican-American Generation and the Politics of Wartime Los Angeles, 1941–1945," *Social Science Quarterly*, vol. 65 (June 1984); Gerald Nash, *The American West Transformed: The Impact of the Second World War* (Bloomington: Indiana University Press, 1985), chapter 7, "Spanish-Speaking Americans in Wartime"; and Robin Fitzgerald Scott, "Wartime Labor Problems and Mexican Americans in the War," in Manuel P. Servin, ed., *The Mexican-Americans: An Awakened Minority* (2d ed., Beverly Hills: Glencoe Press, 1974).

6. Senator Dennis Chavez, in *Congressional Record*, 78th Congress, 2d sess. (June 16, 1944), p. 6156; see also Jesus Chavarria, "On Chicano History: In Memoriam, George I. Sanchez, 1906–1972," in Americo Paredes, ed., *Humanidad: Essays in Honor of George I. Sanchez* (Los Angeles: Chicano Studies Research Center Publications, UCLA, 1977), pp. 41–57.

7. See Louis Ruchames, *Race, Jobs and Politics: The Story of FEPC* (New York: Columbia University Press, 1953), pp. 19–20; and Rodolfo Acuna, *Occupied America: A History of Chicanos* (New York: Harper and Row, 1981), pp. 234–44, 316–29.

8. Carey McWilliams, *North from Mexico: The Spanish-Speaking People of the United States* (Philadelphia: J. B. Lippincott Company, 1948), pp. 275–76. For a more positive view of the CIAA, see Nash, *American West Transformed*, pp. 123–25.

9. See the printed correspondence between Texas governor Coke R. Stevenson and Ezequiel Padilla, Mexico's foreign minister, in their *The Good Neighbor Policy and Mexicans in Texas* (México, D.F.: Department of State for Foreign Affairs, 1943). See also former foreign minister Isidro Fabela's *Buena y mala vecindad* (México, D.F.: 1958); Alonso S. Perales, ed., *Are We Good Neighbors?* (San Antonio: Artes Graficas, 1948), which contains speeches and declarations on the question; and Ernesto Galarza, "Trabajadores mexicanos en tierra extraña," *Problemas agricolas e industriales de México*, vol. 10 (January–June 1958), pp. 1–84.

10. See Coordinator of Inter-American Affairs, *Inter-American Activities in the United States—Spanish and Portuguese Speaking People in the United States*

(Washington, D.C.: 1943); Coordinator of Inter-American Affairs, *Spanish-Speaking Americans in the War: The Southwest* (Washington, D.C.: Coordinator of Inter-American Affairs and Office of War Information, 1943); George I. Sanchez, ed., *First Regional Conference on Education of Spanish-Speaking People in the Southwest* (Austin: University of Texas Press, 1946); and McWilliams, *North from Mexico,* pp. 276–77; Nash, *American West Transformed,* p. 124.

11. For example, see the following writings published at the time: George I. Sanchez, *Forgotten People: A History of New Mexicans* (Albuquerque: University of New Mexico Press, 1940); Sanchez, *First Regional Conference;* George I. Sanchez, "Pachucos in the Making," *Common Ground,* vol. 4 (1943); and Alonso S. Perales, *Are We Good Neighbors?* See also Kibbie, *Latin Americans in Texas.* For a discussion of the ideological influence of George I. Sanchez, see Ralph C. Guzman, "The Political Socialization of the Mexican-American People" (Ph.D. diss., University of California, Los Angeles, 1970), pp. 156–66; and Paredes, *Humanidad,* passim.

12. On Pachucos, see the statement of Ed Duran Ayres to E. W. Oliver, Foreman, Los Angeles County Grand Jury, 1942 (photostatic copy); as well as the *Los Angles Times* (March 22, 1943); *Los Angeles Examiner* (June 17, 1943), *Los Angeles Daily News* (June 8, 1943). For direct observations, see Perales, *Are We Good Neighbors?,* p. 27; Carey McWilliams, "Los Angeles' Pachuco Gangs," in *New Republic,* vol. 108, no. 3 (January 18, 1943), pp. 76–77. On the Sleepy Lagoon case, see *The Sleepy Lagoon Case* (Los Angeles: Citizen's Committee for the Defense of Mexican American Youth, 1942). For a psychohistorical interpretation of the Zoot Suit events, see Mauricio Mazon, *The Zoot Suit Riots: The Psychology of Symbolic Annihilation* (Austin: University of Texas Press, 1984). The quote is from Paul Coronel, "The Pachuco Problem," *The Mexican Voice,* vol. 3, no. 10 (1943), p. 3. The most informative source on the Mexican American Movement is its publications, *The Mexican Voice,* vol. 1 (1938)–vol. 3 (1944); and *Mexican American Forward,* vol. 1 (1945–1947).

13. See "Statement of Frank Paz," in Perales, *Are We Good Neighbors?,* pp. 111–14; McWilliams, *North from Mexico,* pp. 279–80.

14. See Dennis Chavez, "The Good Neighbor Policy and the Present Administration" (Address, Los Angeles, California), October 19, 1944, Perales, *Are We Good Neighbors?,* pp. 134–38; see also, "Fair Employment Practices Act Hearings. . . . March 12, 13, and 14, 1945," in Perales, *Are We Good Neighbors?,* pp. 92–138; Fair Employment Practices Act Hearings, Subcommittee of the Committee on Education and Labor, United States Senate, 79th Congress, 1st sess., in Perales, *Are We Good Neighbors?,* pp. 104–11; Dennis Chavez, in *Congressional Record* (June 16, 1944), p. 6156; see also Tobias Duran, "Social Reform Politics in New Mexico: The Fair Employment Practice Act of 1949" (unpublished manuscript, n.d.); and Emilio Zamora,

"The Failed Promise of Employment Opportunity during the War: The Mexican Worker in the Texas Gulf Coast Oil Industry" (unpublished manuscript, n.d.).

15. See Dr. Carlos E. Castaneda, "Statement on Discrimination against Mexican-Americans in Employment," in Perales, *Are We Good Neighbors?*, pp. 59–63; Carlos E. Castaneda, "The Second Rate Citizen and Democracy," in ibid., pp. 17–20; Gerald D. Nash, *American West Transformed*, chapter 7, and particularly pp. 122–23. See Ruth Lucretia Martinez, "The Unusual Mexican: A Study in Acculturation" (Master's thesis, Claremont Colleges, 1942), p. 24, for the quote on alleged attitudes of Anglo workers as reported by employers.

16. See the direct observations of Morin, *Among the Valiant*, pp. 277–80; Tuck, *Not with the Fist*, pp. 145–72; and Woods, *Mexican Ethnic Leadership*, pp. 63–115.

17. See Patricia Morgan, *Shame of a Nation* (Los Angeles: Committee for Protection of the Foreign Born: 1954); Mark A. Chamberlin, et al., *Our Badge of Infamy* (Los Angeles: Committee for Protection of the Foreign Born, 1959); and Grebler, et al., *Mexican American People*, pp. 517–37.

18. On labor, see Tim D. Kane, "Structural Change and Chicano Employment in the Southwest, 1950–1970: Some Preliminary Questions," *Aztlan*, vol. 4 (Fall 1973); Tim D. Kane, "Chicano Employment Patterns: An Analysis of the Effects of Declining Economic Growth Rates in Contemporary America," *Aztlan*, vol. 10 (Fall 1979); Antonio Rios-Bustamante, "Las clases sociales Mexicanas en Estados Unidos," *Historia y Sociedad*, numero 20 (1978); and Juan Gómez-Quiñones, "An Imperfect Promise: Mexican Labor in the United States, 1940–1965" (unpublished manuscript, 1987).

19. Kibbie, *Latin Americans in Texas*, pp. 271–72. See also "The Mexican American: A National Concern," by Ernesto Galarza, and "The Mexican Americans—Their Plight and Struggles," (anonymous) in *Political Affairs* (May 1949).

20. Manuel Gamio, *Mexican Immigration to the United States* (Chicago: University of Chicago Press, 1930), p. 53. For warm and bittersweet recollections of childhood, see Ernesto Galarza, *Barrio Boy* (New York: Ballantine, 1972).

21. Tuck, *Not with the Fist*, p. 52. For data on Mexican students during the times, see Ruth Lucretia Martinez, "The Unusual Mexican"; and Stephen Reyes, "A Survey of the Problems Involved in the Americanization of the Mexican American" (Master's thesis, University of Southern California, 1957).

22. Tuck, *Not with the Fist*, p. 53; see also the section in which Tuck discusses nativism and the experiences of a consul, pp. 168–72.

23. Ibid., p. 221; see also Morin, *Among the Valiant*.

24. See Galarza, "Mexican American"; Guzman, *Roots without Rights;*

and George I. Sanchez, "The American of Mexican Descent," *The Chicago Jewish Forum*, vol. 20 (Winter 1961–1962).

25. On PAPA, see Ozzie G. Simmons, *Anglo-Americans and Mexican Americans in South Texas* (New York: Arno Press, 1974), pp. 543–44; Francis Jerome Wood, "Mexican Ethnic Leadership in San Antonio, Texas" (Ph.D. diss., Catholic University of America, 1949), pp. 110–11. The quote from PAPA is in ibid., p. 110.

26. See Ralph Guzman, *The Political Socialization of the Mexican American People* (New York: Arno Press, 1976), pp. 185–202.

27. See Jack E. Holmes, *Politics in New Mexico* (Albuquerque: University of New Mexico Press, 1967); Carolyn Zeleny, "Relations Between the Spanish Americans and Anglo-Americans in New Mexico" (Ph.D. diss., Yale University, 1944); and E. B. Fincher, "Spanish Americans as a Political Factor in New Mexico, 1912–1950" (Ph.D. diss., New York University, 1950), passim.

28. On Dennis Chavez, see Chavez, *Memorial Addresses Delivered in Congress* (Washington, D.C.: United States Government Printing Office, 1963).

29. On conditions and figures of New Mexico politics, see Maurilio Vigil, *Los Patrones: Profiles of Hispanic Political Leaders in New Mexico History* (Washington, D.C.: University Press of America, 1980); and F. Chris Garcia and Robert D. Wrinkle, "Urban Politics in a State of Varied Political Cultures," in Wrinkle, ed., *Politics in the Urban Southwest* (Albuquerque: University of New Mexico Press, 1971). For officeholders, see *New Mexico Blue Book* (Secretary of State, various dates); and *Roster of State of New Mexico Elective State, Legislative District and County Officials* (Secretary of State, various dates).

30. See Joseph M. Montoya, "Woe Unto Those Who Have Ears But Do Not Hear," *Congressional Record*, vol. 117, part 2 (May 6, 1971), pp. 13811–14; Holmes, *Politics in New Mexico*, p. 246; John Littlewood and Frederick Aten, *Joseph M. Montoya, Democratic Senator from New Mexico* (Washington, D.C.: Grossman Publishers, 1972); and Vigil, *Los Patrones*.

31. Fernando V. Padilla and Carlos B. Ramirez, "Patterns of Chicano Representation in California, Colorado, and Nuevo Mexico," *Aztlan*, vol. 5 (Fall 1974), pp. 225–29. See also Flaviano Chris Garcia, "Manitos and Chicanos in Nuevo Mexico Politics," *Aztlan*, vol. 5 (Fall 1974), 177–88.

32. See Ernest B. Fincher, *Spanish Americans as a Political Factor in New Mexico, 1912–1950*, pp. 242–67; and Nancy L. González, *The Spanish Americans of New Mexico: A Pride of Heritage* (Albuquerque: University of New Mexico Press, 1977), passim.

33. See *Arizona Year Book* (Phoenix: n. p., several dates); Carey McWilliams, *North from Mexico*, p. 276; C. R. Granberry, *Texas Legislative Manual, Forty-Seventh Legislature* (Austin: Von Boeckmann-Jones Co., 1941), pp. 339–49; and Padilla and Ramirez, "Patterns of Chicano Representation," p. 206.

34. See Saul Alinsky, *Rules for Radicals: A Practice Primer for Realistic Radicals* (New York: Random House, 1971); and Alinsky, *Reveille for Radicals* (1946; New York: Vintage Books, 1969); see also Charles Levine, "Understanding Alinsky: Conservative Wine in Radical Bottles," *American Behavioral Scientist*, vol. 17 (November–December 1973), pp. 279–84; and Robert Pruger and Harry Speht, "Assigning Theoretical Models of Community Organizing Practice," *The Social Service Review*, vol. 43, no. 2 (June 1969), pp. 123–35.

35. See Tobias Duran, "Social Reform Politics in New Mexico: The Fair Employment Practice of 1949"; and for the increasing concern over discrimination, see Clyde A. Miller, "Community Wages Total War on Prejudice," *The Nation's Schools*, vol. 37, no. 1 (January 1944).

36. For radical efforts, see recollections provided by Jon Weiner, "The Communist Party Today and Yesterday: An Interview with Dorothy Healey," *Radical America*, vol. 11 (May–June 1977); and Jesus Mena, "Testimonio de Bert Corona, Struggle Is the Ultimate Teacher," in *201, Homenaje a la Ciudad de Los Angeles* (Los Angeles: Los Angeles Latino Writers Association, 1982). For analysis of the Congress, see Juan Gómez-Quiñones, "The New Century and New Challenges"; for a contrasting view, see Alberto Camarillo, "The Development of a Pan-American Civil Rights Movement: The 1939 Congress of Spanish Speaking People" (unpublished manuscript, 1986).

37. There is scant mention of ANMA in *Fourth Report of Un-American Activities in California* (Sacramento: Joint Fact Finding Committee, 1955); and interestingly, there is a mention of the Spanish-Speaking Peoples Congress, on p. 109 of the 1948 Report; but there is no mention of either in the *Fourteenth Report* (1967). For ANMA, see Liliana Urrutia, "An Offspring of Discontent: The Asociación Nacional Mexico-Americana, 1949–1954," *Aztlan*, vol. 15 (Spring 1984); and Mario T. Garcia, "Mexican American Labor and the Left: The Asociación Nacional Mexico-Americana, 1949–1954," in John A. Garcia, et al., eds., *The Chicano Struggle: Analyses of Past and Present Efforts* (Binghamton, N.Y.: Bilingual Press, 1984), pp. 65–86.

38. For observations on the times and climate, see Owen Lattimore, *Ordeal by Slander* (New York: Bantam, 1950). See also Seymour Martin Lipset, "The Radical Right and McCarthyism"; Richard Hofstader, "The Pseudo-Conservative Revolt"; and Talcott Parsons, "Social Strains in America"; all three are in Daniel Bell, ed., *The Radical Right* (Garden City: Doubleday, 1963). See also Robert Griffith, *The Politics of Fear: Senator Joseph R. McCarthy and the Senate* (Amherst: University of Massachusetts Press, 1970); Alan D. Harper, *The Politics of Loyalty: The White House and the Communist Issue, 1946–1952* (Westport: Greenwood Press, 1969); and Athan Theoharis, *Seeds of Repression: Harry S Truman and the Origins of McCarthyism* (Chicago: Quadrangle Press, 1971).

39. See *El Espectador* (1937–1947); see also Enrique M. López, "Chicano

Anglo Relations in Ontario, California, 1937–1947" (unpublished manuscript, June 1984).

40. See "Los Angeles Community Service Organization, 20th Anniversary" (pamphlet, March 5, 1967, Commerce Hyatt House, City of Commerce); Beatrice Griffith, "Mexican-Americans Enter L.A. Politics," *The Mirror* (May 6, 1949); Mike Glazer, "LA CSO History" (Los Angeles: Community Service Organization, 1965); and Guzman, "Political Socialization," pp. 245–56.

41. See Beatrice Griffith, "Viva Roybal—Viva America," *Common Ground*, vol. 10 (Autumn 1949), pp. 61–69. For the symbol Roybal became in five years, see Martin Hall, "Roybal's Candidacy and What It Means," *Frontier* (June 1954); see also Kaye Briegel, "The History of Political Organizations among Mexican-Americans in Los Angeles since the Second World War" (Master's thesis, University of Southern California, 1967). Roybal is a native of New Mexico and descendant of a settler family. A selection of Edward R. Roybal material is available at the Special Collections section, University Research Library, UCLA.

42. Interview with Antonio Rios, Los Angeles, June 8, 1971 (typescript); and Interview with Antonio Rios and Manuel Aragon, KNBC, Los Angeles, September 14, 1972 (video).

43. Eugene Rodriguez, Jr., *Henry B. González: A Political Profile* (New York: Arno Press, 1976), passim.

44. See Ozzie G. Simmons, "Anglo-Americans and Mexican-Americans in South Texas: A Study in Dominant-Subordinate Group Relations" (Ph.D. diss., Harvard University, 1951), pp. 543–44; and Rodriguez, *Henry B. González*, pp. 32–33.

45. Rodriguez, *Henry B. González*, pp. 30–47; and Edwin Larry Dickens, "The Political Role of Mexican Americans in San Antonio" (Ph.D. diss., Texas Tech University, 1969), passim.

46. Rodriguez, *Henry B. González*, pp. 50–52, 64–73, 74–82, and 84–177.

47. On the American G.I. Forum, see its regular newsletters, Forum News Bulletin and *Forumeer*; its basic document, the American G.I. Forum of Texas, "The Constitution of the American G.I. Forum of Texas" (McAllen, 1963); the authorized history, Henry A. J. Ramos, *A People Forgotten, A Dream Pursued, The History of the American G.I. Forum* (American G.I. Forum, 1983); see also Carl Allsup, *The American G.I. Forum: Origins and Evolution* (Austin: Center for Mexican-American Studies, University of Texas Press, 1982); and Guzman, "Political Socialization," pp. 147–49.

48. On LULAC in this period, see the League of United Latin-American

Citizens, "The Constitution and By-Laws of The League of United Latin-American Citizens" (Austin: 1955); *LULAC News*; Adela Sloss-Vento, *Alonso S. Perales, His Struggle for the Rights of Mexican Americans* (San Antonio: Artes Graficas, 1977); Robert A. Cuellar, *A Social and Political History of the Mexican-American Population of Texas 1929–1963* (San Francisco: R and E Research Associates, 1974); and Edward D. Garza, "LULAC (League of United Latin American Citizens)" (Master's thesis, Southwest Texas State Teachers College, San Marcos, 1951).

49. On the Alianza Hispano-Americana, see its newsletter *Alianza* (1951–1955); Kaye Briegel, "Alianza Hispano-Americana and Some Mexican-American Civil Rights Cases in the 1950s," in Manuel Servin, ed., *The Mexican Americans: An Awakened Minority*; José Hernández, *Mutual Aid for Survival: The Case of the Mexican American* (Malabar: Robert E. Krieger, 1983), pp. 45–67; and Kaye Briegel, "La Alianzo Hispano-Americana: A Fraternal Insurance Society, 1894–1965" (Ph.D. diss., University of Southern California, 1973).

50. See statement of Archbishop Robert E. Lucy, in Perales, *Are We Good Neighbors?*, pp. 11–16; and of Reverend John J. Birch, in ibid., pp. 53–57; and for assessments of the church, see Reverend John A. Wagner, "The Role of the Christian Church," in Julian Samora, ed., *La Raza: Forgotten Americans* (Notre Dame: University of Notre Dame Press, 1966); Patrick H. McNamara, "Dynamics of the Catholic Church: From Pastoral to Social Concern," in Grebler and Sister De Prague Reilly, "The Role of the Churches in the Bracero Program in California" (Master's thesis, University of Southern California, 1969). For statements and documents, see also Antonio M. Stevens Arroyo, ed., *Prophets Denied Honor: An Anthology on the Hispanic Church in the United States* (New York: Orbis Books, 1980). A particularly active priest was Father Robert, O.S.B. (George Hinds Dodson), of East Los Angeles, a descendant of the California Dominguez family.

51. See Edward Drewry Jervey, *The History of Methodism in Southern California and Arizona* (Los Angeles: 1960); Bertha Blair, et al., *Spanish-Speaking Americans: Mexicans and Puerto Ricans in the United States* (New York: National Council of Churches, 1959); and Grebler, *Mexican-American People*, pp. 486–507.

52. For an overview of labor and trade unions, see Juan Gómez-Quiñones, "An Imperfect Promise: Mexican Labor in the United States, 1940–1965" (unpublished manuscript, 1987).

53. Note in *Alianza* (July 1951), p. 42; and Ralph Estrada, "New Horizons and New Techniques," *Alianza* (March 1955), pp. 7–8.

54. See Allen J. Matusow, *The Unraveling of America: A History of Liberalism in the Sixties* (New York: Harper and Row, 1984); Eric Goldman, *The Crucial Decade and After: America, 1945–1960* (New York: Vintage, 1960);

and William L. O'Neill, *Coming Apart: An Informal History of America in the 1960s* (New York: Quadrangle, 1975).

55. On MAPA in the early stages, see Guzman, "Political Socialization," pp. 143–50; and John R. Martinez, "Leadership and Politics," in Samora, pp. 52–53.

56. On PASSO, see Guzman, "Political Socialization," pp. 146–47; Martinez, "Leadership and Politics," *La Raza,* pp. 52–58; Robert A. Cuellar, "A Social and Political History of the Mexican-American Population, 1929–1963" (Master's thesis, North Texas State University, 1969), pp. 41–68; and Daniel Valdes y Tapia, *Hispanos and American Politics* (New York: Arno Press, 1976), pp. 166, 167.

57. "Kennedy Patronage, Latin American Policies Under Fire," *Congressional Quarterly Weekly,* vol. 19 (June 23, 1961), p. 1042.

58. See John Staples Shockley, *Chicano Revolt in a Texas Town* (Notre Dame: University of Notre Dame Press, 1974); and Cuellar, *Social and Political History,* passim.

59. See Sanchez, "American of Mexican Descent"; and Thomas B. Morgan, "The Texas Giant Awakens," *Look* (October 8, 1963). On Edward R. Roybal, see "Biography of Edward Roybal," prepared by the congressman's staff (Washington, D.C., n.d.). On Henry B. González and Elijio de la Garza, see Rodriguez, *Henry B. González;* "Congressman Henry B. González," prepared by the congressman's staff (Washington, D.C., 1981); and "Biography of E. Kika de la Garza," prepared by the congressman's staff (Washington, D.C., n.d.). On Senator Joseph Montoya, see Maurilio E. Vigil, *Los Patrones;* and John Littlewood and Frederick Aten, *Joseph M. Montoya.* For Manuel Lujan, see Sven Erik Holmes, *Manuel Lujan, Jr.: Republican Representative from New Mexico* (Washington, D.C.: Grossman Publishers, 1972).

60. James A. Atkins, *Human Relations in Colorado: A Historical Record* (Denver: Colorado Department of Education, 1968), p. 105. For some insight into the antecedent context, see Daniel Valdes y Tapia, *Hispanos and American Politics* (New York: Arno Press, 1976), passim.

61. See R. Guzman, *Political Socialization;* E. B. Fincher, "Spanish Americans"; and R. Cuellar, "A Social and Political History"; for references to city and county electoral politics. See also T. Phillip Wolf, "Urbanization in New Mexico: With Emphasis on Electoral Patterns"; Leonard E. Goodall, "Emerging Political Patterns in Southwestern Cities"; and John M. Claunch, "The Mexican-American in El Paso"; all in Clyde J. Wingfield, ed., *Urbanization in the South West* (El Paso: Texas Western Press, 1968). For elected offices, see *The Book of States: Supplement I, February 1965: State Elective Officials and the Legislatures* (Chicago: 1965), pp. 3, 24, and 25; see also Frank M. Jordan, comp., *Roster of Federal, State, County and City Officials* (Sacramento, 1964), pp. 1–26; and *Texas Almanac, 1961–1962* (Dallas, 1961).

62. See Jack E. Holmes, *Politics in New Mexico*, pp. 21–29; Ozzie G. Simmons, *Anglo-Americans and Mexican Americans in South Texas*, pp. 270–338; and Evan Anders, *Boss Rule in South Texas: The Progressive Era* (Austin: University of Texas, 1982), pp. 241–83; and V. O. Key, *Southern Politics* (New York: Vintage, 1949), pp. 271–76.

63. William Kornblum, *Blue Collar Community* (Chicago: University of Chicago Press, 1974), pp. 115–79; Julian Samora, "Mexican Americans in a Midwest Metropolis: A Study of East Chicago" (UCLA, Mexican American Study Project, Advance Report, 1967); and Louisa Ano-Nuevo Kerr, "The Chicano Experience in Chicago, 1920–1970" (Ph.D. diss., Loyola University, Chicago, 1976), passim.

64. For San Antonio politics, see Edwin Larry Dickens, "The Political Role of Mexican Americans in San Antonio," in David R. Johnson, et al., eds., *The Politics of San Antonio: Community, Progress, and Power* (Lincoln: University of Nebraska Press, 1983); and Robert Caro, *The Years of Lyndon Johnson: The Path to Power* (New York: Vintage Books, 1981), passim. For the few comments of a "friend" of the community, see John A. Ford, *Thirty Explosive Years in Los Angeles County* (San Marino: Huntington Library, 1961).

65. "Objectives of CMAA," *Eastside Sun* (May 10, 1956); and Paul M. Sheldon, "Community Participation and the Emerging Middle Class," in Samora, pp. 139–40. For the Congress of Mexican American Unity, there is a collection of material in my possession.

66. See for example, *The Civil Rights Status of Spanish Speaking Americans in Kleberg, Nueces, and San Patricio Counties, Texas, A Special Report of the Texas State Advisory Committee to the U.S. Commission on Civil Rights, July 1967* (Washington, D.C.: U.S. Government Printing Office, 1967); United States Commission on Civil Rights, *Mexican Americans and the Administration of Justice in the Southwest: A Report* (Washington, D.C.: Superintendent of Documents, March 1970); and Grebler, part six, "Political Interaction," pp. 556–70.

67. Observations on leadership and organizations are found in nearly all of the written material from and on the period. In viewing Mexican American leaders, the observation by Eric F. Goldman is helpful.

Harold Taylor, president of Sarah Lawrence College, noting the way that charges of Communism were being used to beat down any independence in thinking, got off a definition of a patriotic American as one who tells all his secrets without being asked, believes we should go to war with Russia, holds no political view without prior consultation with his employer, does not ask for increases in salary or wages, and is in favor of peace, universal military training, brotherhood, and baseball. (*Crucial Decade*, p. 162)

68. For the situation of Mexican Americans, see: John H. Burma, "The

Civil Rights Situation of Mexican Americans," in Jitsuichi Masuoka and Preston Valien, eds., *Race Relations: Problems and Theory* (Chapel Hill: University of North Carolina Press, 1961), pp. 155–67; and Gladwin Hill, "The Political Role of Mexican Americans," in Arnold Rose and Caroline Rose, eds., *Minority Problems* (New York: Harper and Row, 1965).

69. For an analysis of unrest, see: Allen J. Matusow, *Unraveling of America*; and Hugh Davis Graham and Ted Robert Guss, *Violence in America, Historical and Comparative Perspectives* (New York: Signet, 1969), passim. My initial electoral campaign participation dates from the 1960s, thus, I had direct observation in reference to many efforts in California. For some assessment of problems and discontent, see Grebler, *Mexican-American People*, pp. 517–41; *Hearings Before the United States Commission on Civil Rights* (San Francisco: January 1960; Washington, D.C.: Government Printing Office: 1960); U.S. President's Commission on Immigration and Naturalization, *Whom Shall We Welcome* (Washington, D.C.: Government Printing Office, 1953); Helen Rowan, *Mexican Americans in the Southwest: A Report Prepared for the U.S. Commission on Civil Rights* (Washington, D.C.: 1968); and Carlos M. Alcala and Jorge G. DeAngel, "Project Report: De Jure Segregation of Chicanos in Texas Schools," *Harvard Civil Rights-Civil Liberties Law Review*, vol. 7 (March 1972).

70. For some pre-1960 election data, see: Raymond Wolfinger, "Some Consequences of Ethnic Politics," in Kent Jennings and L. Harmon Ziegler, eds., *The Electoral Process* (Englewood Cliffs: Prentice-Hall, 1966); and Gabino Rendon, *Voting Behavior in a Tri-Ethnic Community* (San Francisco: R and E Association, 1977).

71. For Mexican American voter mobilization in Kennedy's behalf, see the direct observations of Louis Weshler and John Gallagher, "Viva Kennedy," in Rocco J. Tresolini and Richard T. Frast, eds., *Cases in American National Politics and Government* (Englewood Cliffs: Prentice-Hall, 1966); and the brief statement, twenty years later, in Pastora San Juan Cafferty and William C. McCready, eds., *Hispanics in the United States* (New Brunswick: Transaction, 1985), p. 245.

72. For MAPA, c. 1967–68, see MAPA (newsletter), November 11, 1968; "By-Laws of the Mexican American Political Association as Amended 1967"; and "Roster of Officers of the Mexican American Political Association as of February 22, 1968," all in mimeographs. See also Eduardo Quevedo, et al., "Open Resolution to the President of the United States and Executive Departments and Agencies by National Hispanic and Mexican American Organizations on Civil Disobedience and Riot Investigations," in Kaye L. Briegel, "The History of Political Organizations Among Mexican Americans in Los Angeles Since World War II" (Master's thesis, University of Southern California, Los Angeles, 1967), pp. 63–65; Ralph Guzman, "Politics and

Policies of the Mexican American Community," in Eugene P. Dvorin and Arthur I. Misner, eds., *California Politics and Policies* (Palo Alto: Addison-Wesley, 1966), pp. 350–84; and Kenneth Burt, *The History of the Mexican American Political Association and Chicano Politics in California* (Sacramento: MAPA, 1982).

73. See "Kennedy Patronage, Latin American Policies Under Fire," *Congressional Quarterly Weekly,* vol. 19 (June 23, 1961), pp. 1042–43; Marvin Alinsky, "The Mexican Americans Make Themselves Heard," *The Reporter,* vol. 36 (February 9, 1967), pp. 45–48; and "Another Civil Rights Headache—Plight of Mexican American," *U.S. News and World Report,* vol. 60 (June 6, 1966), pp. 46–48. For voter data, see Mark Levy and Michael Kramer, "Patterns of Chicano Voting Behavior," in F. Chris Garcia, ed., *La Causa Politica: A Chicano Politics Reader* (South Bend, Ind.: University of Notre Dame Press, 1974).

74. On the 1966 meeting, walkout, and consequent activity, see "Walkout in Albuquerque," *Carta Editorial,* vol. 3, no. 12 (April 8, 1966); Rowland Evans and Robert Novak, "Inside Report . . . the Mexican Revolt," *Washington Post* (March 31, 1966). See also Paul Beck, "Mexican American Walkout Mars U.S. Job Conference," *Los Angeles Times* (March 29, 1966); "Text of President's News Conference," *Washington Post* (May 21, 1966); Robert Thompson, "President Pledges Aid to Mexican Americans," *Los Angeles Times* (April 1, 1966); and Marvin Alisky, "The Mexican Americans Make Themselves Heard," *The Reporter,* vol. 36 (February 9, 1967), pp. 45–48.

75. For the El Paso conference, see *Testimony Presented at the Cabinet Committee Hearing on Mexican American Affairs* (Washington, D.C.: Interagency Committee on Mexican Americans, 1967); and Henry A. J. Ramos, *A People Forgotten . . . , pp. 92–112. See also The Presidents Remarks at the Installation of Commissioner Vicente T. Ximenes and a Cabinet Report on the Mexican American Community* (Washington, D.C.: Government Printing Office, 1967).

76. On the effects of the War on Poverty, see Biliana Maria Ambrecht, "Politicalization as a Legacy of the War on Poverty: A Study of Advisory Council Members in a Mexican American Community" (Ph.D. diss., University of California, Los Angeles, 1972); and V. Kurtz, "Politics, Ethnicity, Integration: Mexican Americans in the War on Poverty" (Ph.D. diss., University of California, Los Angeles, 1970). On the politics of 1966 and 1968 in Los Angeles, see Biliana Ambrecht and Harry Pachon, "Continuity and Change in a Mexican American Community: East Los Angeles, 1965–1972" (paper presented at the American Political Science Association, New Orleans, Louisiana, September 4–8, 1973).

77. On population between 1960 and 1970, see José Hernández, et al.,

"Census Data and the Problem of Conceptually Defining the Mexican American Population," *Social Science Quarterly,* vol. 53 (March 1973); The Mexican American Population Commission of California, "Report: Mexican American Population in California" (photostatic copy) (San Francisco, 1971). On grievances see "Another Civil-Rights Headache—Plight of Mexican American," *U.S. News and World Report* (June 6, 1966), p. 47. For an assessment of where the community stood in the mid-1960s, see Helen Rowan, "A Minority Nobody Knows," *Atlantic Monthly* (June 1967), pp. 47–52; and Samora, *La Raza,* passim. For a comparative and critical assessment of trends in the civil rights movement from a Chicano perspective, see Nick C. Vaca, "The Negro Movement as an Anti-revolution, *El Grito,* vol. 2 (Winter 1969).

78. On schooling, see *Summary of the Proceedings of the Twelfth Southwestern Conference: Social and Educational Problems of Rural and Urban Mexican American Youth* (Los Angeles: Occidental College, April 6, 1963). On problems of Mexican American youth, for extensive discussion on identity and on need for cross state cooperation, see "Report of the Southwest Conference in Interstate Inter-Group Relations" (Phoenix, Arizona, April 10–12, 1964); see also Walter Fogel, *Education and Income of Mexican-Americans in the Southwest,* Advance Report 1 (Mexican-American Study Project, University of California, Los Angeles, 1965), particularly table 5, p. 8.

79. On a major issue of employment discrimination, see "Railroad Unions Being Scrutinized by FEPC," *Forum News Bulletin* (October 1956); "Sen. Chavez Enters Railway Brotherhood Clause Tiff," *Forum News Bulletin* (November 1956); and "New Mexico Forums Win," *Forum News Bulletin* (January 1958). For discrimination in schools and schooling, see *Minerva Delgado, et al. v. Bastrop Independent School District of Bastrop County, Texas* (June 1948); Carlos M. Alcala and Jorge C. Rangel, "De Jure Segregation of Chicanos in Texas Schools," *Harvard Civil Rights and Civil Liberties Law Review,* vol. 7 (March 1972); George I. Sanchez and V. E. Strickland, *Study of the Educational Opportunities Provided Spanish-Named Children in the Texas School Systems* (Austin: University of Texas, 1974); and Gladys R. Leff, "George I. Sanchez: Don Quixote of the Southwest" (Ph.D. diss., North Texas State University, 1976).

Chapter 3

1. For a single-volume comprehensive description and assessment of the community during the sixties, see Leo Grebler, et al., eds., *The Mexican American People: The Nation's Second Largest Minority* (New York: Free Press, 1976), passim. For Mexican American Kennedy voter turnout, see: Louis Weshler and John Gallagher, "Viva Kennedy," in Rocco J. Tresolini, and

Richard T. Frast, eds., *Cases in American National Politics and Government* (New York: Prentice-Hall, 1966); and see comments in Pastora San Juan Cafferty and William C. McCready, eds., *Hispanics in the United States* (New Brunswick: Transaction, 1985). For an analysis of unrest across the country, see Allen J. Matusow, *The Unraveling of America: A History of Liberalism in the 1960s* (New York: Harper and Row, 1984); and Hugh Davis Graham and Ted Robert Gurr, *Violence in American, Historical and Comparative Perspectives* (New York: Signet, 1969). For impact of the Kennedy–Johnson programs on the community, see Biliana Maria Ambrecht, "Politicalization as a Legacy of the War on Poverty: A Study of Advisory Council Members in a Mexican American Community" (Ph.D. diss., University of California, Los Angeles, 1973).

2. For reference to this, see Senator Joseph M. Montoya, *The Congressional Record*, vol. 117, part 2 (May 6, 1971), pp. 13811–14; and for surrounding events, see "Walkout in Albuquerque," *Carta Editorial*, vol. 3, no. 12 (April 8, 1966). For an early electoral student effort, see Committee for a Democratic Vote, "Accomplishments in the 1964 Campaign" (unpublished report, Los Angeles: 1964). On the politics of 1966 and 1968 in one community, see Biliana Maria Ambrecht and Harry Pachon, "Continuity and Change in a Mexican American Community: East Los Angeles, 1965–1972" (paper presented at American Political Science Association, New Orleans, Louisiana, September 4–8, 1973). For an assessment of where the community stood in the mid-1960s, see "Another Civil-Rights Headache," *U.S. News and World Report* (June 6, 1966), p. 47; and Helen Rowan, "A Minority Nobody Knows," *Atlantic Monthly* (June 1967), pp. 47–52. On population between 1960 and 1970, see José Hernández, et al., "Census Data . . . ," *Social Science Quarterly*, vol. 53; José Hernández, et al., "Report: Mexican American Population Commission" (1973). See also Nick C. Vaca, "The Negro Movement as an Anti-revolution," *El Grito*, vol. 2, no. 2 (Winter 1969). On the rhetoric of the Chicano "movement," see John C. Hammerbach, et al., *A War of Words: Chicano Protest in the 1960s and 1970s* (Westport, Conn.: Greenwood Press, 1985). On issues and events, see Armando B. Rendon, *Chicano Manifesto: The History and Aspirations of the Second Largest Minority in America* (New York: Collier Books, 1971).

3. The "movement" newspapers are the most readily available source for events and issues. For printed collections of statements, see: Luis Valdez and Stan Steiner, eds., *Aztlan: An Anthology of Chicano Literature* (New York: Vintage, 1972); Philip D. Ortego, ed., *We Are Chicanos* (New York: Washington Square Press, 1973); Edward Simmen, ed., *Pain and Promise: The Chicano Today* (New York: Mentor, 1972). For a poll on preferred designations, see "A Box Full of Ethnic Labels," *Los Angeles Times* (July 25, 1983). For a discussion of the term *Chicano*, see Tino Villanueva, "Prologo," part

1, "Sobre el termino 'Chicano,'" in Tino Villanueva, comp., *Chicanos: Antología histórica y literaría* (México, D.F.: Fondo de Cultura Economica, 1980), pp. 7–67. For an advocacy of terms, see Tom Pino and Daniel Valdez, "Ethnic Labels in Majority–Minority Relations," *Journal of Mexican American Studies*, vol. 1, no. 1 (Fall 1970), pp. 16–30. For the denunciation of the movement by the established leadership, see Henry B. González, *Congressional Record, House of Representatives* (April 22, 1969); Eligio de la Garza, "Reverse Racism," *Congressional Record, House* (April 28, 1969); Edward R. Roybal, "Cabinet Committee on Opportunities for Spanish-Speaking People," *Congressional Record, House* (December 16, 1969); and Joseph P. Montoya, "The Silent People No Longer," *Congressional Record, Senate* (November 17, 1967). The statements of federal officials were recorded and were accessible; the statements of organizational representatives were not, and among them were those by all major groups. On class interaction within the movement, see Armando Navarro, "The Evolution of Chicano Politico," *Aztlan*, vol. 5 (1974), pp. 80–81. For an endorsement of the movement by the established leadership, see Joseph Montoya, *Congressional Record, Senate* (October 29, 1971); for a Chicano perspective on the Black movement, see Nick C. Vaca, "The Negro Movement as an Anti-revolution." On the movement's evolution between the late 1960s and early 1970s, see Armando Navarro, "Evolution of Chicano Politics," pp. 57–84; see also C. Muñoz, *Youth, Identity, Power* (New York: Verso, 1989).

4. For a statement by Chavez, see John R. Moyer, "A Conversation with Cesar Chavez," *Journal of Current Social Issues*, vol. 9 (November–December 1970). The literature on the UFW and Cesar Chavez is considerable and nearly all laudatory; see: Jacques Levy, *Cesar Chavez: Autobiography of La Causa* (New York: Norton, 1975); and Dick Meister and Anne Loftis, *A Long Time Coming: The Struggle to Unionize America's Farm Workers* (New York: Macmillan, 1977). For articles in the contemporary national press, see *Look* magazine (April 1969), *Christian Century* (February 18, 1970), and *Ramparts* (July 1966). For the origins of the union, see Sam Kushner, *Long Road to Delano* (New York: International Publishers, 1975).

5. The Plan de Delano (typescript, n.d., photostatic copy); the plan is sometimes reprinted with the title of "Farm Worker's Manifesto." For commentary and a printed version, see Valdez and Steiner, *Aztlan*, pp. 197–218; for an early printing of the Plan and excellent photos, see *Basta, La Historia de Nuestra Lucha* (Delano: Farmworkers Press, 1966).

6. For a critical assessment of Cesar Chavez in politics, see Harry Bernstein, "Farm Union: Why Didn't It Burgeon?" *Los Angeles Times* (December 6, 1982); and "Cesar Chavez," *El Laberinto* (University of Iowa), vol. 12, no. 3 (May 1985). For a view from within the union, see Dolores Huerta,

"Dolores Huerta Talks About Republicans, Cesar, Children, and Her Home Town," *La Voz del Pueblo* (November–December 1972).

7. For the interpretation of events by those working close to the Johnson administration, see Henry A. J. Ramos, *A People Forgotten, A Dream Pursued: The History of the American G.I. Forum* (American G.I. Forum, 1983), pp. 92–112; in contrast, see Armando B. Rendon, *Chicano Manifesto*, pp. 114–37.

8. On the conference and Plan de la Raza Unida, see *La Raza* (November 15, 1967); in contrast to this coverage, see *Forumeer* (October 5, 1967); and for what some meant by "La Raza," see Jorge Lara Brand, "What Is La Raza," *La Raza Yearbook* (September 1968). For the views of Ernesto Galarza in the midsixties, see "La mula no nacio arisca . . . ," *Center Diary* (September–October 1966).

9. On the Southwest Council of La Raza, see Y. A. Cabrera, *Emerging Faces: The Mexican-Americans* (Dubuque, Iowa: William C. Brown, 1971), pp. 34–36. For the view of the community and of the needs which served as its premise, see Ernesto Galarza, Herman Gallegos, and Julian Samora, *Mexican-Americans in the Southwest* (Santa Barbara: McNally and Loftin, 1969), passim; and Henry Santiesteban, "Southwest Council of La Raza Balance Sheet," *Agenda*, no. 1 (Summer 1973), pp. 16–17. For news reports on the funding of the SWCLR, see *Christian Science Monitor* (May 3, 1968 and July 31, 1968); and the *New York Times* (June 17, 1968), p. 24.

10. On MALDEF, see MALDEF, *Diez Años* (MALDEF: San Francisco, 1978); and MALDEF, "Bylaws and Incorporation Statement" (photostatic copy, 1967).

11. On the Crusade for Justice and Rodolfo González, see: *La Raza* (July 10, 1968); Rodolfo Corky González, "What Political Road for the Chicano Militant," *The Militant* (March 30, 1970); *El Gallo: La Voz de la Justicia*, vol. 1, no. 6, to vol. 12, no. 2 (January 1968 to March–April 1980); Christine Marin, *A Spokesman of the Mexican American Movement: Rodolfo "Corky" Gonzales and the Fight for Chicano Liberation 1966–1972* (San Francisco: R and E Research Association, 1977); and Armando A. Navarro, "Evolution of Chicano Politics," p. 76.

12. For the Poor People's March and the Plan del Barrio, see *La Raza* (July 10, 1968) and *La Raza Yearbook* (September 1968).

13. On the Alianza, see: Reies Lopez Tijerina, "Letter from the Santa Fe Jail," *El Grito Del Norte* (September 26, 1970); *Mi Lucha por La Tierra* (México, D.F.: Fondo de Cultura Economica, 1978); Father Robert G. Garcia, "The Alianza: A Hope and a Dream" (statement), Subcommittee on Rural Development, U.S. Congress, House (June 12, 1967); Peter Nabokov, *Tijerina and the Court House Raid* (Albuquerque: University of New Mexico

Press, 1969); and Richard Gardner, *Grito! Reies Tijerina and the New Mexico Land Grand War of 1967* (Indianapolis: Bobbs-Merrill, 1970).

14. For the Alianza interpretation of the Treaty of Guadalupe Hidalgo, see *The Spanish Land Grant Question Examined* (Albuquerque: Alianza Federal, 1966); and Clark S. Knowlton, "The New Mexican Land War," *The Nation* (June 17, 1968). For the impact of the treaty, see Richard Griswold del Castillo, "The Chicano Movement and the Treaty of Guadalupe Hidalgo," in Juan R. Garcia, et al., *In Times of Challenge: Chicanos and Chicanas in American Society* (Houston: Mexican American Studies Program, University of Houston, 1988).

15. For coverage on the Tijerina trial and Constitutional Party, see *La Raza* (August 15, 1968).

16. On the decline of the Alianza, see Reies Lopez Tijerina, *Mi lucha por la tierra*, passim.

17. In the author's possession are files of over fifty interviews and extensive typed or printed material. On the student movement, see Juan Gómez-Quiñones, *Mexican Students for La Raza* (Santa Barbara, La Causa Publications, 1978); and Carlos Muñoz and Mario Barrera, "La Raza Unida Party and the Chicano Student Movement in California," *Social Science Journal*, vol. 19 (April 1982). For 1970s mobilization, see Carlos M. Haro, *The Bakke Decision: The Question of Chicano Access to Higher Education* (Los Angeles: Chicano Studies, University of California, Los Angeles, 1977).

18. See Chicano Coordinating Council on Higher Education, *El Plan de Santa Barbara* (Oakland: La Causa Publications, 1969). On Mexican Americans and educational achievement, see Ron W. Lopez and Darryl D. Enos, *Chicanos and Public Higher Education in California* (Joint Committee on the Master Plan for Higher Education, California Legislature, Sacramento: December 1972); United States Commission on Civil Rights, *Ethnic Isolation of Mexican Americans in the Public Schools of the Southwest*, Report 1 (Washington, D.C.: U.S. Government Printing Office, April 1971); United States Commission on Civil Rights, *The Unfinished Education. Outcomes for Minorities in the Five Southwestern States: Mexican American*, Report 2 (Washington, D.C.: U.S. Government Printing Office, October 1971); United States Commisison on Civil Rights, *The Excluded Student—Educational Practices Affecting Mexican Americans in the Southwest*, Report 3 (Washington, D.C.: U.S. Government Printing Office, May 1972); United States Commission on Civil Rights, *Mexican American Education in Texas: A Function of Wealth*, Report 4 (Washington, D.C.: U.S. Government Printing Office, August 1972); and United States Commission on Civil Rights, *Teachers and Students—Differences in Teacher Interaction with Mexican American and Anglo Students*, Report 5 (Washington, D.C.: U.S. Government Printing Office, March 1973).

19. On the Brown Berets, see the organization's newspaper *La Causa*,

vol. 1 (1970) and vol. 2 (1971); David Sanchez, *Expedition through Aztlan* (La Puente, Calif.: Perspectiva Press, 1978); and Sanchez, *Material for the Chicano Activist* (mimeographed, 1970). For a statement by a counterpart group, see Black Beret organization, "The Black Berets," in F. Chris Garcia, ed., *La Causa Política: A Chicano Politics Reader* (South Bend, Ind.: University of Notre Dame Press, 1974), pp. 405–6.

20. On late sixties women's activities, see: *Carta Editorial* (1967–1970); *Encuentro Femenil*, vol. 1, no. 1 (Spring 1973), and vol. 1, no. 2 (1974); *Las Hijas de Cuauhtemoc* (unnumbered edition, c. 1970); *Regeneración*, vol. 1 and 2 (1970–1971); Enriqueta Longeaux y Vasquez, "The Women of La Raza," *La Raza* (July 1969); "'Chicanas' in the Movement," *La Raza* (December 1969); Patricia Hernández, "Lives of Chicana Activists: The Chicano Student Movement," in Magdalena Mora and Adelaida R. del Castillo, eds., *Mexican Women in the United States: Struggles Past and Present* (Los Angeles: Chicano Studies Research Center, University of California, Los Angeles, 1980); and Sonia Lopez, "The Role of the Chicana within the Student Movement," in Rosaura Sanchez, et al., *Essays on la Mujer* (Los Angeles: Chicano Studies Research Center, University of California, Los Angeles, 1977).

21. On the Los Angeles "blowouts," see coverage in "Inside East Side, The Chicano Movement," *La Raza* (March–June 1968); and Dial Torgerson, "Brown Power Unity Seen Behind School Disorder," *Los Angeles Times* (March 17, 1968); Ray Santana and Mario Esparza, "East Los Angeles Blowouts," in *Parameters of Institutional Change: Chicano Experience in Education* (Hayward Southwest Network, 1974); and Gerald Rosen, "The Development of the Chicano Movement in Los Angeles from 1967 to 1969," *Aztlan*, vol. 4 (Spring 1973), pp. 155–83.

22. For coverage, see: *El Gallo, La Raza,* and *La Verdad* (March–July 1969); and *El Grito del Norte*, vol. 2, no. 9 (July 1969).

23. Plan de Aztlan (handwritten manuscript, March 1969). Committee original is in my possession; I served on the drafting committee with four other members, among them Luis Valdez and Jorge Gonzalez. For the printed plan and program, see *La Verdad* (San Diego), vol. 1 (June 1969). This issue also contains the poem by Alurista, "Bronce Breath," which was a basic point of departure and a synthesis of early interpretive comments by R. "Corky" Gonzalez. Regrettably and erroneously, in some anthology reprints of the Plan, at the end there appears a meaningless phrase "To hell with the nothing race," which may have been inserted by someone who did not understand Spanish. Two *lemas* were circulated for the bottom on the printed plan: one "Por La Raza, Para La Raza," which harkens back to the 1911 *congreso;* and the other "Dentro de la Raza todo, Fuera de la Raza nada," which harkens to "Dentro de la revolucion . . ." The historical and contemporary content

of these two phrases is very distinct from "To hell . . . ," allegedly inserted by a non-Mexican in a version circulated by the "radical caucus."

24. For statements at the time on schooling–education, see: Southwest Network (Armando Valdez, ed.), *Parameters of Institutional Change: Chicano Experiences in Education* (1974); and Chicano Coordinating Council on Higher Education, *El Plan de Santa Barbara, A Chicano Plan for Higher Education* (Oakland: La Causa Publications, 1969). At the state and national level, there were several efforts to form professional groups of persons in higher education. See Reynaldo Flores Macias, ed., *Perspectivas en Chicano Studies Papers*, presented at the Third Annual Meeting of the National Association of Chicano Social Science (Los Angeles: Chicano Studies Center, University of California, Los Angeles, 1977); and *Directory of Fellows 1977–1978* (Berkeley: National Chicano Council on Higher Education, 1980). For the effort in education, see Guadalupe San Miguel, *"Let All of Them Take Heed": Mexican Americans and the Campaign for Educational Equality* (Austin: University of Texas Press, 1987).

25. For eyewitness accounts, photographs, and statements on the moratorium, see: *La Raza*, vol. 1 (October 1970), p. 32; and Armando Morales, *Ando Sangrando* (Los Angeles: Congress of Mexican American Unity, 1974), pp. 91–122. See also Herbert Marcuse, "Riot and Representation: The Significance of the Chicano Riot" (photostatic copy, pamphlet, n.d., n.p.); "Inaction, Growing Militancy Viewed as Causes of Riots," *Los Angeles Times* (August 31, 1970); and William J. Drummond, "How East LA Protest Turned into Major Riot," *Los Angeles Times* (September 16, 1970). For a critique, see Antonio Camejo, "Lessons of the Los Angeles Chicano Protest," *The Militant*, vol. 3, no. 38 (October 16, 1970).

26. On the death of Ruben Salazar, see: Hank Lopez, "Overkill at the Silver Dollar," *The Nation* (October 19, 1970); and José Angel de la Vera, "1970 Chicano Moratorium and the Death of Ruben Salazar," in Manuel Servin, ed., *The Mexican Americans: An Awakened Minority* (Beverly Hills: Glencoe Press, 1974). For writings by Ruben Salazar, see *Stranger in One's Land* (Washington, D.C.: U.S. Commission on Civil Rights, U.S. Government Printing Office, May 1970).

27. On the origins of La Raza Unida and the leadership, see: "The Del Rio Mexican American Manifesto to the Nation (March 30, 1969)" (photostatic copy, n.d., n.p.); José Angel Gutiérrez, *A Gringo Manual on How to Handle Mexicans* (Crystal City: Wintergarden Publishing, n.d.); "Mexicanos Need to Control Their Own Destinies," in *La Raza Unida Party in Texas* (New York: Pathfinder Press, 1971); *El Político* (El Paso: Mitla Publications, 1972); and "Aztlan: Chicano Revolt in the Winter Garden," *La Raza*, vol. 1, no. 4 (1971), pp. 34–37. See also George Rivera, "Social Change in the Barrio: The Chicano Movement in South Texas," *Aztlan*, vol. 3 (Fall 1972). The

most complete coverage of the party available is the one by LRUP activist Ignacio M. Garcia, *United We Win, The Rise and Fall of La Raza Unida Party* (Tucson: Mexican American Studies and Research Center, University of Arizona, 1989).

28. On Crystal City, see Armando G. Gutierrez and Herbert Hirsch, "Political Maturation and Political Awareness: The Case of the Crystal City Chicano," *Aztlan*, vol. 5 (1974); and John Staples Shockley, *Chicano Revolt in a Texas Town* (South Bend, Ind.: University of Notre Dame, 1974), passim.

29. On the thinking and tactics of La Raza Unida, see: Armando Navarro, "El Partido de la Raza Unida in Crystal City: A Peaceful Revolution" (Ph.D. diss., University of California, Riverside, 1974).

30. On the 1972 El Paso Conference, see: *The Militant* (September 22, 1972); Richard Santillan, *La Raza Unida* (Los Angeles: Tlaquito Publications, 1973), pp. 148–50; and John L. Espinosa, "Raza Unida Conference: Unidos Quedaremos," *La Luz* (October 1872), pp. 10–12. The major statement was "Draft of Constitution of La Raza Unida Party adopted as governing instrument for La Raza Unida Party in the El Paso Convention" (September 1972). R. Santillan's work graphically conveys not only a narrative of events, but also the thoughts, feeling, attitudes, and words of LRUP.

31. On La Raza Unida in California, see Alberto Juárez, "The Emergence of El Partido de la Raza Unida California's New Chicano Party," *Aztlan*, vol. 3, no. 2 (Fall 1972); Richard Santillan, *La Raza Unida* (Los Angeles: Tlaquito Publications, 1973); and Richard Santillan, "The Politics of Cultural Nationalism: El Partido de La Raza Unida in Southern California 1969–1978" (Ph.D. diss., Claremont Graduate School, 1978).

32. *Los Angeles Times* (November 18, 1971); for a view favorable to LRUP, see Santillan, *La Raza Unida*, pp. 84–85. Brophy benefited from a widely reported incident immediately prior to the election in which he claimed that his home had been fired into.

33. *Los Angeles Times* (August 30, 1973, and August 16, 1974). The reference to the Democrat is in the August 30, 1973, issue. See also *Los Angeles Times* (November 22, 1972).

34. On the past incorporation efforts, see: Reynaldo F. Macias, et al., *A Study of Unincorporated East Los Angeles* (Los Angeles: Chicano Studies Research Center, University of California, Los Angeles, 1973); *Los Angeles Times* (August 16, 30, and November 16, 1974); Jaime Raigoza, "The East Los Angeles Cityhood Measure," *Campo Libre*, vol. 1, no. 1 (Winter 1981), pp. 1–23; and Frank del Olmo, "Defeat of East LA Plan Laid to Fear of High Property Tax," *Los Angeles Times* (November 7, 1974).

35. See Tony Castro, *Chicano Power: The Emergence of Mexican America* (New York: Saturday Review Press, 1974), pp. 94–100.

36. *Los Angeles Times* (November 22, 1972); and *Los Angeles Times* (February 9, 1973). On the major issue of reapportionment, see Richard Santillan, *California Reapportionment and the Chicano Community* (Claremont: Rose Institute, Claremont Men's College, 1981).

37. *Los Angeles Times* (January 16, 1973); see also issues of the *Times* for February 21, 1973, and September 3, 1973.

38. José Angel Gutierrez, "Chicanos and Mexicanos under Surveillance, 1940–1980," *Renato Rosaldo Lecture Series Monograph*, vol. 2, series 1984–85 (Spring 1986); see also Ward Churchill and James V. Wall, *Agents of Repression: The FBI's Secret War Against the American Indian Movement and the Black Panther Party* (Boston: South End Press, 1988).

39. On art and critiques of cultural expression, see the extensive bibliography in Shifra M. Goldman and Tomas Ybarra-Frausto, *Arte Chicano* (Berkeley: Chicano Studies Library, 1985).

40. The available sources on these organizations and their activities are the newspapers of the organizations.

41. For an assessment of this literature, see Antonio Rios Bustamente, *Mexicans in the United States and the National Question* (Santa Barbara, Calif.: La Causa, 1978).

42. On the SWP and its involvement, see issues of *The Militant* (1967–1978); see specifically: Elizabeth Barnes, "Bourgeois Democracy and the Struggle for Socialism," *The Militant* (June 27, 1969), p. 4; Peter Camejo, *How to Make a Revolution in the U.S.* (New York: Merit Publishers, 1969); Tony Camejo, "A Contribution on the Chicano Struggle," *Young Socialist Alliance Discussion Bulletin No. 3*, vol. 3, no. 6 (December 22, 1969); Norman Hodgett, "Information and Proposals on the Mexican-American Struggle," *Socialist Workers Party Discussion Bulletin*, vol. 27, no. 6 (July 1969); Gus Horowitz, "P. L.'s Attack on Black Nationalism," *The Militant* (January 31, 1969), p. 7; Willie Petty, "Third World People and the Struggle Against the War," *Young Socialist Alliance Discussion Bulletin No. 2*, vol. 13, no. 5 (December 15, 1969); Della Rossa, "The Chicano Movement in Los Angeles," *Socialist Workers Party Discussion Bulletin*, vol. 27, no. 10 (August 1969); Della Rossa, "West Coast Chicanos Hit Viet War," *The Militant* (January 16, 1970), p. 3; Joel Britton, "Report to the Political Committee on the Chicano Movement" (photostatic copy, New York, February 24, 1970); Juan Suarez (pseudonym), "On the Mexican Question" (typescript, Internal Bulletin, Los Angeles City Convention, 1949). For reference to SWP intervention in a Chicano Studies program see Gustavo V. Segade, "Identity and Power: An Essay on the Politics of Culture and the Culture of Politics in Chicano Thought," *Aztlan*, vol. 9 (1978), pp. 90–91.

43. The most readily available source on CASA is the newspaper *Sin Fronteras* (1974–1978); there are also available documents, the *Reglamento*

and *Who We Are,* a lengthy report on two dozen labor organizing efforts and various typescript assessments of reasons leading to the closure of the organization. One published study on CASA—David Gutierrez, "CASA in the Chicano Movement: A Study of Organizational Politics and Ideology in the Chicano Community, 1968–1978" (unpublished paper, Stanford University, Department of History, 1984)—is marred by errors of facts and misinformed analysis; for an informed commentary, see Arturo Santa María Gomez, *La izquierda norteamericana y los trabajadores indocumentados* (México D.F.: Ediciones de Cultura Popular, Universidad Autonoma de Sinaloa, 1988).

44. On the August Twenty-ninth movement, see *Fan the Flames: A Revolutionary Position on the Chicano National Question* (Los Angeles: ATM, 1976); issues of *Revolutionary Cause* (1976–77); and *The Red Banner, The Theoretical Journal of the August Twenty-Ninth Movement (ML),* vol. 1 (Winter 1976–77). On the League of Revolutionary Struggle, see *Forward,* vol. 1–vol. 7 (1979–87).

Chapter 4

1. On voter characteristics, see Rudolph O. de la Garza, "Voting Patterns in Bi-cultural El Paso: A Contextual Analyses of Mexican American Voting Behavior," *Aztlan,* vol. 5 (1974), pp. 235–60; Donald M. Freeman, "Party, Vote, and the Mexican American in South Tucson," in F. Chris Garcia, ed., *La Causa Politica: A Chicano Politics Reader* (South Bend, Ind.: University of Notre Dame Press, 1974); Mark Levy and Michael Kramer, *The Ethnic Factor: How Minorities Decide Elections* (New York: Simon and Schuster, 1973), pp. 73–85, 248–51; Clifton McCleskey and Bruce Merrill, "Mexican American Political Behavior in Texas," *Social Science Quarterly,* vol. 53 (March 1973), pp. 783–98; Clifton McCleskey and Dan Nimmo, "Differences between Potential, Registered and Actual Voters: The Houston Metropolitan Area in 1974," *Social Science Quarterly,* vol. 49 (June 1968), pp. 103–14; Robert R. Brischetto and Rodolfo de la Garza, *The Mexican American: Political Participation and Ideology* (Austin: Center for Mexican American Studies, University of Texas at Austin, 1983); and Dick Kirschten, "The Hispanic Vote—Parties Can't Gamble that the Sleeping Won't Awaken," *National Journal,* vol. 19 (1983), p. 2410. On districts, see Richard Hamner, "Hispanics and Redistricting," *National Hispanic Journal,* vol. 2, no. 2 (Winter 1982); Robert R. Brischetto and Willie Velasquez, *The Hispanic Electorate* (Washington, D.C.: Hispanic Policy Development Project, 1984); and Southwest Voter Research Institute, "The Hispanic Vote in 1988: U.S., California, Texas, and New Mexico" (San Antonio, Tex.: SVRI, Fall 1988).

2. On the 1968 elections, see Mark Levy and Michael Kramer, "Patterns

of Chicano Voting Behavior," in F. Chris Garcia, *La Causa Política: A Chicano Politics Reader* (South Bend, Ind.: University of Notre Dame Press, 1974).

3. On the McGovern campaign, see the brochures "72 Year of the People," as well as those entitled "McGovern es Mejor Para Nostros" and "Justice, Education, Jobs"; the "McGovern 8-Point Position in the Chicano Community"; and the work by a major participant, Gary W. Hart, *Right from the Start* (New York: Quadrangle–New York Times Book Co., 1973). The demands made on the campaign by the Latino Caucus were communicated by a letter from Joe J. Bernal and Herman Badillo to the Honorable George McGovern, August 9, 1972 (photostatic copy); for a statement on the community by George McGovern a year before the primary, see "The Mexican Americans—Neglected Fellow Citizens," *Congressional Record*, 92nd Congress, 1st sess., Senate, vol. 117, no. 55 (April 21, 1971).

4. On politics between 1972 and 1974, see *SSA-Adelante*, Democratic National Committee, Division of Spanish Speaking Affairs; and Maurilio Vigil, *Chicano Politics* (Washington, D.C.: University Press of America, 1978), passim.

5. See Frank C. Lemus, *National Roster of Spanish Surnamed Elected Officials* (Los Angeles: Chicano Studies Research Center, University of California, 1974); *Directory of Democratic Spanish Surnamed Elected Officials*, Division of Spanish Speaking Affairs, Democratic National Committee (October 1975); and Arthur D. Martínez, *Who's Who: Chicano Officeholders 1977–1978* (Silver City: Western New Mexico University, 1978); NALEO, *1984 National Roster of Hispanic Elected Officials* (Washington, D.C.: NALEO, Education Fund, 1984); and "U.S. Hispanic Elected Officials Climb to 3,202," *Hispanic Link Weekly Report* (September 23, 1985). For specific background information and legislation sponsored by congressional representatives, see United States Congress, *Congressional Directory* (Washington, D.C.: Government Printing Office, 1974). For an analysis of Mexicans in the federal bureaucracy in the early seventies, see Rudolph Gomez, "Mexican Americans in American Bureaucracy," in Frank L. Baird, ed., *Mexican Americans: Political Power, Influence or Resource* (Lubbock: Texas Tech University, 1977), pp. 11–19; and Harry Pachon, "Hispanic Underrepresentation in the Federal Bureaucracy: The Missing Link in the Policy Process" in Armando Valdez, et al., *The State of Chicano Research on Family, Labor, and Migration* (Stanford, Calif.: Stanford Center for Chicano Research, 1983).

6. On Mexicans in the Republican Party, see Tony Castro, *Chicano Power: The Emergence of Mexican America* (New York: Saturday Review Press, 1974), pp. 198–214; Maria D. Garcia Fonseca, "Conferencia del Liderazgo Hispano 1985 de la Republican National Hispanic Assembly," *Noticias del Mundo* (September 9, 1985); Velma Montoya, "Latinos Are Shifting in Their Basic Concerns," *Los Angeles Times* (January 25, 1984); and Peter Sherry, "The

Ambiguity of Mexican American Politics," in Nathan Glazer, ed., *Clamor at the Gates: The New American Immigration* (San Francisco: Institute for Contemporary Studies Press, 1985), pp. 241–55. For a prescription as to how Republican appointees should act, see notarized statement by Lupe L. Franco, "Mexican-American Appointees" (April 25, 1972; photostatic copy); and Jessica Lee, "GOP Reveals $300,000 Plan to Win Over Hispanic Voters," *USA Today* (April 24, 1986); Stephen Goode, "Cathi Villalpando, Special Assistant to the President," *Nuestro* (January–February 1985), pp. 16–18.

7. On Mexicans and the Democratic Party, see *Directory of Democratic Spanish Surnamed Elected Officials* (Washington, D.C.: Division of Spanish Speaking Affairs, Democratic National Committee, October 1975); "Latino Democrats Approve National Organization," press release, Office of Representative Edward R. Roybal, November 4, 1975; "Latino Representation in Congress Remains Low: Progress at National Level Debatable," *Nuestro* (March 1982), pp. 19–21; Daryl Lembke, "Mexican-American Governors, Ethnic Barriers Fall in Southwest Elections," *Los Angeles Times* (November 17, 1974); see also Richard Santillan, "The Latino Community in State and Congressional Redistricting, 1961–1985," *Journal of Hispanic Poltics*, vol. 1, no. 1 (1985).

8. See Division of Spanish Speaking Affairs, Democratic National Committee, "Things to Keep in Mind about Hispanic Community" (handout, n.d.); Frank del Olmo, "Ford-Carter Race: Latins Looking Not Yet Buying," *Los Angeles Times* (September 29, 1976). A graphic depiction of underrepresentation is the *1970 California Roster of Federal, State, County and City Officials*, compiled by the secretary of state (Sacramento: Office of Documents, 1970).

9. "Minutes, Democratic National Convention, Latin Caucus, July 10–14, 1972" (mimeographed copy); and see Division of Spanish Speaking Affairs, Democratic National Committee, *SSA Adelante* (July, August 1976).

10. For development within the DNC, see its newsletter; and on delegates, see "Con su voto, with your vote," *Democratic National Committee, Newsletter* (Summer 1984), p. 3.

11. See the reports of the Southwest Voter Registration Project.

12. On the Southwest Voter Registration Education Project, see David V. Cruz, "Takeover in Texas," *Nuestro*, vol. 2, no. 7 (July 1978), pp. 11–12; and Southwest Voter Registration Education Project, "Latino Political Participation, January 20, 1976" (handout). On MALDEF voting priorities and projects, see MALDEF, "Bylaws and Incorporation Statement" (photostatic copy); and *Diez Anos* (San Francisco: MALDEF, 1978).

13. On National Association of Latino Elected and Appointed Officials (NALEO), see introduction to NALEO, *1984 National Roster of Hispanic Elected Officials* (Washington, D.C.: NALEO, Education Fund, 1984); as

well as NALEO, *National Report* (newsletter), vol. 7, no. 4 (January–March 1987); and Patricia C. Ramirez, "NALEO and the Caucus," *Agenda* (March–April 1979), p. 7.

14. On trade unions and the electoral process, see Labor Council for Latin American Advancement (LACLAA), *La Voz Latina* and *Organize Today—Victory Tomorrow*, Officers Report, 6th national membership meeting, St. Louis, September 24–27, 1986; and Juan Gómez-Quiñones, "Realization and Growth with Progress in Doubt, Mexican Labor in the United States, 1965–1985" (unpublished manuscript).

15. On national lobbies, see Christine Sierra, "The Political Transformation of a Minority Organization, The Council of *La Raza* 1965–1980" (Ph.D. diss., Stanford University, 1982); and "A Citizen Lobby for the Spanish Speaking," *Agenda* (Third Quarter 1975); Moises Sandoval, "The Struggle Within LULAC," *Nuestro* (September 1979), pp. 30–32; Moises Sandoval, *Our Legacy: The First Fifty Years* (Washington, D.C.: League of United Latin American Citizens, 1979); Ron Ozio, "The Hell with Being Quiet and Dignified, Says Ruben Bonilla," *Nuestro* (September 1979), pp. 31–32.

16. On El Congreso (National Congress of Hispanic American Citizens), see Manuel Fierro, "An Open Letter to President Ford," *La Luz*, vol. 5, no. 1 (March 1976), pp. 8–9.

17. On professional and business organizations, see *A Guide to Hispanic Organizations* (New York: Philip Morris, 1979); as well as publications such as Office of Minority Business Enterprise, *Directory of Private Programs Assisting Minority Business, 1970* (Washington, D.C.: Government Printing Office, 1970); and the annual reports of NDEA.

18. On Congress, see *Congressional Hispanic Caucus Report*, 1987; and Susan Welch and John Hibbing, "Hispanic Representation in the U.S. Congress," *Social Sciences Quarterly*, vol. 65, no. 2 (June 1984).

19. On state elected officials and elections, see Maurilio E. Vigil, "Hispanics in Public Office," *Hispanics in American Politics, The Search for Political Power* (Washington, D.C.: University Press of America, 1987), pp. 77–110; see also Tatcho Mindiola, "Chicano and Black Legislators in the 67th Legislative Session" (photostatic copy of the transcript of an analysis presented to the Texas Mexican American Legislative Caucus, c. 1982).

20. A collection of newspaper articles on local elected officials and elections is in the author's possession. For general accounts, see Maurilio E. Vigil, *Hispanics in American Politics*, and Susan A. MacMannus and Carol A. Cassel, "Mexican Americans in City Politics: Participation, Representation and Policy Preferences," *Urban Interest*, vol. 4 (Spring 1982).

21. Interview with Jesús García on Chicago politics, Los Angeles, August 27, 1986.

22. On appointed officials, see various newspaper articles and Vigil, *Hispanics in American Politics*. Officials have been appointed to modest positions since the nineteenth century.

23. On population and voter characteristics and projections, see "Voting and Registration in the Election of November 1984," *Population Characteristics*, series P-20, no. 405 (Washington, D.C.: U.S. Department of Commerce, Bureau of the Census, March 1986); and Robert D. Wrinkle and Lawrence W. Miller, "A Note on Mexican American Voter Registration and Turnout," *Social Science Quarterly*, vol. 65, no. 2 (June 1964).

24. For the electoral college influence potential, the basic initial analysis was *The Electoral College and the Mexican-American: An Analysis of the Mexican-American Impact on the 1972 Presidential Election* (photostatic copy of typescript, c. 1972). This was issued by the Mexican American Bar Association, the Mexican American Population Commisison, and the League of United Latin American Citizens and Public Advocates. See also Andrew Hernández, "The Latin Vote in the 1976 Presidential Elections" (San Antonio: Southwest Voter Registration Education Project, 1977); Choco González Meza, "The Latin Vote in the 1980 Election: Political Research Report" (San Antonio: Southwest Voter Registration Education Project, January 1981); and Mary Lenz, "The Emerging Hispanic Vote," *The Texas Observer* (February 20, 1987), p. 11. On electoral politics, 1976–1984, see Vigil, *Hispanics in American Politics*.

25. On the Voting Rights Act, see "Voting," *Congressional Quarterly Weekly*, vol. 40, no. 26 (June 26, 1982); Roberto and José Aragon, "Needed a Chicano Voting Rights Act Now," *Regeneración*, vol. 5, no. 1 (1970); and Public Law 89-110-August 6, 1985, 42USC, Sec. 1973C (1982).

26. On the middle class and its politics vis-à-vis movement groups, see Navarro, "The Evolution of Chicano Politics," p. 79. For an overview of organizations, see Henry Santiesteban, "A Persepctive on Mexican American Organizations" in Gus Tyler, ed., *Mexican Americans Tomorrow: Educational and Economic Perspectives* (Albuquerque: University of New Mexico Press, 1975), pp. 164–202. For an overview of groups, see César Caballero, *Chicano Organizations Directory* (New York: Neal-Schuman, 1985) and Sylvia Alicia González, *Hispanic American Voluntary Organizations* (Westport, Conn.: Greenwood Press, 1985).

27. On national organizations, see Amaury Cruz, "LULAC Reports New Stance," *Nuestro* (April 1982), pp. 13–15; *The Forumeer* (May 1973). For book-length studies, see Carl Alsop, *The American G.I. Forum: Origins and Evolution* (Austin: Center for Mexican American Studies, University of Texas, 1982); Moises Sandoval, *Our Legacy: The First Fifty Years* (Washington, D.C.: LULAC, 1979), passim; and Benjamin Márquez, "The Politics of Race and

Class: The League of United Latin American Citizens in the Post World War II Period," *Social Sciences Quarterly*, vol. 68 (March 1987).

28. On the interagency, see "Cabinet Committee on the Spanish Speaking: Its Information and Its History," *La Luz*, vol. 1, no. 1 (1972), pp. 18–19.

29. On IMAGE, see Henry Santiesteban, "Image Rapidly Growing Group," *Agenda*, no. 1 (Summer 1973), p. 12.

30. See *A Guide to Hispanic Organizations* (New York: Philip Morris, 1979); Robert Montemayor, "Attorneys: Developing the Power Base," *Hispanic Business* (May 1985), pp. 24–35; Herman Gallegos, "Hispanics Need a Strategy for the 90s," *Hispanic Business* (February 1985), p. 10; and "100 Influentials and Their Assessment of the Critical Hispanic Issues," *Hispanic Business* (September 1985), pp. 18, 33.

31. On women in politics, see the special issue of *Intercambios Femeniles*, vol. 2, no. 3 (Autumn 1984); and Virginia Escalante, et al., "Inside the World of Latinas," *Los Angeles Times* (August 7, 1983). For political progress of Latinos and women, see Cal Clark, Janet Clark, and José Z. García, "Policy Impacts on Hispanics and Women: A Case Study," in Mariam Lief Palley and Michael B. Preston, eds., *Race, Sex, and Policy Problems* (Lexington, Ma.: Lexington Books, 1979).

32. On the churches, see John A. Wagner, "The Role of the Christian Church," in Samora, *La Raza*, pp. 27–45; and César E. Chávez, "The Mexican American and the Church," *El Grito*, vol. 1, no. 4 (Summer 1968), pp. 9–12. For a collection of church-related documents, see Antonio M. Stevens Arroyo, ed., *Prophets Denied Honor: An Anthology on the Hispanic Church in the United States* (Mary Knoll, N.Y.: Orbis Books, 1980).

33. On the Catholic church, see Arroyo, *Prophets Denied Honor*, pp. 117–50, and 313–30; "Los Padres, Hispano Priests Organize," *La Luz*, vol. 5 (May 1973), pp. 6–9; Frank del Olmo, "Latino Community, With Church's Help, Is on Move," *Los Angeles Times* (photostatic copy, 1986?); Moises Sandoval, "The Latinization of the Catholic Church," *Agenda* (November–December 1978), pp. 5–7; and Andres G. Guerreró, *A Chicano Theology* (Maryknoll, N.Y.: Orbis Books, 1988).

34. Peter Sherry, "Neighborhood COPS," *The New Republic* (February 6, 1984), pp. 21–23, and Louis Torres, "East Los Angeles Neighborhoods Unite," *Nuestro* (August 1980), p. 23; L. D., "Levantando La Voz," *The Texas Observer* (July 17, 1987); David R. Johnson, et al., eds., *The Politics of San Antonio* (Lincoln: University of Nebraska Press, 1983), particularly pages 175–76; and Calvin Trillin, "U.S. Journal: San Antonio, Some Elements of Power," *New Yorker* (May 2, 1977), pp. 94–97.

35. For ongoing developments, see *Hispanic Business* and *Hispanic Link Weekly*, as well as SWVRP's newsletter.

36. "Latino Groups Huddling on 88 National Agenda," *Hispanic Link Weekly Report* (August 17, 1981); Peter Appelhome, "San Antonio Mayor in Drive to Unify Hispanic Americans," *New York Times* (June 26, 1987); and Frank del Olmo, "Latino Political Millennium Isn't at Hand," *Los Angeles Times* (July 2, 1987).

37. See Carlos Vásquez and Manuel García y Griego, *Mexican-U.S. Relations: Conflict and Convergence* (Los Angeles: Chicano Studies Research Center, University of California, Los Angeles, 1983); Tatcho Mendiola and Max Martinez, eds., *Chicano-Mexicano Relations* (Houston: Mexican American Studies Program, University of Houston, 1986), passim; Rodolfo de la Garza and Karl M. Schmitt, "Texas Land Grants and Chicano-Mexican Relations: A Case Study," *Latin American Research Review*, vol. 21 (1986); Roberto E. Villareal, "Ethnic Leadership and American Foreign Policy: The Hispanic Experience," *The Borderlands Journal*, vol. 9 (Spring 1986); and Armando B. Rendon, "Latinos: Breaking the Cycle of Survival to Tackle Global Affairs," in Abdul Azis Said, ed., *Ethnicity and U.S. Foreign Policy* (rev. ed., New York: Praeger, 1981).

38. The status of the community in the eighties may be judged by the responses examined in Robert R. Brischetto, "Mexican American Issues for the 1984 Presidential Election," *Southwest Voter Registration Education Project*, Public Opinion Report no. 1 (San Antonio, 1984).

Chapter 5

1. On demographic analysis, see census materials and C. H. Teller, et al., *Cuantos Somos: A Demographic Study of the Mexican-American Population* (Austin: Center for Mexican American Studies, University of Texas, 1977). In the general ten-year census the U.S. Census office identifies Spanish *surname* individuals, but not specifically Mexican descent population who are referred to as Latinos or Hispanics, and of whom approximately 70 percent are of Mexican descent. For this and other reasons, census figures lack precision in reference to Chicanos. However, the U.S. Census does make 15 percent sample surveys that refer to Mexican origin. See Emily G. McKay, "Hispanic Demographics: Looking Ahead" (Washington, D.C.: National Council of La Raza, 1986); and Lori S. Orum, *The Education of Hispanics: Status and Implications* (Washington, D.C.: National Council of La Raza, 1986).

2. On the economic status, as well as the demographic, educational, and familial, see *The Changing Profile of Mexican America: A Source Book for Policy Making* (Claremont: Tomas Rivera Center, 1985); and *Projections of Hispanic*

Population for the United States: 1990 and 2000 (Palo Alto: Center for Continuing Study of the California Economy, 1982).

3. On the politics of Mexican immigration, see Richard D. Lamm and Gary Imhoff, *Immigration Time Bomb* (New York: Truman Talley Books–E.P. Dutton, 1985); and Nathan Glazer, ed., *Clamor at the Gates: The New American Immigration* (San Francisco: Institute for Contemporary Studies Press, 1985). On changes in the law, see the Immigration Reform and Control Act of 1985 (Simpson-Rodino) 99th Congress, 2d sess., House of Representatives, Report 99-1000, October 14, 1986; INA 1986-U.S. Government Interpreters Release (November 3, 1986, and November 17, 1986); and "The Immigration Nightmare," *The Wall Street Journal*, November 10, 1986. For background, see Antonio Rios Bustamante, ed., *Mexican Immigrant Workers in the United States* (Los Angeles: Chicano Studies Research Center, University of California, Los Angeles, 1981), particularly Juan Gómez-Quiñones, "Mexican Immigration to the United States and the Internationalization of Labor 1848–1980"; and Arturo Santamaría Gómez, *La izquierda norteamericana y los trabajadores Indocumentados* (México, D.F.: Ediciones de Cultura Popular, Universidad Autonoma de Sinaloa, 1988).

4. On the border and Mexican Americans, see Stanley Ross, *Views across the Border* (Albuquerque: University of New Mexico Press, 1978); Juan Gómez-Quiñones, "El Paso de Juárez, Past and Continuing Frontier" (unpublished manuscript, 1985); and Oscar Martínez, *Troublesome Border* (Tucson: University of Arizona, 1988).

5. On Chicano attitudes toward Latin American policy, see David R. Ayon and Ricardo Anzaldua Montoya, "Latinos and U.S. Policy toward Latin America," in Abraham F. Lowenthal, ed., *Latin America and Caribbean Contemporary Record, 5: 1985–1987* (New York: Holmes and Meier, 1987), pp. 126–42.

6. On Mexicano-Chicano relations, see Carlos Vásquez and Manuel García y Griego, eds., *Mexican–U.S. Relations: Conflict and Convergence* (Los Angeles: Chicano Studies Research Center, University of California, Los Angeles, 1983); and Tatcho Mendiola and Max Martínez, eds., *Chicano-Mexicano Relations* (Houston: Mexican American Studies Program, University of Houston, 1986). Yet if the fields of culture and education are to be the preferred areas of interaction, will Chicano scholars have only limited acceptance for their interests in Mexico? In the United States, in recent years, there has been a proliferation of "Mexican Studies." A few Chicanos have been at the forefront in this endeavor. Specifically, Chicano scholars have published important studies in the areas of Mexican immigration, the U.S.–Mexico border, and U.S.–Mexican relations. They face, however, strong discrimination from the Anglo scholars who hitherto have monopolized Mexican studies.

Index

Acosta, Oscar, 158
Activism: church involvement in, 64–65; in the mid-1960s, 102; liberal response to, 51–52. *See also* Alianza Federal de Pueblos Libres; Chicanismo; County and municipal political activity; Federal programs; International activity; Middle class; National campaign activity; La Raza Unida Party; United Farm Workers; Youth
Aguirre, Robert, 136
Alatorre, Richard, 136, 165, 170
Alianza Federal de Pueblos Libres, 115–18. *See also* Leaders and leadership; La Raza Unida Party
Alianza Hispano-Americana, 35, 63–64, 66. *See also* American Council of Spanish-Speaking Organizations; Chicanismo; National campaign activity; Political Association of Spanish-Speaking Organizations; Poor People's March
Alinsky, Saul, 49, 180

American Coordinating Council on Political Education (ACCPE), 70, 73
American Council of Spanish-Speaking Organizations, 55, 65–66
American G.I. Forum, 37, 60–62, 181. *See also* American Council of Spanish-Speaking Organizations; Civil rights; Equal Employment Opportunities Commission; Federal programs; Middle class; National campaign activity; Political Association of Spanish-Speaking Organizations; Texas
Anaya, Ruben, 170
Anaya, Toney, 118, 169–70, 172
Apodaca, Jerry, 118, 169–70
Aragon, José, 164
Aragon, Manuel, 96–97
Arizona: electoral efforts in, 70; political experience in, 48. *See also* Alianza Hispano-Americana
Asociación Nacional México Americana (ANMA), 50–51

255